AREA STUDIES

AND

SOCIAL SCIENCE

INDIANA SERIES IN MIDDLE EAST STUDIES

MARK TESSLER, GENERAL EDITOR

AREA STUDIES

AND

SOCIAL SCIENCE

STRATEGIES FOR

UNDERSTANDING

MIDDLE EAST POLITICS

Edited by

Mark Tessler

with

Jodi Nachtwey and Anne Banda

INDIANA UNIVERSITY PRESS   BLOOMINGTON & INDIANAPOLIS

This book is a publication of

Indiana University Press
601 North Morton Street
Bloomington, Indiana 47404-3797 USA

www.indiana.edu/~iupress

Telephone orders   800-842-6796
Fax orders   812-855-7931
Orders by e-mail   iuporder@indiana.edu

Library of Congress Cataloging-in-Publication Data

Area studies and social science : strategies for understanding Middle East politics / edited by Mark
Tessler with Jodi Nachtwey and Anne Banda.
p.   cm. — (Indiana series in Middle East studies)
Includes bibliographical references and index.
ISBN 0-253-33502-7 (alk. paper). —
ISBN 0-253-21282-0 (pbk. : alk. paper)
1. Social sciences—Research.   2. Area studies.
3. Middle East—Study and teaching.   I. Tessler, Mark A.
II. Nachtwey, Jodi.   III. Banda, Anne.   IV. Series.
H62.A6626   1999
300'.7'2—dc21   98-33866
1   2   3   4   5   04   03   02   01   00   99

CONTENTS

Contents

INTRODUCTION: THE AREA STUDIES CONTROVERSY

Mark Tessler, Jodi Nachtwey, and Anne Banda

Growing tension between regional specialists and discipline-oriented social scientists has emerged as a major issue in the fields of international, comparative, and area studies. At the heart of the controversy is an important disagreement about social science epistemology, about what constitutes, or should constitute, the paradigm by which scholars construct knowledge about politics, economics, and international relations in major world regions. This controversy is the result not only of shifting intellectual currents within many social science disciplines but also of external factors, such as changing priorities for U.S. government and private foundation funding. With emphasis increasingly placed on scholarship that is global in perspective and informed by social science theory, these developments have threatened regional studies programs or, at the very least, placed these programs on the defensive.

The area studies controversy, as it is known, has been particularly intense in political science. Thus, in an article entitled "Political Scientists Clash over Value of Area Studies," *The Chronicle of Higher Education* reported the charge that "a focus on individual regions leads to work that is mushy" (Shea 1997). The most important criticism reviewed in the article is the contention that area specialists are hostile to social science theory, meaning that they have no interest in either the development or application of insights which transcend particular times and places. A related criticism is that their research lacks conceptual sophistication and methodological rigor. Similar complaints have been presented in *PS: Political Science & Politics*, a quarterly publication of the American Political Science Association. In June 1997, for example, the journal featured a section containing three articles on "Controversies in the Discipline: Area Studies and Comparative Politics." Articles in the prominent scholarly journal *Daedalus* have also explored this issue. They note that while the controversy may be most pronounced in political science, it is by no means limited to that discipline (Slow 1997; Bender 1997).

Against the background of these tensions and controversies, the present volume offers a collection of essays and research reports by scholars who are grounded in both area studies and their respective social science disciplines. All are Middle East specialists and nearly all are political scientists, although the disciplines of economics and history are also represented. In most cases, authors either take a self-conscious look at some portion of their past scholarship or present the results of a current research project, making explicit and then evaluating the relationship of this work to both their academic discipline and the field of Middle East studies. The essays were first presented at a conference at the University of Wisconsin-Milwaukee, where they formed the basis for an interdisciplinary discussion of the area studies controversy.

The Middle East is by no means the only world region for which these concerns are relevant. On the contrary, the area studies controversy involves criticisms directed at all area studies research. Thus, while a focus on the Middle East offers an excellent opportunity to examine this controversy, this collection seeks to do more than illuminate the foundations of political research in one particular region. The volume's larger purpose is to explore the relationship between area studies and theoretical social science as paradigms for the study of any major world region. By presenting some of their scholarly work and then discussing the ways in which this research is informed by, and contributes to, both theoretical and area-specific considerations, the contributors to this volume provide a basis for thinking about how and for what purposes scholars seek to produce knowledge about a particular country or region. All of the authors conclude that scholarship is especially productive when informed by disciplinary considerations, and by a concern for theory in particular, while at the same time being fully grounded in the real-world circumstances of the countries or regions under study. The essays also show that research which draws upon and integrates social science and area studies perspectives has yielded valuable results in the study of the Middle East.

AREA STUDIES AND DISCIPLINARY SOCIAL SCIENCE

The tension between area studies and disciplinary social science is not new. Discipline-oriented scholars, who place emphasis on the development of general theoretical insights, have for many years argued that the work of area specialists lacks rigor, and, above all, that it is not scientific in that it favors description over explanation, lacks analytical cumulativeness, and shows no interest in parsimony and generalization. Area studies research, these critics also contend, is overly preoccupied with detail and specificity. Though rich in factual information about particular places or particular times, it offers little to those with broader interests, applied, as well as theoretical.

Analytically oriented social scientists have also received their share of criticism. They have been charged with faddishness and oversimplification, with engaging in sterile debates about conceptual and theoretical frameworks, and with constructing highly abstract models that provide little real insight into the complex behavior patterns or events they purport to explain. Discipline-oriented scholars may not be drowning in minutiae, as critics charge is the case with area specialists, but their work is often perceived to be irrelevant, having little or no connection to real world situations. This is the case in particular for international and cross-cultural research, where, according to area specialists, insights uninformed by a knowledge of the languages, cultures, and histories of particular regions are highly unlikely to be meaningful or even accurate.

Posed in these terms, the intellectual divide between the two scholarly approaches may be overstated. Neither area studies nor disciplinary social science should be viewed in such stereotypical terms. Each is more diverse and tolerant than this portrait might suggest, and many scholars have recognized the value of incorporating insights from both paradigms. Nevertheless, this should not obscure the very real tension that has long existed, as will be readily attested by those who have witnessed the contentious debates surrounding personnel decisions in many university social science departments. The divide has also been reflected in scholarly journals, with disciplinary journals and area journals rarely having the same contributors, or even appealing to the same readers. Even with tolerance and mutual respect, which unfortunately have not always been present, area specialists and discipline-oriented social scientists have, to a very significant degree, inhabited two different scholarly worlds.

Several recent developments have sharpened the divide between these two perspectives, and, as noted, placed area specialists on the defensive. In disciplines like political science and economics, for example, increasing sophistication in quantitative data analysis and the popularity of rational choice theory as an approach to model building have created new orthodoxies and diminished the importance attached to foreign language proficiency and overseas research experience. Rational choice theory, in particular, sees behavior as rooted in the self-interested cost-benefit calculations made by all men and women, and it is accordingly skeptical about the inclusion of cultural factors in explanations of behavior.

At the other end of the spectrum, trends associated with postmodernism in some disciplines, most notably anthropology and sociology, have called into question the possibility of objective scholarship and led some to condemn cross-cultural field work on both intellectual and political grounds. Also known as "reflexivity" or the "reflexive turn," this intellectual orientation asserts that since all knowledge is a product of the interaction between observer and observed, the quest for research findings that are intersubjectively transmissible, the foundation of science and cumulativeness, is inevitably doomed to failure. Objective social science, in other words, is said to be an illusion. Admittedly, some trends associated with postmodernism are much less absolute, calling simply for greater self-awareness regarding the subjective elements of data collection and field work, including those pertaining to the researcher's motivations. Others, however, insist that there is no possibility of empathetic understanding or even accurate observation across lines of culture. The same is said to apply to divisions based on race, gender, and other critical social categories.

A concern with "Orientalism," which is not new, has also had something of a chilling effect on area studies scholarship. The charge here is that many area specialists consider behavior to be determined primarily by cultural influences, and that they accordingly place the people they study outside of science by seeking to explicate the unique culture and history that makes them behave as they do. Among the results of such research have been studies with titles like "The Arab Mind" and "Temperament and Character of the Arabs," which critics of Orientalism condemn as stereotypical, one-dimensional, reductionist, and deterministic (Said 1978, pp. 309–311). In response to such criticism, reflecting a desire to avoid the stereotyping about which critics of Orientalism quite properly complain, a tendency has developed to question the value of any research that gives prominent attention to cultural and historical factors when studying non-Western societies. This tendency, once again, places area studies scholarship on the defensive.

Challenges to area studies have also been based on considerations of relevance. Specifically, area studies is said to be a product of the Cold War, developed with federal funds in the 1950s and 1960s in order to ensure that the United States would possess the knowledge about Third World countries needed to compete effectively with the Soviet Union. This global confrontation was often described at the time as "the struggle for men's minds." While most area specialists did not see their scholarly mission in such terms, support for the study of less commonly taught languages and for overseas research in developing countries was made possible by an American government and several private foundations that saw strategic value in the collection of detailed information about Third World societies. Support for the study of Second World societies and languages, said to be necessary so that the United States would know its enemy, was also provided. The National Defense Education Act, passed by the U.S. Congress in 1958, was particularly important. The graduate fellowships it provided for advanced training in foreign languages and area studies laid a foundation for the entry into American universities of a large new corps of regional specialists.

Today, however, new global realities, coupled as they are with a concern for reducing the federal budget in the United States, have led many to argue that area studies is an anachronism. An influential expression of this view was provided by Stanley Heginbotham, vice president of the Social Science Research Council (SSRC), who in a 1994 article called for less attention to in-depth studies of regional particularisms and more attention to themes of global relevance (Heginbotham 1994). The SSRC subsequently refocused its program of "area" research grants and announced that it would henceforth encourage "thematic" studies addressed to such global concerns as ethnic conflict and transitions to democracy, preferably to be examined in comparative investigations within or even across world regions.

The Ford Foundation, the Mellon Foundation, and the MacArthur Foundation have all begun to move in this direction as well. The Ford Foundation, for example, which provided major support for the establishment of area studies programs in the 1950s and 1960s, in December 1996 announced a new grants program devoted to the "revitalization" of area studies. Apparently judging the training and research associated with area studies to be in need of reform, the foundation is encouraging area programs to reexamine their goals and is offering assistance to those prepared to move in new directions. Ford also joined with the MacArthur Foundation several years ago to encourage research on global rather than regional problems, and the Mellon Foundation has taken a similar approach in its program on cross-regional issues.

The end of American-Soviet rivalry is only one part of the new reality that critics of area studies cite in order to justify their calls for attention to global rather than regional issues. Other trends, some associated with the end of the Cold War and some reflecting the revolution in communications and information technology, are also transforming the environment within which scholarship takes place. One important consideration is that political and economic liberalization is breaking down national barriers and forcing an increasing number of countries, whether they wish it or not, to deepen their involvement in the world economic and political system. However different might be their cultures and histories, events and developments in countries around the world are increasingly subject to the same global influences.

Similarly, the communications revolution is breaking down isolation and fostering the development and worldwide dissemination of common cultural forms and shared behavioral norms. Francis Fukuyama calls this "The End of History" (Fukuyama 1992). According to this argument, a process of global integration and linguistic and cultural consolidation is taking place. Western culture and the English language will play an increasingly important role in the non-Western world, just as a continuing expansion of the dominant languages and cultures in these regions will further reduce, and perhaps eventually eliminate, the great diversity that has marked Third World societies in the past. According to critics of area studies, these trends are another reason why it is no longer important for Western scholars to acquire detailed information about the history, culture, or languages of most developing countries.

Area specialists have begun to respond to this constellation of charges and challenges. At the center of their response are two interrelated arguments: first, the research agenda of many area specialists has a strong theoretical focus and, accordingly, the alleged division between area studies and disciplinary social science is highly exaggerated; and second, the kind of substantive knowledge associated with area studies not only *can* contribute to the development of social science theory, it is in fact essential.

Many scholars working under the umbrella of area studies are concerned with, and have in fact produced, broadly generalizable theoretical insights. A good example, and one which shows that this is by no means a new phenomenon, is the work on cultural pluralism by Crawford Young, a political scientist and Africanist at the University of Wisconsin-Madison (Young 1976 and 1993). Although trained as an area specialist and using a traditional case study methodology, Young has nonetheless made major theoretical contributions to our understanding of how political identities are formed and subsequently change. The theoretical contributions of numerous other area specialists could be similarly cited, including Barrington Moore, Theda Skocpol, Lucian Pye, Lloyd and Suzanne Rudolph, Leonard Binder, John Waterbury, Albert Hirschman, Guillermo O'Donnell, and Philippe Schmitter, among many others.

Reflecting on this situation, John Creighton Campbell, an Asia specialist at the University of Michigan, asserted that "most of the things that people say about area studies are silly. . . . Most of the stuff that people say area studies should be doing is what area studies is already doing" (Shea 1997, p. 13). The same point was made by Peter Hall and Sidney Tarrow, political scientists at Harvard and Cornell, respectively. Writing in 1998, Hall and Tarrow rejected the claim that area specialists focus only on detailed descriptions of individual nations or regions. They noted that many scholars concerned with theory, including Charles Tilly, Benedict Anderson, Donald Horowitz, and Michel Crozier, have drawn upon "deep and context-rich knowledge of a particular society or region to develop propositions of general applicability." Thus, they concluded, the charge that area specialization is incompatible with theoretical inquiry is "little more than a misleading rhetorical exercise" (Hall and Tarrow 1998, p. B5).

Area specialists frequently argue not only that their work is compatible with a concern for social science theory, but that the quest for theory cannot be pursued meaningfully without attention to the kind of contextual knowledge that area studies research provides. They note, for example, that theory construction often begins with observation, with the delineation of variance that hypotheses are then formulated to explain. Further, the hypotheses themselves will have explanatory power only to the extent that they are neither trivial nor obvious. Finally, hypotheses cannot be tested without the development of measures that are valid within the social and cultural context from which data are drawn. All of this, however, requires an ability to recognize, understand, and evaluate the facts on the ground, which is precisely the kind of knowledge associated with area studies.

An argument along similar lines is advanced in relation to rational choice theory by Robert Bates, a political scientist and African specialist at Harvard. Bates's own work on African markets, like that of Young on cultural pluralism, illustrates the theoretical contributions that can and often do grow out of area studies research (Bates 1981 and 1989). In addition, however, Bates contends that the kind of knowledge produced by area specialists is essential for the development of social science theory. To illustrate this point, he cites the work of several anthropologists and states that without the kind of cultural knowledge produced by their studies it would be impossible to evaluate the significance of the alternative behaviors among which individuals must choose, and hence to apply rational choice theory (Bates 1997).

Hall and Tarrow write in the same vein when responding to the charge that globalization has made area studies increasingly irrelevant. Expressing concern about recent trends in political science and economics, they take issue with claims that "rational-choice analysis (which uses econometric models and game theory to study how people make decisions) can explain the behavior of Japanese politicians and bureaucrats without much reference to Japanese culture" (Hall and Tarrow 1998, p. B4). Thus, like Bates, they insist that while rational choice theory may provide a useful conceptual framework for analyzing decision processes, this framework can be applied to particular cases only if information about the meaning and importance attached to alternative courses of action is available.

Some scholars add that this is precisely what discipline-oriented social scientists do when they study their own society and culture, and so it is puzzling that they should have difficulty understanding why it is essential for the development of theory that applies to other parts of the world. According to one account, this in fact makes culture the "master concept of all social science." Meaningful social inquiry, this argument continues, requires that one "immerse oneself in one's subject, learning the language, living with the people, and getting to understand the society so thoroughly as a participant that it problematizes one's own place as an objective observer" (Suehiro 1997, pp. 20–27). This point of view is cited in an article by Chalmers Johnson, a prominent Asianist from the University of California. Johnson goes on to write that "this is what social scientists do naturally when studying their own culture, and it is what they *must* do in order to study another culture. There is no alternative or rational-choice shortcut" (Johnson 1997, p. 172).

Disagreement about the value of case studies, a mode of inquiry strongly identified with the research of area specialists, reflects a methodological dimension of the area studies debate. Some social scientists have argued that case studies are either inherently atheoretical or, at best, useful only for *generating* testable hypotheses. As early as 1963, Donald Campbell and Julian Stanley characterized the case study as a "one shot" methodology that "is of no scientific value" (Campbell and Stanley 1963). Arend Lijphart's influential article in the *American Political Science Review* several years later expressed similar, if somewhat less categorical, reservations about the theoretical value of case studies (Lijphart 1971). Yet area specialists insist that in-depth case studies are fully compatible with systematic social science inquiry. Clifford Geertz, for example, writing in response to early criticisms, justified case studies as necessary to provide the "thick description" without which the complex interrelationships among social processes and events cannot be meaningfully unraveled (Geertz 1973).

Introduction

More recently, area specialists, as well as some others, not only have continued to insist that case studies offer an opportunity to test research hypotheses, they have also proposed innovations designed to enhance the value of case studies for broader comparative and theoretical inquiry. Many of these innovations, including contributions by Harry Eckstein, Alexander George, and Robert Yin, are summarized in a useful article by David Collier. Collier reports that in-depth case studies can be extremely useful in hypothesis testing and theory building, and he notes in this connection that some social scientists have "dramatically recanted" their earlier charge that such research is without scientific merit (Collier 1991, p. 23). Collier also reports that case studies have been used effectively in rational choice analysis, as in the work of Christopher Achen and Duncan Snidal, for example (Achen and Snidal 1989).

Beyond these arguments about epistemological and methodological considerations, area specialists often make several additional observations, some calling attention to the strengths of their own approach and others to the deficiencies they find in social inquiry that is excessively abstract and theoretical. With respect to the former, they insist that many of the intellectual considerations which generated support for area programs in the past are as relevant today as ever. These include the importance of interdisciplinary scholarship, since complex real-world problems rarely fall entirely within the purview of a single discipline. They also include a need to transcend ethnocentrism and Western bias, not only to ensure accuracy and relevance but also so that insights derived from the study of one region or culture might contribute to innovative thinking about other regions or cultures. Intellectual considerations of this sort, as well as strategic calculations associated with the Cold War, led the Social Science Research Council and the Ford Foundation to invest heavily in area studies programs in the 1960s (Ward and Wood 1974), and area specialists insist that these concerns are no less important than in the past.

Area specialists also sometimes insist in this connection that the significance of their investment in acquiring research skills be recognized and appreciated. For example, few social science Ph.D. programs require more than four or five courses in formal theory and quantitative methods; this is usually considered adequate to prepare students for "scientific" research. By contrast, twice that number of courses is necessary to establish proficiency in many less commonly taught languages. Area specialists rightly claim that the effort and accomplishment reflected in such preparation is, at the very least, no less praiseworthy than the training in social science research methods that others have acquired, and which they themselves have very often acquired as well.

So far as the work of discipline-oriented scholars is concerned, there are complaints both about a double standard and about relevance. Area specialists note, for example, that many of these scholars produce descriptive and atheoretical studies of American society and politics. They are, in effect, American area specialists. There is nothing wrong with this, of course. On the contrary, this research is often quite valuable. The complaint is that the work of these

"Americanists" is valued and considered mainstream by political science, economics, and other social science disciplines, while the same appreciation is not extended to area specialists who do descriptive work or study contemporary issues in other parts of the world, especially the non-Western world.

More serious, perhaps, is a contention that it is actually disciplinary research, rather than scholarship associated with area studies, which most often is of little real-world relevance. This charge has been leveled at both quantitative analysis and rational choice theory. A recent article by Johnson, for example, argues that mathematical formulas are no substitute for significance and then suggests that the latter is frequently lacking in quantitative social science. In this connection, Johnson endorses the view of Martin Anderson, who writes that "the main problem is not that much of the writing of academic intellectuals is too mathematical, but that it is insignificant, unimportant, trivial. If the ideas were significant and important ones couched in the language of mathematics, that would be fine, for presumably it could be reworked into English. But if the writing is devoid of any merit, expressing it in plain English would expose the intellectual sham" (Anderson 1992, p. 101).

With respect to rational choice theory, Johnson states that he cannot think of a single book "in which rational choice theory has been applied to a non-English-speaking country with results even approximately close to the claims made for the method" (Johnson 1997, p. 173). Similar criticism has been advanced by others. For example, as noted, Hall and Tarrow challenge the claim that political behavior in Japan can be fully understood without reference to Japanese culture. David Hollinger offers a more sweeping condemnation, accusing the rational choicers "of failing to illuminate anything of genuine significance . . . of avoiding the complexities of the real world" (Hollinger 1997, pp. 347–348).

THE VOLUME

The purpose of reviewing these claims and counterclaims is not to cast doubt on the intrinsic value of either area studies or discipline- and theory-oriented social science. Nor is it to invite discussion about which perspective offers the more appropriate guide to social research in the fields of comparative and international studies. It is rather to identify the context within which the present volume seeks to make a contribution. Beyond this, it may be observed that the controversy about area studies and disciplinary social science is actually quite healthy. It forces those associated with each perspective to reflect on their assumptions and practices, and from the resulting self-examination will hopefully emerge conceptual and methodological refinements on the one hand and greater tolerance and respect for diversity on the other.

This book seeks to contribute to the realization of these objectives. Moreover, and more specifically, it seeks to demonstrate that social science theory and area studies are not incompatible or even in competition with one another, and that political science and other disciplines will be best served by encouraging research that draws in a meaningful way on both scholarly perspectives. This view is shared by the contributors to this volume, who seek through their essays and research reports to show that work of this sort can be done, is being done, and is of significant value.

Other considerations relating to research in the Middle East and other developing areas are also illustrated by this collection. One of these involves the diversity of research methods that permit the integration of theoretical and area studies concerns. As the chapters show, these include traditional in-depth case studies, often involving intensive overseas fieldwork, systematic comparative studies based on multiple cases, studies involving the analysis of aggregate nation-level data or of individual-level public opinion data, and studies in which the data base is provided by documents or historical experiences and events. The chapters also provide a basis for reflecting on issues of conceptualization and conceptual equivalence across cultures. Do such notions as civil society, feminism, and religiosity, for example, carry the same meaning and have the same explanatory utility when applied in different social, cultural, or political settings? These concepts, as well as several others, are examined in one or more of the chapters to follow.

Finally, there is significance in the particular theoretical and substantive issues addressed by the chapters, which, taken together, provide a valuable overview of politics and international relations in the Middle East. Among these issues are democratization and political development, state-society relations, political economy and public policy, politically salient dimensions of culture, including gender and religion, and both international relations in general and the Arab-Israeli conflict in particular. On the one hand, this diversity illustrates the broad range of topics for which the concerns of this volume are pertinent. On the other hand, the chapters offer insights and findings that contribute to an understanding of politics and international relations not only in the Middle East but in other developing areas as well. In this connection, the volume encourages and will inform efforts to integrate scholarly perspectives in the study of other world regions. It also encourages the incorporation of the Middle East into research efforts that are cross-regional or even global.

With these objectives in mind, the essays collected here represent an effort by Middle East specialists with disciplinary as well as area expertise to situate their scholarship within the context of current debates about the relevance of area studies. In differing ways and from their differing perspectives, each contributor inquires about the relationship between theory-oriented social science and area studies, offering conclusions that shed light both on the state of research about Middle East politics and on the perspective that should inform political scientists and others who undertake to carry out this research.

Lisa Anderson makes two interrelated points about the sometimes troubled relationship between the discipline of political science and research on Middle East politics. On the one hand, she objects that the scholarly agenda of American political science is too narrow and fails to give adequate attention to many of the topics that are most relevant for an understanding of political life in the Middle East and other developing areas. This tends to marginalize and alienate those political scientists working in the region. Further, it denies to the discipline the valuable contributions that these scholars might make. For example, Anderson suggests that "the study of Hamas [might] tell us a lot about rational choice theory." On the other hand, while she acknowledges that Middle East specialists have sometimes been slow to draw upon the investigatory tools of analytical social science, Anderson notes many political scientists working in the Middle East have indeed been moving in this direction, making their research more rigorous, systematic, and theoretically focused.

John P. Entelis concentrates on the issue of democratization and is concerned with generalizable causal relationships. Focusing on a single country, Algeria, Entelis uses a case study methodology to evaluate the relative explanatory power of propositions derived from three different conceptual frameworks, which he labels culture, conspiracy, and civil society, respectively. His goal is to explicate political dynamics at the national level and, in particular, to account for the failure of Algeria's experiment in democratization. His conclusion is that attention to considerations of culture is necessary but insufficient to achieve these objectives, and that both a concern for theory and in-depth information about the Algerian experience are necessary for a proper analysis. This leads Entelis to argue that the kind of case study he has undertaken can "contribute to the development of generalizable social science insights, and correspondingly, that the case itself can be illuminated by social science theory."

Augustus Richard Norton, codirector of an ongoing research project on civil society in the Middle East and North Africa, examines the analytical value of applying the concept of civil society to the study of Arab politics. Although the concept has been borrowed from research in other world regions, he concludes that it is indeed useful for understanding state-society relations in the Middle East. Norton also addresses some of the concerns about governance explored by Entelis. He argues that the persistence of authoritarianism in the Middle East cannot be attributed to cultural factors but is rather a consequence of specific government policies and of established patterns of leadership more generally.

Jodi Nachtwey and Mark Tessler draw upon feminist theory from political science and other disciplines to shed light on the attitudes of Muslim Arab women toward Islamist political movements and their platforms. They analyze public opinion data from several Arab countries not only to test analytical insights derived from the theoretical literature but also to assess the explanatory power of competing hypotheses and to identify the conditions, if any, under which each obtains. Nachtwey and Tessler demonstrate the utility of disciplinary tools for the investigation of topics, such as determinants of support for political Islam, that are usually considered to be within the purview of area studies. In addition, they show that such topics offer opportunities for productive research aimed at discerning generalizable causal relationships.

Introduction

Clement M. Henry examines the politics of banking in the Middle East and North Africa. Employing a political economy framework, he shows how attention to the politics surrounding economic policy-making can shed light on issues of governance. He also incorporates a useful civil society perspective by examining the ways that businessmen and others with an interest in financial matters participate and exercise influence within the political process. Henry's contribution involves the systematic comparison of a number of cases, thus enabling the analysis to take place at both the within-country and the between-country level. He argues that drawing upon both area studies knowledge and social science theory provides "a way to track developments of civil society in the Middle East and North Africa and to anticipate political change in a way that is more coherent and comparative."

Political economy is also the focus of economist Magda Kandil, who applies economic theory pertaining to factor mobility to the issue of labor migration in Egypt. Kandil examines both the domestic "push" and the external "pull" factors that influence an individual's decision to migrate. She also discusses the impact of migrant remittances on the Egyptian economy, again grounding her work in relevant theory as well as data from the Egyptian case. Kandil concludes that her research shows how "theories and methods from the discipline of economics can be utilized to increase our understanding of critical issues facing developing countries in the Middle East and elsewhere."

Two chapters deal with the Arab-Israeli conflict. In both instances, the research reported has a clear theoretical focus and uses this important Middle East case to develop insights that are likely to apply to inter-state disputes in other world regions. In the first of these chapters, Mark Tessler and Jodi Nachtwey present a statistical analysis that examines the degree to which religious orientations shape popular attitudes toward the Arab-Israeli conflict. Using public opinion data from five Arab countries, they test statistical models that relate various kinds of religious sentiments to attitudes about the conflict. Their findings contribute to the development of general theory by shedding light on the differences and similarities between the Middle East and the West.

In the next chapter, historian Laura Zittrain Eisenberg examines Arab-Jewish negotiating experiences dating as far back as World War I in order to identify the obstacles to success in such diplomatic initiatives. The result is a model that organizes "a decades-long history of erratic Arab-Jewish negotiations into a meaningful analytical whole," and which, Eisenberg concludes, has both practical and theoretical value. With respect to the former, it illuminates the conditions that must be fulfilled if diplomacy aimed at conflict resolution is to make progress. With respect to the latter, Eisenberg uses the Middle East case to develop explanatory insights that are "generalizable to other cases of prolonged conflict and to repeated negotiation attempts around the globe."

The last two chapters address issues of international relations more generally, moving beyond a concern with regional conflicts to focus on economic and diplomatic relations among states. Laurie A. Brand, in the first of these chapters, examines the factors shaping Jordan's economic and diplomatic relations with neighboring countries. She reports that much of the theoretical literature in international relations offered her little guidance because of its preoccupation with military alliances and big power relations. On the other hand, theoretical insights from the political economy literature, combined with in-depth knowledge of the Jordanian case, proved to be extremely useful. This led Brand to focus on domestic economic exigencies and structures, which, she concludes, do a much better job of explaining and predicting the foreign policy behavior of a country like Jordan than do traditional explanations based on military strength or superpower politics.

Bahgat Korany returns to the volume's point of departure by responding to some of the criticism that has been aimed at area studies scholarship. Reviewing international relations research relating to the Middle East, Korany demonstrates that a concern with theory has long been one of the preoccupations of area specialists working in the region and that these scholars make a critical contribution by testing social science theory in the Middle East and other non-Western regions. Without this contribution, progress toward the development of generalizable insights, including the delineation of conditionalities associated with causal relationships, would be impossible.

Taken together, these essays demonstrate that area studies scholarship is not inherently atheoretical, uninformed by the canons of systematic social science research, or uninterested in insights that transcend a given world region. On the contrary, the serious study of particular cultures and regions is fully compatible with the kind of scholarly inquiry associated with academic disciplines. Moreover, these essays show that the substantive knowledge, linguistic ability, and cultural sensitivity that are the traditional strengths of area studies are as essential as ever. However theoretical and social scientific might be its focus, no program of scholarship carried out in a particular country or region will produce valid results unless it is informed by area expertise. Neither the strategies and calculations of groups and governments nor the attitudes and behavior of ordinary citizens can be adequately understood without a knowledge of the context within which these actors reside. Indeed, key concepts cannot even be applied sensibly without such contextual knowledge.

In making these arguments, this book offers a progressive rather than a defensive response to the critics of area studies, recognizing the value of the approach they advocate and calling for tolerance and mutual respect. The volume does more than articulate general principles about pluralism and scholarly integration, however. It demonstrates, with analytical essays and exemplars of research by students of the Middle East, how the principles it champions can be, and have been, respected in practice. Moreover, it seeks to show not only that the scholarly paradigms of area studies and disciplinary social science are both important, but that significant contributions can result when programs of research are informed by the two perspectives.

Since these concerns are relevant not only for social scientists interested in the Middle East, but for those concerned with other geographic and cultural areas as well, the volume's contributions offer a stimulus and a model for increasing the value of research about any country or region. They illustrate the wide array of topics and the methodologies for which this perspective is appropriate, none of which, of course, is limited to the Middle East. With respect to topical focus, the book addresses numerous issues related to politics, economics, public policy, and international relations. With respect to methodology, it includes case studies, comparative studies, historical research, and both aggregate and individual-level quantitative data analysis.

Graduate students as well as scholars will find the work collected in this volume instructive. Both individually and taken together, the chapters will help to orient students preparing for research in the Middle East or other regions, contributing to their ability to conceptualize and design scholarly investigations to be carried out in another part of the world. Toward this end, contributions to this volume demonstrate how programs of research can and should draw upon both area studies knowledge and the theoretical insights of social science disciplines, and how this kind of intellectual integration can take place when examining particular topics and employing particular research methods.

Finally, for undergraduate students, the book offers specific and concrete information about many important topics, most of which are relevant for an understanding of politics and international relations in many world regions. More important than specific factual information or particular analytical insights, however, is an appreciation of the scholarly enterprise by which this information and these insights are produced. By self-consciously shedding light on the research process, with particular emphasis on intellectual and epistemological concerns, this volume will help students recognize and evaluate the strategies guiding investigation of the issues being addressed.

In conclusion, the book demonstrates that meaningful research in particular countries and regions is impossible without in-depth knowledge of the domestic political, social, and cultural environment. At the same time, the necessity for such knowledge does not imply that disciplinary concerns and the pursuit of generalizable insights are unimportant. The contributors to this volume share these values. In addition, however, they not only reject the "either-or" rhetoric that characterizes much of the current area studies debate, they seek as well to demonstrate the value of research that draws upon and integrates the two analytical perspectives. Their contributions to this volume support their commitment to tolerance and scholarly integration with concrete and diverse illustrations of how these principles can be put into practice.

REFERENCES

Achen, Christopher, and Duncan Snidal. 1989. "Rational Deterrence Theory and Comparative Case Studies." *World Politics* 41 (2): 143–169.

Introduction

Anderson, Martin. 1992. *Imposters in the Temple: American Intellectuals Are Destroying Our Universities and Cheating Our Students of Their Future*. New York: Simon & Schuster.

Bates, Robert. 1997. "Area Studies and the Discipline: A Useful Controversy." *PS: Political Science & Politics* XXX (2): 166–169.

———. 1989. *Beyond the Miracle of the Market: The Political Economy of Agrarian Development in Kenya*. Cambridge: Cambridge University Press.

———. 1981. *Markets and States in Tropical Africa: The Political Basis of Agricultural Policies*. Berkeley: University of California Press.

Bender, Thomas. 1997. "Politics, Intellect, and the American University." *Daedalus* (Winter).

Campbell, Donald, and Julian Stanley. 1963. *Experimental and Quasi-Experimental Designs for Research*. Chicago: Rand McNally.

Collier, David. 1991. "New Perspectives on the Comparative Method." In *Comparative Political Dynamics: Global Research Perspectives*. Dankart Rustow and Kenneth Paul Erickson, eds. New York: Harper-Collins.

Fukuyama, Francis. 1992. *The End of History and the Last Man*. New York: Free Press.

Geertz, Clifford. 1973. "Thick Description: Toward an Interpretative Theory of Culture." In *The Interpretation of Cultures*. Clifford Geertz, ed. New York: Basic.

Hall, Peter, and Sidney Tarrow. 1998. "Globalization and Area Studies: When Is Too Broad Too Narrow?" *The Chronicle of Higher Education*, 23 January.

Heginbotham, Stanley. 1994. "Rethinking International Scholarship." *Items* 48 (2–3): 33–40.

Hollinger, David. 1997. "The Disciplines and the Identity Debates, 1970–1996." *Daedalus* (Winter).

Johnson, Chalmers. 1997. "Preconception vs. Observation, or the Contributions of Rational Choice Theory and Area Studies to Contemporary Political Science." *PS: Political Science & Politics* XXX (2): 170–174.

Lijphart, Arend. 1971. "Comparative Politics and Comparative Method." *American Political Science Review* 65 (September).

Said, Edward. 1978. *Orientalism*. New York: Pantheon.

Shea, Christopher. 1997. "Political Scientists Clash over Value of Area Studies." *The Chronicle of Higher Education*, 10 January.

Slow, Robert. 1997. "How Did Economics Get That Way and What Way Did It Get?" *Daedalus* (Winter).

Suehiro, Akira. 1997. "Thinktanks and the Evolution of 'Chiiki Kenkyu,' Japan's Area Studies." *Social Science Japan* (February).

Ward, Robert, and Bryce Wood. 1974. "Foreign Area Studies and the Social Science Research Council." *Items* 48 (4): 53–58.

Young, Crawford. 1993. *The Rising Tide of Cultural Pluralism: The Nation-State at Bay?* Madison: University of Wisconsin Press.

———. 1976. *The Politics of Cultural Pluralism*. Madison: University of Wisconsin Press.

AREA STUDIES

AND

SOCIAL SCIENCE

1. Politics in the Middle East
Opportunities and Limits in the Quest for Theory

Lisa Anderson

In a 1996 issue of the newsletter of the Comparative Politics section of the American Political Science Association, Barry Ames, a noted rational choice theorist, wrote:

> From my perspective as a Latin Americanist, the state of comparative politics looks pretty good. Latin American political science, at least, is undergoing a renaissance. The return of competitive politics has renewed interest in parties, public opinion, elections, and legislative behavior; the stuff, in other words, of modern political science (Ames 1996, p. 12).

From my perspective as a student of the Middle East and North Africa, this observation is striking in two respects. First, its remarkably upbeat and optimistic tone is quite a departure from the anxious and jaded style ordinarily assumed by most of my own regional studies associates.

Far more important and troubling, however, is the second remarkable aspect of Ames's observation: the surprisingly complacent equation of the institutions of modern politics with the subjects of modern political science. Is modern political science not possible in the absence of the institutions of competitive politics? Are those of us who study politics where "parties, public opinion, elections, and legislative behavior" are notable mostly by their absence to be relegated to "premodern" political science? Are the authoritarian regimes and kinship networks, the kings, cliques, and clients we struggle to understand, unfit subjects for political scientists, and appropriately assigned to the obscurity of second-rate journals as "mere area studies"? This essay is devoted to an exploration of these questions through examination of the recent tribulations of students of political democratization in the Middle East and North Africa.

I must note at the outset that in marked contrast to Ames's satisfaction, I am neither satisfied with the present state of my field nor fully confident that I can outline a solution to the problems I identify, although, as I hope to show, there may be reasons for guarded optimism. My unease may have unduly influenced my assessments of my own work and that of some of my colleagues, however, and if I seem somewhat uncharitable, my chagrin is born of the conviction that we must work harder to ensure that the study of Middle East politics is not isolated from the mainstream of American political science. Neither our comprehension of the Middle East nor our aspiration to a universal science of politics profits from failure to be both geographically inclusive and theoretically rigorous.

A decade or so ago, many of us who worked in the Middle East and North Africa thought we would not have to address the question of the "modernity" of the institutions we study and the techniques we use to do so. Political democratization promised to solve problems not only for Middle Eastern citizens who yearned for personal freedom and equality but for American political scientists who sought professional respectability and acceptance. By producing institutions instantly recognizable to other American political scientists, democratization was to promote not only the rule of law in political life in the Middle East, but the generalization of the scientific method in political science.

American political science developed in the study of American politics. Just as the practice of American politics has long been thought by most Americans to set the standard for politics in the free world (or perhaps in the aftermath of the collapse of communism, in the whole world), the science of politics in the United States has been thought by most political scientists to set the standard for the scientific study of politics everywhere else. The intimate association of American politics and American political science has meant that many of the most highly developed, most refined, most visible, and most prestigious research areas are those associated with American politics: political parties and political participation, voting and mass behavior, legislative and judicial institutions. As should instantly be apparent, for most of the Middle East and North Africa, these issues and the methods developed to explore them are of relatively little consequence. By contrast, the issues which consume the Middle East and North Africa—questions of monarchical succession, tribalism, military government, nationalism, state formation, political violence, for example—are of largely historical interest to most Americanists.

Despite or perhaps because of their self-evident significance in industrial democracies, export of the questions, methods, and techniques associated with the study of American politics has always been more difficult than their exponents anticipated. Modernization theorists a generation ago had dismissed the mismatch between their theory and the empirical realities of the "developing areas" as an anachronistic artifact of "traditions" that would soon be the purview only of historians (as they are in American politics) or anthropologists and other students of exotica. In much the same spirit of giddy optimism, we students of democratization in the Middle East succumbed remarkably easily to the vain hope that reality would catch up to theory before we would be required to consider the limitations of the theory itself.

The last decade has turned out to be instructive and sobering. Political democratization did not happen in most of the Middle East, and those of us who set out to support and study it were left in many respects normatively disappointed, politically unprepared, and scientifically isolated. I will take each of these results in turn.

NORMATIVE COMMITMENTS AND DISAPPOINTMENTS

Among the several heartening and invigorating qualities of the literature on transitions to democracy that emerged from southern Mediterranean and Latin American studies in the early 1980s was the willingness—indeed, insistence —of its authors to make explicit normative commitments. As the influential volumes edited by Guillermo O'Donnell and Philippe Schmitter declared:

> The first general and shared theme [of the studies] is normative, namely that the insaturation and eventual consolidation of political democracy constitutes per se a desirable goal. . . . we all agreed that the establishment of certain rules of regular, formalized political competition deserved priority attention by scholars and practitioners (O'Donnell and Schmitter 1986, p. 3).

No longer did scientific respectability require studiously "objective" researchers who carefully designed their projects to ensure that they met the highest standards of "value-neutrality." Suddenly, being a little "engagé" was not only permissible but desirable.

For those of us who studied Middle East politics, this was a particularly liberating development. Most of us had spent our professional development practicing and refining our public posture not only of scientific objectivity but political "evenhandedness." The possibility of actually caring about the outcome of a political process and, still more remarkable, admitting it, constituted a major shift in our terms of reference. Yet, for many of us, part of the enormous attraction of the agenda represented by human rights and democracy was the prospect that we could utilize our knowledge and skills in political activity on behalf of, and in collaboration with, our colleagues, informants, and friends in the region. Thus did I seize the opportunity to join the Board of Human Rights Watch when that organization established the last (and what seemed to be the most intractable) of its regional committees, on the Middle East, in the mid-1980s, and many of my colleagues openly embraced similar causes and organizations.

What little extra impetus our participation might have given these efforts was not enough to guarantee their triumph, however, and the failure of the human rights movements and the democratization efforts to bear immediate and substantial fruit was probably more disappointing than it would have been had we not gotten our hopes up in the first place. And, now that we have allowed ourselves the luxury of caring, that disappointment may be coloring our assessment of the current scene. Nonetheless, the prospects for democracy seem exceptionally bleak as we survey the remnants of so many of the democratic experiments, from the spectacular crash-and-burn of Algeria's liberalization to Tunisia's more subtle but no less profound transformation into a police state, from Egypt's backsliding into electoral manipulation to the obvious reluctance of the Palestinian authorities to embrace human rights.

WISHFUL THINKING, PREDICTION, AND EXPLANATION

It is probably fair to say that only the most cynical among us really expected these outcomes (and I hope it is fair to say, even fewer of us welcomed them). This raises a troubling question: if we did not expect these results, how well equipped are we to explain them? Most of the scholarly work on the liberal political and economic experiments of the last few years in the Middle East and North Africa paid little attention to explanation. Most of us were content to describe rather than to analyze and, in my view, we made little progress since my similarly cranky broadside of 1990, when I complained that Middle East political science was largely anecdotal, descriptive, and obsessed with current events (Anderson 1990).

Two efforts to link regional political developments with general propositions in contemporary political science may serve to illustrate the problem with painful clarity. In the late 1980s, I wrote an article hailing the Tunisian National Pact of 1988 as an important step on the road to democracy, comparable to the Pact of Moncloa in Spain, on which it was said to have been modeled. By the time my article appeared in print in 1991, it was all too obvious that Tunisia was not on its way to a Spanish-style transition and that the National Pact had played a very different role in Tunisia than its apparent counterpart in Spain (Anderson, 1991). Why? In Spain, as in most of the Latin American countries where political pacts were effective instruments in furthering democratic transitions, the pacts brought together political actors with independent bases of power in the society and economy and institutionalized and symbolized the compromise that had been brokered among them. In Tunisia, by contrast, virtually all the signatories of the pact represented dependencies of the perennial ruling party; far from a compromise or bargain among equals, the pact was an effort to create the appearance of political pluralism in the absence of political actors with autonomous social and economic power. As a result the pact could not play the role its Spanish and Latin American homologues played, and it quickly became little more than a symbol of dashed hopes among liberal intellectuals. The lesson that political institutions and mechanisms are abstracted from their economic and social context only at great peril is one I shall never forget.

At the same time, however, the equal and opposite temptation—to elaborate that very context at the expense of identifying the universal or generic qualities of particular concepts or institutions—is no better a solution, as was demonstrated by the highly touted project on "Civil Society in the Middle East," conceived and run by the team of political scientists Augustus Richard Norton and Farhad Kazemi. To their credit, both Norton and Kazemi are active members of the American Political Science Association and through the Conference Group on the Study of the Middle East, much of the work that went into this project enjoyed early exposure at annual APSA meetings. In commissioning the essays that were published in the two-volume set of the same name, however, Norton ultimately abandoned any pretense of a common definition of its central notion, "civil society." His discomfort is evident in his insistence that

> though scholars of the Middle East may debate civil society existentially, theoretically, conceptually, normatively, and ontologically, the simple fact is that civil society is today part of the political discourse in the Middle East. Scholastic debates notwithstanding, civil society is the locus for debate, discussion, and dialogue in the contemporary Middle East (Norton 1995–1996, p. 25).

Small wonder that the contributors retreated to description—albeit often very good, detailed, thoughtful, and perceptive description—instead of developing the common analytical, existential, theoretical, conceptual, or ontological framework that would have permitted, perhaps required, comparison with other times and places in the world, thereby enabling formulation and testing of explanatory hypotheses.

Between these two extremes is what is in my estimation the best single book to appear on the apparent democratization trend in the Muslim world in the last decade, *Democracy without Democrats*, an elegant collection of essays explicitly linking a variety of hypotheses about the nature of democratization and Middle Eastern cases (Salamé 1994). Perhaps tellingly, it includes only one American political scientist—John Waterbury—among its dozen contributors, however, and it is unlikely that more than a handful of the card-carrying members of the American Political Science Association have even heard of the volume, much less read and appreciated it. The reverse, however, is evidently not true. The editor, Ghassan Salamé, an estimable scholar and teacher of international relations in Paris, is a well-read and sophisticated consumer of contemporary American political science. His citations include not only American political scientists, historians, and economists who work on the Middle East, including Waterbury, Leonard Binder, Farhad Kazemi, Dankwart Rustow, Peter von Sivers, and Alan Richards, but American political scientists who do not work on the Middle East, including Schmitter and Adam Przeworski. Among the very perceptive essays in this volume are contributions by geographers, economists, and sociologists based in the Middle East and Europe, whose fine-grained appreciation of the nuance of politics in the region does not preclude sophisticated engagement with debates in political science about electoral engineering, political pacts, class politics, and rational bargaining.

Of course, for the last five or ten years at least, students of politics in the Middle East have had the excuse that current events have been unusually interesting: the end of the Cold War, the regional realignments signaled in the Persian Gulf war, the transformations marked in the Oslo peace agreements, the domestic challenges these agreements have met in both Israel and the Arab world have all had analysts of Middle East politics understandably mesmerized. In the meantime, however, the discipline of political science has been continuing to develop, and while description of these momentous changes is certainly a useful start, it is unlikely to give us much leverage in establishing general conditions for the success or failure, or even the initiation and consolidation, of processes associated with any of the values we have now declared for—be they peace, or human rights, or democracy, or something else altogether—in the Middle East or anywhere else. Few scholars of the Middle East are in a position to take much satisfaction in the disarray in post-Soviet studies, for we face dilemmas of comparable magnitude without even being fully aware of it. The end of the Cold War had its own particular dynamic in the Middle East and our failure to capture it is a measure of how little we understood its role in shaping politics in the region in the first place.

PROFESSIONAL INVOLVEMENT AND ISOLATION

The perplexity with which so many students of the Middle East approach their field in the late 1990s exacerbates a professional isolation that began much earlier. We are obsessively interested in the specificities of regional politics—the tribal support of Mu'ammar al-Qaddafi, the differential impact of the sanctions in Iraq, the prospects for succession in the Saudi monarchy, the doctrinal foundations of Islamist political activities, the health of numerous ailing political figures—which are obviously crucial to our comprehension and interpretation of those politics. Yet these are not the run-of-the-mill preoccupations of American political scientists, who by contrast are self-consciously at work developing and refining "modern" analytical tools, approaches, and methods. Little does it matter that most of these methods—technical quantitative and statistical methods, survey research and polling, formal modeling and game theory, for example—are so highly developed precisely because they lend themselves to examination of politics in industrial democracies, where census data, election polling, market research, behavioral psychology are all highly refined and easily accessible. These "modern" techniques developed in tandem with—and probably as a direct result of—the development of "modern" politics.

Yet what is the budding statistician to do when confronted with the fact that the figure for the total population of Saudi Arabia, not to say any break out of census data, is a state secret? How does median voter theory contribute to our assessment of the routine election-rigging in Morocco, Tunisia, or Egypt? What is the new institutionalist to do in the absence of clear property rights in the vast public sectors of most of the Middle East?

Obviously, for some students of political science, the answer is to abandon the Middle East and to flex their theoretical and methodological muscle in more fertile terrain—including Ames's Latin America. Those of us who, whether from inertia or affection, do not want to leave the Middle East to the theoretically unambitious or the methodologically uninformed are obliged, however, to consider the extent to which "non-modern" political institutions and behavior are amenable to "modern" scientific analysis. Can rational choice theory illuminate adherence to Hamas, might game theory clarify court politics in Morocco, could statistical analysis shed light on tribal feuds in Yemen?

To some degree the answer is yes. The limited survey research done in the Arab world has had disproportionately high payoffs, as both transient attitude shifts and more profound changes in conceptions of national identity have been revealed and verified (Tessler et al. 1987; Pollock 1992). Similarly, game and bargaining theory has been deployed provocatively to examine the negotiations that produced the Camp David Accords between Israel and Egypt (Telhami 1990). Waterbury's recent book (Waterbury 1993) on public enterprise in Egypt, India, Mexico, and Turkey probably did more to introduce scholars of public choice and collective action to Egypt and Turkey than any other single work, and it suggests potentially fruitful lines of inquiry for many of the students of political and economic liberalization in the Middle East and North Africa.

THE DISCIPLINE AND THE AREA STUDY: ENLARGING "MODERNITY"

If the study of the Middle East is to be enhanced by the approaches and techniques of modern political science, however, political science itself must be strengthened by the study of the Middle East. We must ask ourselves what our intimate knowledge of the Middle East might contribute to the development of the theories and methods of our discipline: what, in other words, can the study of Hamas tell us about rational choice theory? I believe the answer is probably quite a bit. There are already, in fact, theoretically ambitious political scientists working in the many very different veins of positive political economy, feminist theory, constructivist international relations, and other approaches current in contemporary political science, who are drawing on their expertise in the Middle East and North Africa. While there is still no obvious successor to the "transitions to democracy" literature that might serve as a common research agenda through which students of the Middle East will enter cross-regional, genuinely comparative debates about the nature of politics, three areas of inquiry seem particularly promising.

From the perspective of political liberalization, students of the Middle East clearly have much to contribute to discussions of the nature of economic conditions and constraints. Nearly all of the countries of the region have swollen public sectors, ambiguous property rights, a legacy of the soft-budget constraints associated with the rentier state whose effects on politics beg for sustained and systematic comparison with the former communist states of Eastern Europe, Russia, and Central Asia. Similarly, students of identity politics—ethnicity, religion, and nationalism—in the former communist world as well as much of Africa and South Asia have much to learn from and to offer their colleagues in Middle Eastern studies. Some of the most interesting work in these areas is being done by scholars working in the rational choice and collective action schools—particularly at their critical peripheries—and Middle Eastern scholars should be able to contribute productively to the discussions of the nature of rights and property in unregulated or informal economies or the importance of household and kinship in "framing" definitions of rational self-interest.

Similarly, in international relations, the Middle East has the potential to provide a particularly fertile testing ground for theories about the influence of international alliances in shaping domestic politics and about the role of norms in international politics. Astonishingly, despite regular reference to the importance of postwar American aid in shaping politics in South Korea, Taiwan, Greece, and Turkey, no systematic comparison of the influence of the Cold War in East Asia and the Middle East has yet been done. The Middle East also offers a potentially instructive terrain from which to examine changing norms in international relations through a comparison of the regional system that succeeded the collapse of the Ottoman Empire, with its formally sanctioned League of Nations mandates, and the postimperial system among the former Soviet Central Asian republics, with its much greater reliance on the informal influence of international NGOs.

Finally, in a more sociological, "new institutionalist" vein, there is much to be gained in continuing and adapting work begun by students of the state and state formation in, for example, a reexamination of the legacies of colonialism in the Middle East and North Africa. The European mandates in the Middle East reflected not only the imperatives of old-style imperialist rapacity—a long-standing and well-documented charge—but also the growth of the welfare state in much of the world. From the Soviet Union's construction of communism to the Keynesian responses to the interwar crises of capitalism, the norms of the welfare state were adopted throughout much of the industrializing world and they were reflected in the state institutions built in the Middle East and North Africa during that period. Far more than is usually acknowledged of the postwar "socialist" welfare state in the Middle East had its roots in the colonial era, in marked contrast to both European colonialism in sub-Saharan Africa and Japanese colonialism in East Asia.

There is much work in progress from which collective research agendas linking the preoccupations of the area study and the discipline can be built.

Some of this is by relatively well-established scholars, including Kiren Chaudhry's examination of the nature of markets, rents, and political reform (Chaudhry 1989), Gregory Gause's exploration of the nature of sovereignty in the region (Gause 1991), Robert Vitalis's investigation of the nature of class and power (Vitalis 1995), or Timothy Mitchell's critical deconstruction of the Egyptian state (Mitchell 1988, 1991). Perhaps most encouraging, however, are the increasing numbers of Ph.D. dissertations that exhibit both exceptional area expertise and substantial theoretical ambition. As a sampling, these include (but are by no means limited to) Steve King's examination of the micro-consequences of economic privatization in Tunisian local politics (King forthcoming); Vickie Langohr's comparison of Egypt's Muslim Brotherhood and India's BJP (Langohr forthcoming); Marc Lynch's analysis of the international politics of Jordanian national identity (Lynch forthcoming); and Joseph Massad's critical deconstruction of the creation of the postcolonial state in Jordan (Massad forthcoming).

Although I have disparaged the work done by many of the "democracy enthusiasts" in Middle Eastern studies, I must point out that the existence of a cohort of exceptionally talented young scholars willing and able to contribute simultaneously to the area study and the discipline is in part a reflection of genuine advances in the political science of the Middle East associated with the efforts to study and promote human rights and political democracy in the region. The relinquishing of old attachments to "value neutrality" and "scientific objectivity" permitted not only expressions of personal and professional political solidarity with local scholars and academics—see, for example, the work of the Committee on Academic Freedom of the Middle East Studies Association—but what in the colorless language of the education establishment is known as "field development"—scientific training and professional collaboration with local scholars. Nearly half of the contributors to the *Civil Society in the Middle East* volumes, for example, live and work in the Middle East. Just at the moment when political science research is becoming increasing collaborative, American students of the Middle East and North Africa are forging professional and collegial relationships with their European and Middle Eastern counterparts in far greater numbers. This itself will contribute to breaking down the parochialism which has so long characterized American political science, and much of the credit for that must go to American political scientists who see their scientific role as intimately linked to political commitments and responsibilities.

Ultimately, then, the universalistic pretensions that have so long bedeviled American political science in the association of "modern" political institutions and "modern" political science may well be challenged and transcended, through a renewed appreciation of the contribution that area studies can make to the formulation, testing, revision, and refinement of apparently universal scientific generalizations. If that is the outcome of the checkered history recounted here, it will have been well worth the experience.

REFERENCES

Ames, Barry. 1996. "Comparative Politics and the Replication Controversy." *APSA-CP: Newsletter of the APSA Organized Section in Comparative Politics* 17, 1 (Winter).

Anderson, Lisa. 1991. "Political Pacts, Liberalism and Democracy: The Tunisian National Pact of 1988." *Government and Opposition* 26, 2.

———. 1990. "Policy-Making and Theory-Building: American Political Science and the Islamic Middle East." In Hisham Sharabi, ed., *Theory, Politics and the Arab World*. New York: Routledge.

Chaudhry, Kiren. 1989. "The Price of Wealth: Business and State in Labor Remittance and Oil Economies." *International Organization* 43, 1.

Gause, F. Gregory, III. 1991. "Revolutionary Fevers and Regional Contagion: Domestic Structures and the 'Export' of Revolution in the Middle East." *Journal of South Asian and Middle Eastern Studies* 14, 3.

King, Steve. Forthcoming Ph.D. dissertation on the impact of economic privatization on local political alliances in Tunisia, Department of Politics, Princeton University.

Langohr, Vickie. Forthcoming. *Religious Nationalism in Egypt and India: The Muslim Brotherhood and the BJP.* Ph.D. dissertation, Columbia University.

Lynch, Marc. Forthcoming. *Contested Identity, Contested Security: The International Politics of Gardenia Identity.* Ph.D. dissertation, Cornell University.

Massad, Joseph. Forthcoming. *Negotiating National Identity and the Post-Colonial State: The Case of Jordan.* Ph.D. dissertation, Columbia University.

Mitchell, Timothy. 1991. "The Limits of the State: Beyond Statist Approaches and Their Critics." *American Political Science Review* 85, 2.

———. 1988. *Colonizing Egypt.* New York: Cambridge University Press.

Norton, Augustus Richard, ed. 1995–1996. *Civil Society in the Middle East.* 2 vols. Leiden: Brill.

O'Donnell, Guillermo, and Philippe C. Schmitter, eds. 1986. *Transitions from Authoritarian Rule: Tentative Conclusions about Uncertain Democracies.* Baltimore: Johns Hopkins University Press.

Pollock, David. 1992. *The "Arab Street"? Public Opinion in the Arab World.* Washington: Washington Institute for Near East Policy. (Policy Papers; 32).

Salamé, Ghassan, ed. 1994. *Democracy without Democrats? The Renewal of Politics in the Muslim World.* London: I. B. Tauris.

Telhami, Shibley. 1990. *Power and Leadership in International Bargaining: The Path to the Camp David Accords.* New York: Columbia University Press.

Tessler, Mark A., Monte Palmer, Tawfic E. Farah, and Barbara Lethem Ibrahim. 1987. *The Evaluation and Application of Survey Research in the Arab World.* Boulder: Westview.

Vitalis, Robert. 1995. *When Capitalists Collide: Business Conflict and the End of Empire in Egypt.* Berkeley: University of California Press.

Waterbury, John. 1993. *Exposed to Innumerable Delusions: Public Enterprise and State Power in Egypt, India, Mexico and Turkey.* New York: Cambridge University Press.

2. | **State-Society Relations**
Algeria as a Case Study

John P. Entelis

AUTHORITARIANISM AND DEMOCRACY

Two decades ago, Michael Hudson wrote in his path-breaking book on Arab politics: "The central problem of government in the Arab world today is political legitimacy. The shortage of this indispensable political resource largely accounts for the [unpredictable] nature of Arab politics and the autocratic . . . character of all the present Arab governments" (Hudson 1977, p. 2). Despite the passage of time and the movement of the international political economy toward a more democratic and therefore more legitimate world order, many Arab regimes continue to lack in this essential "political resource." The states of North Africa, as well as other Arab states and many countries in the developing world more generally, share a common predicament: public contestation and the right to participate—democracy's core principles (Dahl 1971) —are virtually nonexistent, or at least seriously compromised.

This situation has led to differing assessments. On the one hand, some observers, including Hudson, focus on authoritarianism as the region's main dependent variable (Hudson 1995, p. 61). Notwithstanding the incipient experiments with political liberalization and democratization that were begun in the 1980s, they note with disappointment "the return of the state" and its

Portions of this chapter first appeared in earlier form in the following publications: "Introduction." State and Society in Algeria. Ed. John P. Entelis and Phillip C. Naylor. Boulder: Westview, 1992, pp. 1–30; "Islam, Democracy, and the State: The Reemergence of Authoritarian Politics in Algeria." Islamism and Secularism in North Africa. Ed. John Ruedy. New York: St. Martin's, 1994, pp. 219–251; and "Civil Society and the Authoritarian Temptation in Algerian Politics: Islamic Democracy vs. the Centralized State." Civil Society in the Middle East. Ed. Augustus Richard Norton, 1995–1996, pp. 45–86.

national security (*mukhabarat*) apparatus, which have combined to subvert civil society and thwart democracy's emergence. In the same vein, Jill Crystal makes clear the complex political economy forces which have sustained Arab authoritarian politics these last fifty years (Crystal 1994). On the other hand, there are serious students of the Middle East who believe that Arab authoritarianism is not inevitable. These analysts argue that change is coming, and they sometimes assert that pressures for political liberalization have increased following the Gulf war of 1990–1991 (Brynen, Korany, and Noble 1995). Also associated with this tendency is the work of Augustus Richard Norton and his collaborators (Norton 1995–1996), who assert that a reanimated and revitalized "civil society" is leading to the emergence of a "political society," upon which a viable democracy can in turn be built.

A common concern for comparative and cross-regional political theory informs these competing perspectives. At the heart of this preoccupation is a desire to move away from "exceptionalist," "Orientalist," or "essentialist" explanations of Arab state and society—ones that are either culturally deterministic or externally imposed. In their place, scholars have employed any number of plausible analytical constructs and frameworks in an effort to place Arab political processes within the disciplinary perspective of social science inquiry. Such constructs and frameworks include, inter alia, political culture (Hudson 1995, Entelis 1996), political economy (Chaudhry 1994, Bellin 1995, Anderson 1995, Waterbury 1993, Tessler 1997), civil society (Norton 1995–1996; Bellin 1994), the state (Anderson 1987), authoritarianism (Crystal 1994), religion and politics (Eickelman and Piscatori 1996), political democracy (Salamé 1994; Brynen, Korany, and Noble 1995), neopatriarchy (Sharabi 1988), and class (Amin 1992).

In the final analysis, these analysts assume that the study of Arab politics is no different from the study of politics elsewhere—who gets what, when, and how (Lasswell 1958). In the modern period, political activity in the Arab world has been centered on the behavior of relatively small groups of individuals who have maintained power over long periods of time through uneven combinations of consent and coercion. Is this condition permanent or open to change? Further, in either case, what particular domestic and/or international circumstances are conducive to continuity and/or change? And finally, are the most useful and satisfying answers to these questions provided by insights of disciplinary social science or area studies? Answers to these and related questions can be gained only through empirical research.

North Africa represents an important subregional context for efforts to contribute to comparative empirical theory, and the case of Algeria in particular offers an excellent opportunity to explicate the workings of an authoritarian-democratic dialectic that is common in the Middle East. More specifically, Algeria's experience illuminates the following pattern: authoritarianism and economic crisis lead to an expanded civil society and, if left "untamed," this results in a form of "savage" democracy; this, in turn, brings political repression and fosters a new political economy crisis, which soon degenerates into a revival of military-initiated state repression; and at this point the cycle begins again.

Against this background, the present report examines state-society relations, in Algeria as well as more generally, from the competing perspectives of culture, conspiracy, and civil society. In so doing, it seeks to demonstrate both that the study of a Middle East case can contribute to the development of generalizable social science insights, and, correspondingly, that the case itself can be illuminated by social science theory. While the Algerian case is unique in many ways, its political development is not fully dependent on peculiar cultural factors. On the contrary, it resembles in important respects patterns of political behavior occurring elsewhere. By identifying these patterns and their underlying causal mechanisms, an analysis of the Algerian experience can illustrate the productive interaction between social science theory and empirical reality in the study of the Middle East.

At the same time, Algeria cannot be understood through the lens of comparative empirical theory alone. Historical and other contextual factors must also be considered in order to provide a comprehensive and sensitive explanation of political dynamics in Algeria, both in general and with respect to patterns of authoritarianism and democracy in particular. In this connection, the present analysis provides additional evidence that both area studies *and* social science approaches to inquiry are necessary in order to advance our understanding of Middle Eastern politics.

POLITICAL CHANGE AND STATE-SOCIETY RELATIONS

An overview of state-society relations in the contemporary Arab world will help to place the Algerian case in perspective and will indicate the broader lessons of which it is indicative. Since the early 1960s, politics in the Middle East and North Africa has been characterized by strong state-centered tendencies. For our purposes, the state can be defined as "an organization *within* the society where it coexists and interacts with other formal and informal organizations from families to economic enterprises or religious organizations. It is, however, distinguished from the myriad of other organizations in seeking predominance over them and in aiming to institute binding rules regarding the other organizations' activities" (Azarya 1988, p. 10).

The mass mobilizing state, an all-pervasive bureaucracy, a mass production factory system, and an official national culture have become the hallmarks of state-building in the Arab world. A central feature of this authoritarian system is the role played by the internal security apparatus, the *mukhabarat*. Indeed, a "two-state" system has long operated among the so-called socialist republics (Richards and Waterbury 1990), as well as among the liberal and absolute monarchies of the Arab world. A secret police structure exists alongside a military-bureaucratic structure, with the former dominating everyday life and serving as the ultimate regulator of civil and political existence. Some Arab critics have gone so far as to characterize the mukhabarat state, regardless of its legal and political forms and structures, as little more than a modernized version of the traditional patriarchal sultanate (Sharabi 1988, p. 7).

The growth of the bureaucratic or mukhabarat state has been a major political fact of the contemporary Arab world, and with it has come a pronounced tendency toward authoritarian politics. "Those who control the Arab state," Hudson has observed, "now have more of an advantage over the opposition than was the case three decades ago. Over the same period there has been a separate but not unrelated decline in autonomous political action and expression originating in civil society" (Hudson 1988, p. 161). Most disturbing of all has been the human rights records of these mukhabarat states, which have ranged from troubling to appalling to abysmal.

The fact that some of these autocratic regimes, mainly those of minimally populated states with vast oil wealth, have policy outcomes equal or superior to democratic systems in terms of growth, equity, or quality of life says little about their long-term political legitimacy (Hudson 1988, p. 159). Indeed, the incredible speed with which Kuwait disappeared from the map of nation-states following Iraq's invasion and occupation in August 1990 is testimony to the weak legitimacy that existed in that autocratic microstate, despite its enviable status as one of the world's wealthiest countries.

By the early 1980s, it was assumed that the Arab state had "won the game" vis-à-vis civil society, and also that technocratic norms and political expediency had displaced more ideological and "value-impregnated" formulae as the basis for state-society relations (Hudson 1988, p. 161). Yet this condition of pervasive authoritarianism is not permanent. Indeed, the authoritarian state in North Africa and elsewhere has in recent years been experiencing concurrent crises with the potential to alter its political character in fundamental ways. The crisis of authoritarianism is worldwide, moreover, and has called into question both the legitimacy and the competence of all manner of authoritarian political systems (Pye 1990, p. 5).

With few exceptions (notably in the hydrocarbon and banking sectors), state-owned enterprise has proven to be unprofitable on all accounts. Such ventures have not only failed to meet the sociopolitical and economic agendas for which they were originally intended, but their steep requirements —steady capital flows, high levels of investment, and subsidization—have also gradually undermined national economies (Richards and Waterbury 1990, p. 219). Similarly, large overextended state bureaucracies have been unable to cope with the demands of complex diversified economies, and poorly implemented heavy industrialization initiatives have employed labor and capital inefficiently and been unable to produce for competitive export (Richards and Waterbury 1990, p. 236). Finally, rapid population growth has siphoned the benefits of state-led structural change, absorbing potential income increases.

Across the Afro-Arab world, poor government performance is also reflected in service restrictions or curtailments, in erratic capital flows, and in consumer goods shortages. These problems in turn provoke criticism from diverse quarters and further expose the inability of ruling elites to fulfill expectations of an improved standard of living.

The consequences of and responses to this interrelated political and economic crisis have varied widely, ranging from direct transitions to democracy, as in Eastern Europe, to increased repression, as in China. But whatever the style, content, or configuration of the response, it is clear that authoritarian politics has failed to provide the purposeful efficiency promised by dictatorial rulers and governing one-party states. As elsewhere, the political systems of the Arab world, including those in North Africa, have failed to deliver on their exaggerated promises, demonstrating, ultimately, that the presumed advantage of authoritarian politics for economic development is but a mirage (Pye 1990, p. 7). There has accordingly been a great loss of confidence among both rulers and ruled about the efficacy of state intervention, as well as a serious erosion more generally of the popular legitimacy of most regimes (Bratton 1989, p. 410).

In the hope of reversing or at least slowing these trends, state economic policy is increasingly placing emphasis on the private sector, on the reform of public-sector decision making, on an opening to international capital, and on greater reliance on market forces. The degree of state withdrawal should not be overstated, however. Despite a Maghribi version of perestroika, state autonomy persists. The international dimension partly explains this phenomenon: "Insofar as a country 'opens up' to the rest of the world, the state will have a central role in mediating between the domestic society and international actors" (Richards and Waterbury 1990, pp. 238–239).

Yet the state is indeed retreating, albeit unevenly, and this is the case in the political as well as the economic sphere. The harsh reality of state formation in the Middle East and North Africa is like that in many other regions of the Third World: the apparatus of governance has begun to crumble before it has been fully consolidated. Michael Bratton has made this point in his analysis of sub-Saharan Africa: "There is a crisis of political authority that is just as severe as the crisis of economic production. These two crises are intimately interrelated, each being both a cause and an effect of the other" (Bratton 1989, p. 409). Like its neighbors to the south, North Africa is witnessing a self-perpetuating cycle of change "in which weak states engender anemic economies whose poor performance in turn further undermines the capacity of the state apparatus" (Bratton 1989, p. 409). Were it not for the oil and natural gas wealth of a number of Middle Eastern–North African countries, state authority would have faltered earlier.

State-society relations thus stand at a crossroads in the Middle East and North Africa. The trend of expanding political control has peaked as socioeconomic crises force the state to retreat from overambitious commitments. Based on experience elsewhere, a loosening of regulations governing economic activity can be expected to produce pressures for political liberalization. Moreover, although government willingness to promote economic liberalization has for the most part been reciprocated only partially in the political sphere, competition between the state and civil society has been intensifying since the late 1980s. Poor state performance and the lessening of authoritarian control have enlarged the political space within which associational life and other aspects of civil society are able to thrive. This is illustrated by the situation in the Maghrib, as well as other parts of the Arab world, where Islamic, civic, secular, feminist, student, labor, and farmer groups have had greater opportunities to attract a following, develop a bureaucratic form, and formulate policy alternatives (see Bratton 1989, p. 412).

These political and economic dynamics have the potential to dramatically alter the patterns of state-society relations that have been in existence in North Africa for several decades. And while the relationships between the state and civil society that will emerge are yet to be determined, present-day dynamics are creating both political opportunities and political costs—opportunities for the disenfranchised and costs for the ruling class.

CULTURE, CONSPIRACY, AND CIVIL SOCIETY: THE ALGERIAN CASE IN THEORETICAL CONTEXT

The experience of Algeria is illustrative of this authoritarian crisis. Within the Middle East and North Africa, postindependence Algeria was perhaps the most successful example of the bureaucratic-authoritarian state (Entelis 1986). Supported by impressive hydrocarbon resources, a revolutionary elite created one of the Third World's most centralized systems of command and control aimed at transforming a backward agricultural society into a modern industrialized state—proud and powerful.

Given the visionary objectives of the country's radical leadership, it seemed only natural that the state would assume the leading role in this revolutionary transformation. A sort of "ruling bargain" was struck by the leadership with the Algerian people at independence, "under which the populace gave up its rights to independent political activity in return for the state's provision of social welfare" (Brumberg 1990, p. 120).

Throughout most of independent Algeria's history, civil society and mass organizations were thus subordinated to the state-party apparatus and relegated to roles of recruitment and propaganda. From 1968 until 1989, all mass associations, including those ostensibly representing workers, students, women, and the like, operated under the direct administration of the ruling party, the National Liberation Front (FLN), thereby bolstering the party's image as the sole representative of the country's populace while simultaneously inhibiting the development of any independent political organization or activity. Operating in the service of party and state, these associations worked to mobilize mass support for the ruling elite and devoted little attention to the particular interests of the groups they claimed to represent.

For many within and outside the region, the Algerian technocratic state of the 1970s came to represent the quintessential model of how autonomous development could take place free of interventionist influence from domestic social forces or their global collaborators. By the mid-1980s, however, as world oil and natural gas prices declined, massive industrial projects faltered or collapsed altogether, and population growth soared, it became obvious that something had gone seriously wrong with this bureaucratic-authoritarian model of development.

No single event so revealed the depth of the regime's failure as the nation-wide riots of October 1988, whose scope, destructiveness, and resulting loss of life rocked the Algerian state to its very foundations. Autonomous social forces, long regarded as either impotent or subservient to the regime, emerged with incredible vigor, if not vengeance, to challenge the hegemony of state power. In addition, the resultant legalization of political parties in 1989 allowed a large number of independent interest groups to present themselves as political parties, attesting further to the pervasive nature of associational life in Algerian politics despite the state's program of "depoliticization" and control. All in all, literally thousands of independent associations, professional groupings, and political parties emerged in the two years following the loosening of government restrictions on political activity.

While evidence from several quarters indicates that civil society in North Africa is developing greater powers of autonomy vis-à-vis the state than had originally been assumed, differing regime responses make it difficult to determine whether the region is "at the dawning of a new era in which the state will confine itself to regulating market economies or merely in a period of stock taking and statist regrouping" (Richards and Waterbury 1990, p. 217). In Algeria, as well as the Middle East and North Africa more generally, and also in other parts of the Third World, state capabilities remain impressive and incumbent elites are unlikely to surrender power without a fight.

Wavering between the advantages of increased authoritarianism and the benefits of political openness, the future of these states is unclear, and an understanding of the mechanisms of political change is therefore necessary in order to anticipate future developments. Toward this end, one helpful approach is grounded in the analytic construct of civil society. This competes with two other theoretical perspectives: culture and conspiracy.

A culture approach takes a historically oriented view of Algeria, in which both precolonial habits and practices reinforced by 130 years of French rule are seen as having created an "authoritarian political culture" (APC). This APC, so it is argued, has been further reinforced by over thirty years of one-party socialist rule. According to this perspective, authoritarianism in Algeria reflects a cultural predisposition, and inasmuch as culture changes very slowly, significant developments related to civil society, pluralism, or democracy should not be expected any time soon.

A conspiracy approach is essentially an elitist interpretation of political life, in which ruling elites in the army, bureaucracy, dominant party, and government manage the affairs of state and society and seek to preserve the status quo. Through education and privileged access to power and resources, these elites constitute the authentic and appropriate expression of Algerian politics. To understand current developments in the country, therefore, one simply observes the patterns of elite behavior, giving scant attention to broader social forces, political dynamics, or economic imperatives. In this view, the crisis in Algeria is the result of mismanagement by the president, high army officers, the ruling party, and even the leaders of the Islamist opposition. These actors either misread their cues or miscalculated their collaborators' intentions. Consequently, analysts may assess the future by watching to see whether relevant political actors seek to reestablish preexisting patterns and, if so, how they structure the rules of the political game.

According to the perspectives of both culture and conspiracy, democracy—whether procedural, normative, or substantive—will be impossible to achieve in the Algerian context for at least the near and intermediate future. A different dynamic is posited by the civil society approach, however.

A civil society approach assumes that Algeria has not been standing still these last two centuries, stuck in a near-permanent state of backwardness, retardation, and immobility. Rather, the very opposite is argued—Algeria has been experiencing a dramatic transformation. Internal socioeconomic development, accelerated by exposure to modern education, technology, administration, and communications, has created a dynamic society whose "civil" identities were long suppressed by an authoritarian political order, first imposed by the French and then by a successor state. This approach also emphasizes Algeria's transformation into a modern society, fully capable of participating in the modern world and able to express its popular will through political democracy. When given an opportunity, as in the period from late 1988 until early 1992, the full range of behavioral, institutional, and attitudinal attributes associated with pluralistic life and an animated civil society became evident.

Reanimated civil society provided the impetus for a contentious democracy during this period, one that behaved according to democracy's own rules and thus sought to mediate differences within civil society as part of a broader process of consensus building and expanding political legitimacy. Within this environment, Islamist groups competed equally with others for the hearts, minds, and votes of the Algerian people. That the Islamic Salvation Front (FIS) was more successful than its rivals in these efforts was testimony to the power of its message and the efficacy of its organization, rather than to the fatalistic workings of "culture" or the "conspiratorial" efforts of ruling elites.

CIVIL SOCIETY AND DEMOCRACY IN ALGERIA

While civil society may be a critical factor in Algeria's political transformation, it must be placed within a broader political context in order to adequately account for Algeria's movement toward political liberalization and its subsequent reversion to authoritarianism. To this end, it is useful to analyze the case of Algeria within the broader comparative frameworks of democratic transition theory, civil society development, and counterhegemonic theory.

Civil society, as the site which connects society and the state, is "absolutely indispensable for democracy" because a society that does not have free individual and group expression in nonpolitical matters is unlikely to make an exception for those who are political (Chandhoke 1995, p. 40). It comes as no surprise, therefore, that countries with few civil liberties also have limited political rights. However, civil society as an arena in which sociological space is created and autonomous action enhanced among ordinary citizens is separate from but related to civil society as an arena for political organization and the mobilization of groups seeking to influence or capture political power. As Assad's Syria and Mubarak's Egypt clearly reveal, an expansive civil society can be reflected in the existence of numerous functional, professional, social, cultural, economic, and business associations without there being effective or autonomous political organizations capable of challenging the hegemony of the state. The growth of civil society, by itself, is thus insufficient to guarantee the emergence of either political liberalism or political democracy.

For the latter to take place, groups that see as their primary mission the establishment of an alternative political regime must be permitted to exist. Without political choice or the presence of a viable political alternative, democracy has virtually no meaning. In Algeria, both features of civil society existed from late 1988 to early 1992, although, to be sure, the necessary preconditions for the emergence of those features had evolved over time. That is, a vibrant civil society fostered a dynamic political society that saw the emergence of diverse and contentious political groupings competing for the same political space in their quest for national power. The most effective of these groups were the Islamists.

That such a civil society was possible recalls Gramsci's account of how civil society can emerge within the context of an oppressive state. In a Gramscian sense, "social groups would form on the basis of independently articulated interests and goals, limiting their goals to those which would not threaten the power or legitimacy of the regime. The interpretation and expression of interests would be pursued independently of (though necessarily related to) the structure of state domination and economic relations" (Weigle and Butterfield 1992, p. 4).

The experience of Algeria thus follows the stages of civil society development witnessed elsewhere in formerly authoritarian political systems (Weigle and Butterfield 1992, p. 1). There is first a defensive stage "in which private individuals and independent groups actively or passively defend their autonomy vis-à-vis the party-state." Then there is an emergent stage in which "independent social groups or movements seek limited goals in a widened public sphere which is sanctioned or conceded by the reforming party-state." In a third, mobilizational phase, the legitimacy of the party-state is undermined by independent groups or movements who offer alternative forms of governance to an increasingly politicized society. Finally, in an institutional stage, "publicly supported leaders enact laws guaranteeing autonomy of social action, leading to a contractual relationship between state and society regulated eventually by free elections." In the relatively brief period from October 1988 to the coup d'état of January 1992, Algeria almost completed the fourth and final stage of an emerging civil society. While that process has been halted since early 1992, all of the ingredients that were necessary for the "takeoff" stage of civil and political society remain in place, ready for resurrection.

Algeria's short-lived political opening demonstrates the centrality of the "organization of counterhegemony," an analytical construction that is again consistent with the pertinent theoretical literature in political science. As Adam Przeworski writes:

> a common feature of dictatorships, whatever mix of inducements and constraints they use, is that they cannot and do not tolerate independent organizations. The reason is that as long as no collective alternatives are available, individual attitudes toward the regime matter little for its stability. . . . What is threatening to authoritarian regimes is not the breakdown of legitimacy but the organization of counterhegemony: collective projects for an alternative future. Only when collective alternatives are available does political choice become available to isolated individuals (1991, pp. 54–55).

Continuing, Przeworski observes that at some moment a group within the authoritarian power establishment, or the leader himself, decides to tolerate autonomous organization in civil society. This marks the onset of liberalization, suggesting to civil society that at least some forms of autonomous organizations will not be repressed (Przeworski 1991, p. 56).

In the case of Algeria, this process began modestly with the law of associations of 12 July 1987, and then accelerated with the amended constitution of 1989 that permitted the establishment of independent political organizations, including the FIS. Pressures both from above (failed political economy policies) and from below (the October 1988 riots) help to explain Algeria's push towards liberalization. Further, President Chadli Benjedid and other liberalizers saw the possibility of an alliance with certain forces—Islamists in this case. Finally, power struggles between hardliners and reformers contributed significantly to Algeria's political opening.

What reformers failed to appreciate, however, was the congenital character of civil society—deeply rooted, long developed, anticipatory, and socialized. Given the danger of a reprise of October 1988, they hoped to control the opening of political space. As Przeworski notes, the project of all liberalizers "is to relax social tension and to strengthen their position in the power bloc by broadening the social base of the regime: to allow some autonomous organization of the civil society and to incorporate the new groups into the authoritarian institution" (Przeworski 1991, p. 57). This contingent liberalization usually fails to achieve its objectives, however, because of the "thaw" principle: "a melting of the iceberg of civil society that overflows the dams of the authoritarian regime" (Przeworski 1991, p. 58). And this is precisely what happened in Algeria in 1989–1991. Once repression was removed, the first reaction was an outburst of autonomous organization in the civil society. Almost overnight, independent parties, unions, associations, and newspapers sprang up and demanded the right to be heard.

As scores of autonomous and semiautonomous associations, groups, and movements pressed their claims on the state, authoritarian structures became incapable of responding effectively or fully. A kind of *décalage* emerged between the autonomous organizations of civil society and the closed character of state institutions, with the street the only arena in which newly organized groups could struggle for their values and interests. Inevitably, the struggle for democracy assumed a mass character, and liberalization thus had the consequence of destabilizing the existing order. Mass demonstrations soon undermined the position of the liberalizers in the authoritarian bloc and led to the president's forced resignation by the military on 11 January 1992.

When faced with such conditions, only three alternatives present themselves: incorporate the few groups that can be absorbed and repress everyone else; open up the system to genuine political democracy; or return to the authoritarian stasis. Algeria's military decided on the last, to the tragedy of thousands of killed, wounded, and imprisoned Algerian men and women. In choosing this course, the army was moving to protect its privileged position. It had been discredited in the eyes of most Algerians by its performance in the October 1988 riots, and as a consequence, newly formed autonomous organizations within civil society had to a dangerous degree ignored its interests during a period when the control of national power was being contested.

What those currently struggling to stay in power apparently fail to appreciate, and as experiences in postauthoritarian states elsewhere have shown (Weigle and Butterfield 1992, pp. 5–8), the crisis had its roots in the failure of the incumbent regime to adequately "perform self-defined functions of value formation and interest representation." Despite a plethora of institutional, ideological, and political-economic incentives, the Algerian authoritarian state failed to impose its "value package" on society. Rather, while elements of the socialist discourse found root in populist Islam's own social activist orientation, the official discourse was for the most part conducted in one language while the popular social and cultural discourse functioned in another. In addition, as with other postcolonial regimes where "ruling parties [acted] as state instruments more than citizen representatives" (Vatin 1987, p. 174), the government's persistent claim "to hegemony of interest representation and control of channels of participation" (Weigle and Butterfield 1992, p. 8) became steadily less credible, further widening the value gap between the political elite and populace.

In sum, failure in value formation and interest representation led to incremental political liberalization, which in turn rapidly accelerated and reanimated civil society. The latter fostered a political environment conducive to counterhegemonic organization that challenged the status quo through democratic means. Fearful of complete defeat, hegemonic forces responded by reimposing the authoritarian stasis Civil war ensued.

ALGERIA: HISTORICAL CONTEXT

Algeria's experience resembles that of other North African societies in several ways, but its distinctive history and often traumatic past have also shaped the development of its civil society, including the emergence of political pluralism and the establishment of democratic institutions and practices. An understanding of present-day Algeria thus requires an appreciation of the country's complex political evolution, indicating the need for substantive knowledge as well as a comparative perspective and a grounding in political science theory.

Algeria's historical complexity explains the coexistence of two diametrically opposed yet powerful tendencies in Algerian political history: political authoritarianism (the tendency towards centralized governance) and political democracy (the desire for choice and autonomy). Unlike any other Third World country, with the possible exceptions of South Africa and Palestine, Algeria's 132 years of colonial domination were unique in the brutality and destructiveness, not only in terms of lives lost but also in the impact of colonial domination on the totality of social, economic, and cultural circumstances. The continuous struggle for physical, moral, and cultural survival and assertion during the long years of occupation created a distinctive Algerian identity and political culture—one nurtured in an environment of fear, suspicion, and distrust of all things foreign while reaffirming the primacy of and pride in all things nativistic. This colonial experience not only engendered hostility to France and the West, it also fostered a strong nationalist consciousness and sense of political community. In addition, an underlying fear of (re)separation, (re)dislocation, and (re)destruction left a residue of authoritarianism, in whose name law and order are often invoked.

Further, the nearly eight-year struggle for independence (November 1954–July 1962), in which a bloody revolutionary war of national liberation was conducted countrywide, instilled a powerful sense of populist accomplishment. The Algerian war of national liberation left a deep sense of hard-won pride in the body politic, reaffirming the primacy of a national identity that transcended the internecine quarrels dividing the political elite. In this regard, Algeria's war of independence, although bloody and traumatic, built upon its twin precolonial and colonial legacies to confirm the country's national integrity and populist legitimacy. It also fostered, however, an authoritarian streak that renegade elites have cruelly exploited to the tragic disadvantage of the general public.

In the first two decades of its independence, Algeria's pursuit of an ideology of socialist planning and management further enhanced its sense of historic purpose and sociopolitical uniqueness. Although it would eventually prove to be an economic failure of huge proportions, Algeria's socialist orientation at the time reinforced its sense of populist purpose and its historically developed self-definition in terms of "rugged collectivism," national integrity, and revolutionary ethos. During the thirteen-year rule of Houari Boumediene (1965–1978), these experiences concretized an evolutionary process of nation-building and political development in which participatory politics, albeit from above, advanced significantly.

Finally, Algeria's experience has affected its foreign policy orientation and created yet another distinctive feature in its political history. Employing a strategy of militant "Third Worldism," the country sought to establish abroad what it was working to create at home: namely, a powerful, independent, and secure international political-economic order, free of external control either by global superpowers or by multinational corporations (Mortimer 1970, 1984a, 1984b). Within various regional and international fora, Algeria pursued a policy of political autonomy and economic self-sufficiency that was consistent with its strong sense of national pride and socialist purpose.

On the other hand, exposure to the Western world during both the colonial and postcolonial eras introduced more modern forms of social activism and political participation. Specifically, intensive and sustained periods of travel, study, work, and personal interactions between Algerian and European societies, along with the creation of advanced systems of telecommunications and broadcasting, introduced Algerians to alternative forms of political expression that challenged the authoritarian political order of the state while invigorating preexisting Islamist populist and protodemocratic tendencies.

From Algeria's early modern history, then, the dialectical process of promoting harmony and political unanimity in pursuit of freedom and autonomy has created a bifurcated political culture, one that can inspire both political authoritarianism and political democracy. The long period of colonial domination and the need to maintain a sense of identity at all costs, compounded by the independence war's need to foster cooperation and solidarity in the face of a more powerful enemy, engendered an enduring sense of national identity and political purpose. In addition, however, these experiences also promoted a tendency to justify political control from above as necessary to combat "enemies" of the state, whether of external or internal origin.

Knowledge of Algeria's unique history is necessary not only for a proper analysis of civil society and the country's authoritarian inclinations, but also to understand the emergence of a democratic movement in the late 1980s and early 1990s. That Algeria was able to embark on this process in a spontaneous and comprehensive way, unmatched anywhere in the Arab world, reflects the long and tortuous evolution of its nationhood, political identity, socialist consciousness, and international stature and respect. Without these preconditions, it is highly unlikely that pluralist politics would have emerged as quickly, forcefully, and widely as they did in the 1980s. In this regard, and in a manner similar to its other pathbreaking roles, Algeria's experiment in democracy went beyond anything as yet undertaken in the Arab-Islamic world.

STATE-SOCIETY RELATIONS AND PROSPECTS FOR DEMOCRACY IN NORTH AFRICA

As the case of Algeria has demonstrated, the dramatic failures of command economies and top-down political orders have not ensured a transition to democracy. On the contrary, market forces have yet to overcome entrenched bureaucracies in the Maghrib. Political democracy has often come to mean little more than new slogans, altered party labels, and manipulative discourses unrelated to a fundamental appreciation of individual rights, human liberties, freedom of choice, respect for differences, sociopolitical pluralism, and the legitimacy of majority rule. Yet what is different today is that the forces of globalization have made it more difficult for a political regime to mobilize and dominate a society. The inability of centralized states to move societies forward has been telling, and the limitations of "sheer political will" have not been lost on local populations (Pye 1990, p. 9).

Clearly, the process of transition from crisis to transformation in the Middle East and North Africa is both difficult and long, as the experience of the West illustrates as well. More important, perhaps, is that in all the crises of authoritarianism there emerges a fundamental clash between the world culture associated with globalization and a country's national political culture. The imperatives of globally oriented Western-centric orders—materialism, modernism, mechanism—are frequently at odds with fundamental collective needs for national integrity and a sense of communal self-identity. However, as described by Lucian Pye in general theoretical terms, while the confrontation of particular national values with "universal standards" is inherently destabilizing, it at the same time produces a vital social amalgam for developing states. "The former are essential for economic performance and effectiveness, and the latter are critical for creating national loyalties and distinctive national political styles" (1990, p. 11).

In the Maghrib today, this conflict between the power of "technocratic rationality" and indigenous discourse is deep and widespread. Probably in no other region of the Islamic world does the globalization process take place in the context of such constant battling between two uneven sovereign forces—

the impersonal and universalistic requirements of the world culture as articulated by Westernized national elites, and the particularistic passions of politics and of group identity which find their most visible expression in Islamic revivalist movements. What seems clear is that the direction and extent of political change will be determined by the ways in which particular political cultures come to terms with such conflict. While all cultures are to some degree protective of their indigenous integrity, Maghribi political culture—with Islam at its core—is particularly sensitive to perceived threats from foreign ideas and practices.

Whatever the eventual outcome of this crisis, it is clear that the psychological shock experienced by rulers and followers alike at the failure of authoritarianism is critical to the weakening legitimacy of incumbent authoritarian leaders. It is also crucial in raising levels of political consciousness and education among the masses, so as to prepare them for taking charge of their own political destiny. In North Africa this process is probably most advanced in Algeria and least developed in Morocco.

The failure of authoritarianism is important for additional reasons. First, failure reveals the fallibility of human leadership. Political rulers are not supermen, whatever else King Hassan II, Zine el-Abidine Ben Ali, or Liamine Zeroual—the leaders of Morocco, Tunisia, and Algeria, respectively—may believe. This realization by both elites and masses provides a second, related lesson: namely, as Pye writes, that it is thinkable "to accept the risks of allowing power to be transferred to others who can then have their turn at being fallible" (Pye 1990, p. 15).

To the degree that leaders and their publics absorb these two lessons of failure, "it is possible for the society to realize 'true' democratic politics" (Pye 1990, p. 15). Admittedly, long years of authoritarian rule in Algeria and the rest of the Maghrib do not predispose North Africans to accept the uncertainties of a society organized around democratic politics. Also, certain elements of the traditional political culture are suspicious, if not disdainful, of the spirit of competition and compromise, and such attitudes, whatever their sources or manifestations, inhibit development of the ethos of pluralism and tolerance that is necessary for democratic politics. Yet, in the final analysis, there may be a certain inevitability about the processes of global modernization and the resultant diversification of social, economic, and political life.

And this inevitability may have arrived in the Maghrib sooner than anticipated; the exhaustion of the authoritarian state's technological, bureaucratic, and moral capabilities is becoming increasingly apparent. Until recently, the cost of suppression was lower than the cost of accommodation, but this situation may now be changing, especially in Algeria where the political, moral, and economic costs of a bloody civil war continue to mount. In an important sense, this is the lesson of the Iranian revolution, and, on a smaller scale, the Palestinian *intifada*: that civil society has the intrinsic power to survive and eventually to overcome state power, and that state reliance on modern control technologies cannot substitute indefinitely for political legitimacy.

25

CONCLUSION

The future of North African politics remains uncertain, but insights from both comparative theory and area studies may help researchers understand the implications of recent political events. While the persistence of authoritarianism in the Middle East is often analyzed in culturally deterministic terms, the case of Algeria shows that recent political changes can be understood through the lens of a broader theoretical perspective which highlights the importance of socioeconomic forces and role of civil society. Algeria, like other developing countries, has followed a cycle where political repression, economic crisis, and inadequate interest representation have led to political liberalization, counterhegemonic organization, and renewed political oppression.

Algeria's experience is in some ways unique, however. The wide emergence of pluralist politics and the scope of its democratic experiment go further than that of any other regime in the Arab-Islamic world, and this can only be understood by examining the country's historical experience and the development of its sense of nationhood and political consciousness. The present analysis thus demonstrates that broad comparative theory in conjunction with regional expertise provides the best and most comprehensive approach for studying political change in the Middle East. Further, applying comparative theory to the Algerian case not only clarifies that country's experience, it also contributes to the cumulativeness and generalizability of comparative theory.

A question remains. As we approach the year 2000, are we at the end of an era in the process of regime and state formation? Four decades have passed since the North African nations won independence, and over time disillusionment and frustration have replaced high political, social, and economic expectations. There is a sense that existing systems of rule must be brought to some form of closure, a notion that emerges from both a pervasive general cynicism and the increasing political acumen of the population at large (Richards and Waterbury 1990, p. 329). Yet the present-day political milieu is delicately balanced. In the final analysis, therefore, one needs to ask whether the vigorous expression of associational life can be an effective counterweight to the state in North Africa in general and in Algeria in particular. Despite its animated status, civil society has yet to create a democratic political order. Indeed, nowhere in the Arab world has a multiparty election in a formerly one-party state directly replaced the party in power. The true measure of civil society's autonomy and influence, as well as the true test of Middle Eastern democracy as both concept and condition, will occur only when such transitions take place.

REFERENCES

Amin, Samir. 1992. *Empire of Chaos*. New York: Monthly Review Press.

———. 1991. "The Issue of Democracy in the Contemporary Third World." *Socialism and Democracy* 12 (January): 83–104.

Anderson, Lisa. 1995. "Democracy in the Arab World: A Critique of the Political Culture Approach." In Rex Brynen, Bahgat Korany, and Paul Noble, eds. *Political Liberalization and Democratization in the Arab World*. Vol. 1. Boulder: Lynne Rienner, pp. 77–92.

———. 1990. "Liberalism in Northern Africa." *Current History* 89, 546: 145–175.

———. 1987. "The State in the Middle East and North Africa." *Comparative Politics* (October): 1–18.

Azarya, Victor. 1988. "Reordering State-Society Relations: Incorporation and Disengagement." In Donald Rothchild and Naomi Chazan, eds. *The Precarious Balance: State and Society in Africa*. Boulder: Westview, pp. 3–21.

Bellin, Eva. 1995. Book Reviews of Iliya Harik and Denis J. Sullivan, eds., *Privatization and Liberalization in the Middle East*. Bloomington: Indiana University Press, 1992; and Henri Barkey, ed., *The Politics of Economic Reform in the Middle East*. New York: St. Martin's, 1992. *Comparative Political Studies* (October): 479–483.

———. 1994. "Civil Society: Effective Tool of Analysis for Middle East Politics?" *PS: Political Science and Politics*, 27, 3 (September): 509–510.

Bratton, Michael. 1989. "Beyond the State: Civil Society and Associational Life in Africa." *World Politics* 41, 3 (April): 407–430.

———. 1982. "Patterns of Development and Underdevelopment: Toward a Comparison." *International Studies Quarterly* 26, 3 (September): 333–372.

Brumberg, Daniel. 1991. "Islamic Fundamentalism, Democracy, and the Gulf War." In James Piscatori, ed. *Islamic Fundamentalisms and the Gulf Crisis*. Chicago: American Academy of Arts and Sciences, pp. 186–208.

———. 1990. "An Arab Path to Democracy?" *Journal of Democracy* 1, 4 (Fall): 120–125.

Brynen, Rex, Bahgat Korany, and Paul Noble, eds. 1995. *Political Liberalization and Democratization in the Arab World: Theoretical Perspectives*. Boulder: Lynne Rienner.

Chandhoke, Neera. 1995. *State and Civil Society: Explorations in Political Theory*. Thousand Oaks, Calif.: Sage.

Chaudhry, Kiren Aziz. 1994. "The Middle East and the Political Economy of Development." *Items* 48, 2–3 (June/September): 41–49.

Chhibber, Pradeep K. 1996. "State Policy, Rent Seeking, and the Electoral Success of a Religious Party in Algeria." *Journal of Politics* 58, 1 (February): 126–148.

Crystal, Jill. 1994. "Authoritarianism and Its Adversaries in the Arab World." *World Politics* 46, 2 (January): 262–289.

Dahl, Robert A. 1989. *Democracy and Its Critics*. New Haven: Yale University Press.

————. 1971. *Polyarchy: Participation and Opposition.* New Haven: Yale University Press.

Diamond, Larry, Juan J. Linz, and Seymour Martin Lipset. 1990. "Introduction: Comparative Experiences with Democracy." In Larry Diamond, Juan J. Linz, and Seymour Martin Lipset, eds. *Politics in Developing Countries: Comparing Experiences with Democracy.* Boulder: Lynne Rienner, pp. 1–38.

Eickelman, Dale F., and James Piscatori. 1996. *Muslim Politics.* Princeton: Princeton University Press.

Entelis, John P. 1997. "Political Islam in the Maghreb: The Nonviolent Dimension." In John P. Entelis, ed. *Islam, Democracy, and the State in North Africa.* Bloomington: Indiana University Press.

————. 1996. "Civil Society and the Authoritarian Temptation in Algerian Politics: Islamic Democracy versus the Centralized State." In Augustus Richard Norton, ed. *Civil Society in the Middle East.* 2 vols. Leiden: Brill, pp. 45–86.

————. 1996. *Culture and Counterculture in Moroccan Politics.* Lanham, Md.: University Press of America.

————. 1995. "Political Islam in Algeria: The Nonviolent Dimension." *Current History* 94, 588 (January): 13–17.

————. 1994. "Islam, Democracy, and the State: The Reemergence of Authoritarian Politics in Algeria." In John Ruedy, ed. *Islamism and Secularism in North Africa.* New York: St. Martin's, pp. 219–251.

————. 1992. "Introduction: State and Society in Transition." In John P. Entelis and Phillip C. Naylor, eds. *State and Society in Algeria.* Boulder: Westview, pp. 1–30.

————. 1986. *Algeria: The Revolution Institutionalized.* Boulder: Westview.

Hudson, Michael C. 1995. "The Political Culture Approach to Arab Democratization: The Case for Bringing It Back In, Carefully." In Rex Brynen, Bahgat Korany, and Paul Noble, eds. *Political Liberalization and Democratization in the Arab World.* Boulder: Lynne Rienner, pp. 61–76.

————. 1992. "Democracy and Foreign Policy in the Arab World." *The Beirut Review* 4 (Fall): 3–28.

————. 1991. "After the Gulf War: Prospects for Democratization in the Arab World." *Middle East Journal* 45, 3 (Summer): 407–426.

————. 1988. "Democratization and the Problems of Legitimacy in Middle East Politics." *Middle East Studies Association Bulletin* 22, 2 (December): 157–171.

————. 1977. *Arab Politics: The Search for Legitimacy.* New Haven: Yale University Press.

Labat, Séverine. 1995. *Les Islamistes Algériens.* Paris: Seuil.

Lasswell, Harold Dwight. 1958. *Politics: Who Gets What, When, How.* New York: Meridian.

Levine, Donald H. 1988. "Paradigm Lost: Dependency to Democracy." *World Politics* 49, 3 (April): 377–394.

Mortimer, Robert A. 1984a. "Global Economy and African Foreign Policy: The Algerian Model." *African Studies Review* 27, 1 (March): 1–22.

————. 1984b. *The Third World Coalition in International Politics.* Boulder: Westview.

————. 1970. "The Algerian Revolution in Search of the African Revolution." *Journal of Modern African Studies* 8, 3 (October): 363–387.

State-Society Relations

Norton, Augustus Richard, ed. 1995–1996. *Civil Society in the Middle East*. 2 vols. Leiden: Brill.

Przeworski, Adam. 1991. *Democracy and the Market: Political and Economic Reforms in Eastern Europe and Latin America*. Cambridge: Cambridge University Press.

Pye, Lucian W. 1990. "Political Science and the Crisis of Authoritarianism." *American Political Science Review* 84, 1 (March): 3–19.

Richards, Alan, and John Waterbury. 1990. *A Political Economy of the Middle East: State, Class, and Economic Development*. Boulder: Westview.

Salamé, Ghassan, ed. 1994. *Democracy without Democrats? The Renewal of Politics in the Muslim World*. London: Tauris.

Sharabi, Hisham. 1988. *Neopatriarchy: A Theory of Distorted Change in Arab Society*. New York: Oxford University Press.

Tessler, Mark A. 1997. "The Origins of Popular Support for Islamist Movements: A Political Economy Analysis." In John P. Entelis, ed. *Islam, Democracy, and the State in North Africa*. Bloomington: Indiana University Press.

Vatin, Jean-Claude. 1987. "Seduction and Sedition: Islamic Polemical Discourses in the Maghreb." In William R. Roff, ed. *Islam and the Political Economy of Meaning: Comparative Studies of Muslim Discourse*. Berkeley: University of California Press, pp. 160–179.

Waterbury, John. 1993. *Exposed to Innumerable Delusions: Public Enterprise and State Power in Egypt, India, Mexico, and Turkey*. Cambridge: Cambridge University Press.

Weigle, Marcia A., and Jim Butterfield. 1992. "Civil Society in Reforming Communist Regimes: The Logic of Emergence." *Comparative Politics* 25, 1 (October): 1–23.

3. Associational Life
Civil Society in Authoritarian Political Systems

Augustus Richard Norton

THE PERSISTENCE OF AUTHORITARIANISM

Although the worldwide phenomenon of democratization has inspired a wealth of new scholarship over the last decade, few mainstream scholars of the subject address the Middle East and North Africa.* This is for good reason. The region can be justifiably singled out as a stronghold of authoritarianism where the free expression of political ideas is often ruthlessly suppressed, harassed, and punished. Most of the governments in the region refuse to tolerate more than token political dissent, and they impose strict and usually capricious controls on associational activity so as to de-politicize public life. Unlike Europe, Latin America, Africa, and Asia, only one transition from authoritarianism to democracy has occurred in the Middle East and that was in Turkey, where a remarkable if incomplete transition occurred in the space of less than half a century. Israel was arguably born a democracy, although the political rights of its Arab citizens have often been curtailed. Lebanon's unique system of "consociational democracy" began half a century ago, but it was sidetracked by fifteen years of civil war, and Lebanon's representative institutions are now routinely manipulated by Syria. The vocabulary of democracy is often intoned in presidential circles in Egypt and Tunisia, but this is not language that is meant to be taken too seriously. Incipient experiments in democratization in Jordan and, more problematically, in Kuwait do continue, but with little forward momentum. In Morocco, the king has permitted opposition parties a carefully orchestrated voice in politics. Otherwise, authoritarian rule is the norm in the region.

In future references to the region, I will use the term "Middle East" as inclusive of North Africa.

Nonetheless, the objective challenges facing many governments in the Middle East are formidable; and governmental inefficiency, ineptitude, and corruption are omnipresent complaints across the boundaries of rich and poor states. Understandably, vocal denunciations—from within these states—of governmental abuses are uncommon, a reflection of the high price of speaking out. Nonetheless, some of the opprobrious physical abuses inflicted upon citizens by their governments do not pass unnoticed, thanks largely to the work of indigenous human rights workers (Waltz 1996). Although journalists in the region operate under enormous handicaps, the print media has sometimes challenged government abuses as well, especially in Egypt, Israel, Jordan, Kuwait, Lebanon, Turkey, and Yemen. Nearly every government in the region has signaled its awareness of its challenges by launching carefully orchestrated political reforms, often in tandem with economic reforms. While generalizations must be applied carefully, rich and poor states share some serious problems. The richest governments in the region are less threatened by economic disaster, yet they are, like the poorer governments, viewed with suspicion and disapproval by large segments of the population. In less wealthy states, notably Algeria, Egypt, Iran, Jordan, Morocco, Syria, and Tunisia, the provision of public services is often stretched to the point of disappearance, while increasing demands for jobs in economic systems with already saturated labor pools create the potential for widescale unrest and oppositional mobilization in the near future. Across the region, population growth rates are extremely high (except in Israel), exceeded only by sub-Saharan Africa, thereby accelerating the demands for jobs, public services, education, and health care.

One must guard against the tendency to exaggerate the weight of socioeconomic factors or the resentment of government abuses, as though their combined weight would compel change. Only when people attribute their problems to their political system and begin to believe that there are political solutions to their problems, does deprivation become a serious concern for government. In other words, when problems in society are politicized, people become available for political mobilization (Norton 1987). The governments are facing trouble from the Islamist opposition movements, which are attuned to popular complaints, precisely because of the Islamists' adept mobilization of dissent and efficient response to popular complaints. Economic inequity, unemployment, poor housing, and public services are frequent subjects of complaint and are at the very core of the Islamist opposition indictment of the regimes.

Despite the daunting challenges that they confront, few close observers expect the authoritarian rulers in the Middle East to yield power freely, and they have already demonstrated that they will only dabble with the right to participate. Open political opposition, when permitted, is carefully monitored and quite tame. These are entrenched regimes that are protected by phalanxes of police and security forces. The persistence of authoritarianism poses an intriguing and fundamental set of questions: why do such regimes proliferate and endure in the Middle East and how are they likely to change or reform? In answering this pair of questions, one can fall back on some of the venerable shibboleths of area studies or, instead, employ an analytical lens that reveals some remarkable insights on the relationship between state and society in the Middle East. In this paper, I shall focus on the second approach, using the construct of civil society. I shall argue that by examining civil society, it is possible to gain a fuller understanding of how authoritarianism persists, and why the path of reform in the Middle East is likely to be strewn with boulders. Prior to examining civil society in the Middle East more fully, it is germane to examine the perspective that I reject.

It is commonplace for scholars to attribute the persistence of authoritarianism to deep cultural explanations, especially the impact of Islam, as well as the proclivity for patrimonial rule and patriarchal structure in Middle East societies. Elie Kedourie, for instance, describes Arab society as "accustomed to . . . autocracy and passive obedience" (Kedourie 1992, p. 103). Charles Butterworth, a respected student of Islamic thought, notes that the Arab world lacks a commitment to popular sovereignty. "In sum, then, the absence of an unquestioned, perhaps unquestionable, belief in the fundamental need for popular sovereignty is what primarily explains why political life in the Arab world differs so markedly from political life in the West" (Butterworth 1987, p. 110). Such arguments fail to take into account the conditions under which the modern state system emerged in the Middle East, the political economies of the regimes, or the skilled performance of the Islamist movements as modern political institutions. In this chapter, I shall put aside these essentialist arguments because they offer a skewed analysis of the context for Middle East politics and because they confuse context with consequence. In other words, the dearth of political freedom is not a cultural trait but the result of specific government policies and practices, specifically the tendency to closely monitor, regulate, restrict, and, when necessary, annihilate associational life. Thus, the absence of political freedom in the Middle East is precisely not a cultural artifact, but a modern condition.

PROBLEMS OF LEGITIMACY AND COMPLIANCE

Despite the venerable history of the Middle East, the state is a twentieth-century innovation, and nearly every state in the region was given territorial shape by a European power. The lingering ill effects of twentieth-century designs wrought in London, Paris, and, in recent decades, Washington, include a not unjustified suspicion of Western political models. Equally important, the political economy that underpins many of the Middle Eastern governments has permitted them to purchase support and bribe potential opponents. While most Middle Eastern states do not enjoy the luxury of drawing most of the government budget from oil and natural gas earnings, many of the state coffers are supplemented by oil earnings, subsidies, and other forms of what economists call "rents." As a result, governments in the Middle East are less dependent on direct taxation than most governments in the world. Thus, scholars have argued cogently that for this reason Middle Eastern governments, in general, are less likely to be faced with citizen demands for better, more responsive government. While this argument offers an important explanation for the quiescence of many people in the Middle East, it is not totally elastic. As populations continue to grow and demands on governments expand, most of the governments will be hard pressed to maintain even the present level of per capita spending for nondefense purposes. Reduced government services and entitlements will be functionally equivalent to increased taxes and will further undermine the citizen's respect for government.

The presence of impressive Islamist oppositional movements is a symptom of state failure, and is often epiphenomenal to government policies designed to restrict, if not strangle, associational life. Extensive government restrictions upon associational life have had significantly less effect on the Islamists because the Islamists have succeeded in cloaking themselves in the symbols of their faith, with the result that it is much more difficult to stifle their activities. Instead of presuming that the politicization of Islam is an inevitable historical development—a natural cultural result—it is relevant to contrast the organizing style and strategy of the Islamists to that of their secular opponents. Following Philip Khoury, I argue that these movements must be seen as "the vehicle for political and economic demands, rather than being the 'impulse' behind the demands" (Khoury 1983). The Islamists have also evinced a more profound understanding of the requisites of political mobilization than their adversaries and competitors. In point of fact, many of the Islamist movements have been acutely sensitive to the needs of their constituencies, providing reliable, efficient services to the urban lower class, and winning respect in the urban middle class by their integrity and relative incorruptibility. This is not to deny the Islamists a significant victory in dominating the discourse of reform as well as providing a resonant critique of government performance, but their ideological success is built upon solid populist politics, which are seldom rivaled by non-Islamist opposition parties, or, for that matter, by progovernment parties. Most of the region's governments, seeking to compete with the Islamists as the custodian of sacred symbols, succeed only in demonstrating the political relevance of Islam and ramifying the opposition's challenge.

The Islamists have also largely succeeded in attaining dominance in their depiction of Islam. The whole question of the unity of *din-wa-dawla* (religion and state) is illustrative. In the history of Islamic religion and politics, religion and the state have typically been distinct realms. Although there are more than forty Quranic references that may be interpreted to specify the unity of religion and state, the history of Islam provides only a singular example of *din-wa-dawla* in practice, namely during the life of the Prophet Muhammad (Eickelman and

Piscatori 1996, pp. 46–79). Remarkably, the Islamists' insistence upon the immutability of *din-wa-dawla* has been accepted almost as an article of faith by Western scholars with little regard for the very different empirical record which clearly suggests that in Islam there almost always has been, in practice, a separation between religion and the state.

Obviously, none of this would matter very much if the governments readily gained the compliance of their citizens and enjoyed widespread support. Few governments set out to be intentionally unpopular and those wielding political power certainly understand that willing compliance is preferable to coerced or purchased compliance. The heart of the ideological project mounted by several Middle Eastern states in the 1950s and 1960s was "solidarism," the idea of fostering an integrated, cohesive citizenry. These projects failed, notably in Algeria, Egypt, Iran, Iraq, and Syria. As Alan Richards and John Waterbury note, although the "rhetoric of solidarism" survives, the reality is quite different. Viable organizational alternatives to traditional forms of association were not permitted to survive except as hollow puppets of the state. In the absence of social solidarity, and in order to preserve power, the state has divided its citizens rather than uniting them, falling back on primordial attachments (Richards and Waterbury 1990, pp. 330–352). In theory, the tribe, clan, and sect offer the opportunity of control through socially embedded channels, but at the cost of literally dividing society against itself.

The extreme case may be Iraq. Writing prior to the Gulf war of 1991, Kanan Makiya argued that the intolerance and the ruthlessness of the state exacerbated sectarianism and created the conditions for a horrible bloodletting when the repressive apparatus of the state finally ends. In the weeks following the end of the Gulf war, in 1991, Makiya's prescience was demonstrated in southern Iraq when the majority Shi'ite Muslim population tried violently to cast off Baghdad's control only to be brutally crushed by the still lethal remnants of Iraq's army to the cheers and applause of the Sunni minority that had come to see its survival as inextricably linked to the survival of the regime.

More than other Middle East states, the Iraqi government has depended upon coercion to ensure the people's acquiescence if not the compliance of its citizens. In any political system, whether Saddam's Iraq, al-Sabah's Kuwait, or Mubarak's Egypt, the fundamental question is not only how the few come to rule the many but how those who rule sustain the compliance of the ruled. In other words, the basic question is how does a regime establish legitimacy? Two decades ago, in his seminal analysis of Arab politics as a "search for legitimacy," Michael Hudson demonstrated the centrality of the concept of legitimacy in an attempt to understand politics in the Arab world. Hudson provides a typology of the strategies for building legitimacy, which he labeled personal, ideological, and structural (Hudson 1977, pp. 1–30). The personal or charismatic qualities of a political personality of the caliber of Jamal 'Abd al-Nasir were formidable, but nontransferable. The "search for legitimacy" is the quest for a broader justification for legitimacy, one that will not follow a ruler into the grave.

Associational Life

Those who rule seek to establish a legal and moral basis for their claim to legitimacy. Gaetano Mosca, the Italian theorist famous for his work on political elites, describes this claim as the "political formula" upon which the power of the political class rests. As Mosca emphasizes:

> [This] does not mean that political formulas are mere quackeries aptly invented to trick the masses into obedience. Anyone who viewed them in that light would fall into grave error. The truth is that they answer a real need in man's social nature; and this need, so universally felt, of governing and knowing that one is governed not on the basis of mere material or intellectual force, but on the basis of a moral principle, has beyond any doubt a practical and real importance (Mosca 1939, p. 71).

Hence, in the Middle East, ideologies stressing social solidarity provided an indispensable tool for constructing the political formula of a regime. However, these ideological arguments lost their appeal by the 1970s and they now have few adherents, even in the ruling circles of government. What has clearly eluded many Middle Eastern rulers is institutionalization, or what Hudson refers to as structural legitimacy, which is embodied in a system of nonarbitrary rules and laws. To the contrary, government rule-making continues to be incredibly capricious. Governments largely do what they wish, when they wish, whether by shaping the outcome of elections, selectively enforcing laws, or brutalizing citizens.

While valuable, Hudson's perspective fails to capture analytically the concern that underlies any regime's political formula, namely, the attainment of the broad compliance of the citizenry. In a recent short paper, Ian Lustick provides insight on the question of compliance. He notes that all regimes seek to achieve ideological hegemony, "the establishment of beliefs so much akin to simple common sense that they disappear as contingent beliefs and become the natural 'culture' of the political community" (Lustick 1996). In contrast to the goal of hegemony, support for government in the Middle East is not natural at all, but contingent. Taxes are routinely evaded, building codes are widely ignored, and corruption is part of the cost of doing business or interacting with government. (Scholars who work in the Middle East usually acquire an inexhaustible repertoire of anecdotes about the routine evasion of government authority, as anyone who has shared a dinner table with them can attest.) Governments use a combination of coercion and bribes (e.g., subsidies, jobs, benefits) to win the support of citizens. Support for government is not a tribute to its hegemony, but reflects instrumental calculations and the prospect for coercion and intimidation. The failure of the state to meet social and economic needs amounts to reneging on the "ruling bargain" (Brumberg 1992). According to this tacit bargain, the state would meet the needs of citizens in exchange for the citizens' agreement to curb dissent and avoid challenging the authority of the state. Writing about Egypt, Diane Singerman has argued, since the popular classes enjoy "few legal avenues of opposition . . . , small changes in government policy can ignite direct, illegal opposition to the state" (Singerman 1995, p. 245). When people rush to the streets to challenge and protest cuts in subsidies, as they did in Jordan in August 1996, and as they have done previously in Algeria, Egypt, Iran, Morocco, and Tunisia, they expose the tenuous basis of regime legitimacy. It is precisely because the consent of the governed is tethered by the flimsy string of subsidies that governments have been so reluctant to lift subsidies, even in the face of heavy external pressure.

THE PROSPECTS FOR POLITICAL REFORM

Since hegemony will continue to elude these governments, they are likely to continue on their present course, winning compliance instrumentally when possible, repressing dissent when it is not, and continuing tepid experiments in political reform in order to broaden support. The existing governments are intellectually barren, and judging from their performance in recent years they are not likely to prove creative in terms of renovating their own political formulae. The record of recent "initiatives" in democratization and liberaliza-tion justifies this pessimism. Rather than engendering meaningful political reform, most initiatives have only been designed to buy time, to let off steam, or to quell international criticism. Jordan is the only Arab state, at present, in which serious reform efforts through democratization have been sustained, and even there the institutionalization of reforms is still inchoate and hardly irreversible. Elsewhere in the Arab world, the record is not very reassuring. For several generations some Middle East scholars have speculated about the prospects for democracy in the region, but the record of recent years shows that if the authoritarian governments that predominate in the Middle East seek reform, it is reform without democracy.

If creative ideas about political reform are unlikely to come from the rulers, where will the ideas come from? I argue here that elements in civil society are the most likely source of creative thinking on political reform. In addition, and on the strength of recent evidence, there is reason for confidence that when the iron fist of autocracy loosens its grip on power, the resulting space for political dialogue and debate will be filled by nonviolent groups of men and women intent upon improving their life chances. This is not to argue that civil society in the Middle East will call loudly for democracy. As I show below, this is unlikely to be the case.

In fact, despite their tenuous legitimacy, Middle Eastern governments are not faced with widespread demands for democracy. In general, the middle class is not pushing for democracy and segments of the middle class have worked strenuously to forestall democracy, most dramatically in Algeria where the January 1992 coup d'état was widely applauded in many middle-class circles.

Where experiments in reform have occurred—notably in Egypt, Jordan, Kuwait, Morocco, Tunisia, and Yemen—governments have liberalized, not democratized. Liberalization refers to lifting press restrictions, easing controls on associational life (including the formation of political parties), and easing restrictions on individual mobility; political liberalization has often been linked to economic liberalization. In contrast, democratization connotes accountability, which, in turn, clearly implies the right to choose one's government, but distinguishing liberalization from democratization is far easier in principle than in fact. Programs of liberalization are not easily contained: as press controls are loosened, demands for accountability emerge. Controls on associational life may be selectively lifted, but, even so, the right to organize freely is hard to contain. Thus, programs of liberalization designed to take the pressure off government often threaten to gain their own momentum as people seize the novel opportunity to openly vent demands upon government. This is why liberalization, though analytically distinct from democratization, is an unstable solution to the puzzle of reform, and this is why most Middle Eastern governments have habitually reversed liberalization or limited it so severely so as to render it a mere cosmetic to cover the blemishes of authoritarianism.

Authoritarian governments have amply demonstrated a penchant for preserving a firm grip on power, and given their failure to establish hegemony over society it is not at all surprising that they are loath to concede even a minor share of power to their opponents. This is not hard to understand, but, as we have seen, many scholars, probably a majority, argue that the prevalence of authoritarian government in the Middle East is a legacy of culture, and especially the imprint of Islam, rather than the behavior of the present governments. Underlying these arguments are a series of pathological assumptions about Islam, chief among which is the presumed hostility of Islam for democracy, as well as the Muslim's purported disinterest in the values of a civil society, namely tolerance for the other.

Whether the scholars are comparativists working outside the Middle East or area specialists, there is a persistent skepticism in the literature that Islam can be compatible with democracy (or civil society). Ian Shapiro, who has written impressively on South Africa, writes that "[t]heir Islamic creeds seemed to many in retrospect to be incompatible with the basic prerequisites of democracy." Giovanni Sartori warns that democracy is impossible in nonsecular settings, especially where Islamic fundamentalism is strong: "the international community is ill-advised in asking countries currently facing the tide of Islamic fundamentalism to "certify" their democracy by calling for a vote. In a nonsecularized, warlike setting in which the loser expects to be killed, democracy of any kind is impossible" (Sartori 1995, p. 105). Strictly speaking, Muslims, including Arab Muslims, do argue that sovereignty belongs to God, not to the people. Thus, the doctrine of popular sovereignty as well as the idea of secularism is rejected out of hand. Nonetheless, amongst moderate Islamists, who comprise the majority, there is a trend to justify democracy as a broadened form of consultation or *shura* whereby elections are taken to be a means of consultation (Moussalli). The Islamists have proven to be a very adaptable Realpolitik opposition, arguably no less flexible than the avowedly secular actors. They now openly embrace competitive elections and, implicitly, incremental reform rather than radical transformation. Unfortunately, the scholarship on Islam and politics is much too textual and only a handful of writers have dealt seriously with the dynamic empirical reality of the Islamist movements. A notable exception is *Muslim Politics* by Dale Eickelman and James Piscatori, in which the authors perspicaciously demonstrate that attempts to stereotype the political attitudes of Muslims should be received with appropriate skepticism.

In any case, it is necessary to consider whether a culture of democracy is a precondition for democratization, not to say democracy. Obviously, if a democratic culture is a precondition for democracy, it is difficult to imagine how democracy could emerge in the Middle East or almost anywhere else for that matter. As Dankwart Rustow emphasizes in his landmark 1970 article, democracy is a solution to a political impasse, and it becomes institutionalized as the participants become habituated to the rules. In fact, where Islamist parties have had the opportunity to become habituated to democratic rules of the game, they have embraced the opportunity, notably in Turkey, as well as in Israel, Jordan, Kuwait, and Lebanon.

THE CIVIL SOCIETY CONSTRUCT

The idea of a democratic culture may thus be of limited analytical value in considering the potential for greater democratization in the Middle East. A more useful approach is to examine the role of civil society and its relationship to the state. The civil society construct is a potentially rigorous vehicle for gaining an appreciation of the limitations, perils, and opportunities that are presented to reform-minded politicians in the Middle East, and in this connection it can provide important insights about how and why governments might be transformed. Further, it offers an appropriate conceptual framework for thinking about the role of Islamist movements and for placing them within the context of state-society relations more generally. Finally, the civil society construct offers a valuable tool for comparative research, with the possibility of a broader theoretical contribution as the nature and dynamics of civil society are reformulated in order that the concept may be usefully employed in the Middle East.

Discussions of civil society have come relatively late to the Middle East. In the past decade, civil society enjoyed an impressive revival of attention by scholars and policy-makers (e.g., Jean Cohen and Andrew Arato, Ernest Gellner, John Hall, John Keane, and Adam Seligman). The revival of interest has been partly inspired by the acclaimed, but exaggerated role of civil society in toppling the communist regimes in Central and Eastern Europe in the *annus mirabalis* of 1989. In addition, a series of widely read studies of authoritarian transitions to democracy highlighted the resurgence of civil society as authoritarian regimes liberalized. It was from civil society, Guillermo O'Donnell and Philippe Schmitter argue, that exemplary citizens and groups emerged, who, in turn, gave shape and voice to popular demands for freedom and democracy (O'Donnell and Schmitter 1986).

Scholars of the region have found the concept provocative and some, but by no means all, have adopted civil society as an approach to understanding issues of state and society. The spring 1993 issue of the *Middle East Journal*, a thematic issue devoted to civil society in the Middle East, sold more copies than any other issue in the journal's history and quickly went out of print, despite an unusually large press run. Among scholars in the Middle East, the relevance of civil society has become a lively debate topic, with one school rejecting the concept completely due to its Western provenance and its supposed link to Western projects of domination and manipulation (Bisharah 1995); while another school, often associated with Islamist ideologies, has co-opted and naturalized the concept, arguing that the norms of civil society are already realized in the ideal-typical Muslim society (Moussalli in Norton 1995); while a third, smaller school of scholars and activists exploit the concept to publicize their secular oppositional agenda (Ibrahim 1995); and, finally, a fourth school advocates adopting the concept, including its normative components (al-Sayyid 1995b). These varying and often overlapping perspectives underline that civil society is a polysemous concept. There is no "right" or privileged definition of civil society, any more than there is a definitive definition of democracy. Accordingly, the best procedure is to stipulate a definition and to proceed.

As used in this chapter, civil society refers to the melange of associations, clubs, guilds, syndicates, federations, unions, parties, and groups that provide a buffer between state and citizen. Civil society not only refers to associability, the coming together of individuals on the basis of shared goals and interests, but also to the acceptance of two norms—civility and citizenship. Ideally, civil society is marked by the norm of tolerance, although in practice many individuals and groups fall short, not least in terms of their internal practice of civility. There is wide debate about the importance of civility or tolerance. Shapiro, referring to Tocqueville's and Michael Walzer's claims that civil society organizations do not have to be internally democratic, argues:

> In the end it is not a plausible view, because democratic habits of thought and action have to be learned through practice in everyday life. There is no convincing reason to think that this will occur in an authoritarian political culture. In debates about the relations between civil society and democratic politics, we should eschew questions about how "weak" or "strong" civil institutions might be and turn to the study of how democratic they might be made to be (Shapiro 1993, p. 150).

But, as Hudson asks, how does one measure tolerance? Perhaps an ethic of tolerance is not essential, so long as the political contestants can strike a bargain (Hudson 1996, pp. 94–95). *Ceteris paribus*, there is no doubt that the enculturation of the norm of civility, including tolerance for the other, is an important goal. However, as social scientists we should be looking for the practice of tolerance, not its internalization by individuals. Toleration can emerge from a structure of social control in which the state plays a key regulatory role. When the state performs this role with reasonable impartiality and with respect for fundamental human rights, an ethic of tolerance might be inculcated. The real issue, however, is the actual behavior of men or women, not what is in their hearts (Kazemi and Norton 1996, p. 115). This means that projects of democratization should not be held hostage by the idea that only when the political culture of authoritarianism is replaced by the political culture of democracy is democracy possible.

Citizenship also underpins civil society. To be a part of the whole is a precondition for the whole to be the sum of its parts. Otherwise, society has no coherence; it is just a vessel filled with shards and fragments. Since society is not self-regulating, civil society only exists in relationship to a state, one that respects the rights of the individual and applies the law fairly. Edward Shils has put this well:

> The state lays down laws which set the outermost boundaries of the au-
> tonomy of the diverse spheres and sectors of civil society; so, civil society
> from its side lays down limits on the actions of the state. Civil society and the
> state are bound together by the constitution and by traditions which stress
> the obligations of each to the other as well as their rights vis-à-vis each other
> (Shils 1991, p. 4).

In the absence of a state justly applying the law, many people will seek security in the social units of reproduction—family, clan, or tribe—rather than in the exposed associational promontories of civil society. This implies that it is wholly inappropriate to expect to find close replicas of Western civil society in the Middle Eastern states where autocratic rule prevails. Civil society is not as much absent from the Middle East as different in the Middle East.

CIVIL SOCIETY AND DEMOCRACY

Recent writings on the subject of civil society have made several central claims about the connection between civil society, on the one hand, and democracy and liberalism on the other hand. Writing out of the experience of established Western democracies, many scholars are inclined to depict civil society as synonymous with democracy, if not logically prior to its emergence. Gellner argues that democracy is embodied in civil society: "the ideas associated with this expression are indeed intimately connected with the establishment of a democratic or liberal social order. In fact, 'democracy,' though acceptable as a shorthand code term for participatory and accountable government, carries with it a model which is less useful than the one suggested by 'civil society'" (Gellner 1991, p. 495). Along similar lines, James Turner Johnson claims a causal link between civil society and democracy: "in short, democracy begins from the bottom up, with the creation of a civil society consisting in a complex web of interrelationships and mutual responsibilities formed by the free choice of individuals and by the natural relationships amongst them" (Johnson 1992, pp. 45–46).

Despite these claims, the complex historical record of Western democracy does not permit unequivocal conclusions about causality—whether the democratic egg was laid by the civil society chicken, or vice versa. It is clear, though, that civil society is a necessary condition for the durability of democracy. In the absence of a vibrant civil society alert to the protection of individual rights and capable of protesting the excesses of government, democracy is likely to be fragile indeed. Thus, Walzer argues that civil society and democracy are inextricably connected, and that the survival of democracy turns on the existence of a civil society. "Only a democratic state can create a democratic civil society; only a democratic civil society can sustain a democratic state" (Walzer 1991, p. 302).

Perhaps not surprisingly, some of these same scholars, emphasizing the deep historical roots of Western democracy, and therefore civil society, are inclined to express skepticism about the prospects for civil society or democracy in the Middle East. Gellner expresses the view that "[Muslim societies] are suffused with faith, indeed they suffer from a plethora of it, but they manifest at most a feeble yearning for civil society" (Gellner 1991, p. 506). Hall, influenced by Gellner's claim that the rise of Islamism represents the novel supremacy of "high Islam," the triumph of the religion of the "book" over the religion of popular belief, custom, and individual piety, argues that literalist, high Islam is threatening to civil society, although its ("puritanical") values are complementary to modernity (Hall 1995, p. 22).

Of course, Muslim society is much more heterogeneous and flexible than Gellner's essentialist characterization of Islam would suggest. More to the point, the Islamist movements have established a significant presence in what may aptly be called the informal sector of civil society, the urban networks that crisscross society joining the interstices of the informal economy. There the Islamist movements have fostered the development of an array of voluntary associations which illustrates that the Islamists have a keener grasp of the sociology of urban life in the contemporary Middle East than many professional students of the region or of civil society. These efforts—which are often largely uncontested by either government agencies or the secular opposition— are part of the Islamist's project for building a popular base in society (Sullivan 1995). This is why the Islamists are in a position to benefit if and when associational controls are lifted by government.

If the establishment of civil society is problematic in the Middle East, it is wise to consider explanations other than the presence of Islam. Thus, reflecting on the broader context of developing societies, Hall expresses his doubt that civil society can emerge at all. "Societies facing rapid industrialization and, still more, nation-building often find themselves with politics of such total society novelty—a situation in which, unfortunately, everything is up for grabs—as almost to rule out the possibility of civil society" (Hall, 22). "Another reason is that many Islamic countries are almost swamped by enormous social problems; this is obviously true of Egypt, whose political system, anyway far from liberal, looks as if it will have the greatest difficulty dealing with an immense demographic revolution" (Hall 1995, p. 25).

What of those parts of the world, such as the Middle East, that do not possess vibrant, robust civil societies? Are they doomed to wallow in autocracy, forever rebuffed at the threshold of democracy? In his widely read and acclaimed study of Italy, Robert Putnam seems to suggest that the verdict of natural history was rendered long ago, and that people do not simply get the sort of government that they wish or deserve, but that they get the sort of government that is possible given the historically embedded sociocultural setting (Putnam 1993, p. 80). Civic associations in Italy are deeply rooted in history, and especially in the instruments of credit, according to Putnam. Indeed, Putnam traces Italian civil society to the eleventh century. However, other scholars assume a much shorter gestation period for civil society. Writing about the Spanish transition to democracy, Victor Peréz-Díaz emphasizes that the church in Spain made the journey from authoritarianism to democracy in sixty years (Peréz-Díaz 1995, p. 88). Equally germane is the fact that Catholicism and democracy were viewed by many scholars as incompatible well into the 1970s.

Some thinkers, though sharing the view expressed by Putnam, Gellner, and Walzer that civil society and democracy are inextricably connected, argue that civil society may be fostered and that the emergence of civil society is a sufficient condition for the building of democracy. For instance, David Hamburg, former president of the Carnegie Corporation, argues: "civil society builds democracy, first, by allowing the evolution of democratic values through nonviolent conflict. Groups compete with each other and with the state for the power to carry out specific agendas. Civil society increases the effectiveness of coalitions of individuals for innovative activities, and, within the context of institutionalized competition, tolerance and acceptance of opposition can develop" (Hamburg 1996, p. vi). Even in the intimidating presence of an authoritarian political system, Johnson claims, the promotion of civil society is a stimulant to democracy.

> The experience of Eastern and Central Europe shows that it is not necessary simply to wait passively for such a culture to be created; rather, it can be brought into being by intentional action even within a hostile environment. The implication for persons interested in stimulating the growth of democracy in nondemocratic states, is that the first step should be efforts to create the conditions for the free associational groupings that signify the accomplishment of the first stage in the social contract (Johnson 1992, p. 46).

Johnson is not sufficiently sensitive to the pressures that government may bring to bear on an inchoate civil society. Thus, while a vigorous civil society may fortify a democracy by confronting government, it is by no means clear that a nascent civil society will choose the path of confrontation. In addition, it should be recalled that the much-touted renaissance of civil society in Latin America and in Southern and Central Europe followed rather than preceded government decisions to reform politically. In this sense, the renaissance of civil society was sparked by a change in the political rules of the game, not, directly at least, by the sponsorship of external allies.

Peter M. Lewis offers a more realistic depiction of the relationship between state and civil society, in which he implies that elements of civil society are enmeshed and implicated in the state, and are therefore unlikely to overtly challenge the authority of government:

> Civil society is simultaneously arrayed against the state and engaged with the state in setting the boundaries of public power and guarding its prerogatives. While civil society intrinsically resists state encroachment, the various interests within civil society also seek to influence the state in the exercise of public policy and the allocation of valued resources. This engagement may be either cordial or antagonistic, but it does reflect a common recognition of state sovereignty and (at least implicit) legitimacy. State and civil society are engaged in a dialogue at arm's length (Lewis 1992, p. 36).

Apropos of this dialogue at arm's length, it is important to emphasize that the project of civil society, as least insofar as civil society reflects bourgeois interests, is not democracy. Significant and powerful elements within civil society maintain a strategic alliance with the state. To the extent that these alliances eke out individual rights and create space for other interests to organize, they may inadvertently open the way for democratic initiatives as well as the expansion of civil society. Realistically speaking, the momentum for political reform initiatives will come from those who govern, but these initiatives have often responded to demands from civil society, including women's groups, human rights organizations, the press, and associations of businessmen as well as organized labor. Only infrequently is the goal of these segments of civil society democracy, but typically their demands may be encapsulated as liberalization, including a greater respect for individual rights, freedom to organize, and freedom of the press. An illustrative case was the rise and fall of Law 93 in Egypt, when the press syndicate succeeded (in 1996) in gaining the cancellation of a draconian press law intended, among other things, to stifle reporting on corruption in high places. The press syndicate's strategy was carefully planned in full consultation with well-placed reformist elements within the government and provides a clear example of how authoritarian governments may be induced to pursue liberal goals, in this instance press freedom (Kazemi and Norton 1997).

CONCLUSION

The evidence on the renaissance of civil society in the Middle East is actually more encouraging than many observers seem to presume. Despite extensive government controls on associational life, the regionwide trend is clear: both the numbers of associations and total membership have grown impressively over the past two decades (in some cases by more than 100 percent). As cracks in the edifice of authoritarian rule appear, associations seize the available space. Even fleeting experiments in reform without democracy have prompted the rapid growth of associations, most notably in Algeria (1989 to 1992), where one leading expert claims that the country was on the brink of establishing a contractual relationship between state and society when the military seized power in 1992 (Entelis 1996, p. 48). Other less dramatic examples include Egypt, Jordan, Kuwait, and even Yemen (Norton, ed., 1995 and 1996a for detailed case studies).

Much of the scholarship on civil society, including the studies that I organized in the Civil Society in the Middle East program from 1991 to 1995, focuses on civil society as a middle-class phenomenon. This has resulted in a distortion of the construct of civil society as it has been applied in the Middle East. Specifically, informal associations, networks, and ad hoc self-help groups organized among the urban lower class have received very little attention. Not only does this lacuna represent an incomplete empirical picture, but it excludes a segment of society in which individuals motivated by ideas of generalized reciprocity often exemplify tolerance and civic values (Singerman 1995). In other regions, such as Latin America, these forms of association have actually been inspired defensively by economic restructuring. Thus, Philip Oxhorn observes:

> Most researchers generally agree that a "civil society" of some sort is inextricably intertwined with the fate of democratic political regimes. In Latin America, the historical weakness of civil society is often seen as an important factor in explaining the fragility of political democracy in the region. I will argue that while this has been true in the past, it may not be true in the future. Specifically, as processes of *controlled inclusion* have given way to processes of *coerced marginalization*, new interests and needs have led to the beginnings of civil society in areas that it was absent (Oxhorn 1995, p. 251, emphasis original).

The parallel with the Middle East is reasonably exact, as individuals increasingly confront economic hardship by organizing themselves or by joining others, such as the Islamist movements.

Thoughtful scholars have argued that the concept of civil society is rooted in the Western experience, and removed from its European context the "dream of civil society" has little resonance (Mardin 1995). Of course, in terms of the historical specificity of the concept, civil society is an unabashedly European idea. Nonetheless, there is a powerful heuristic value to the concept and it is hard to imagine any serious discussion of political reform in the Middle East which does not take account of civil society. Moreover, unlike other approaches, such as political culture, or sectoral analyses of the informal sectors, civil society is conceptually rich and analytically rigorous. Most important, by addressing the construct of civil society and its relationship to the state, it is possible to gain a full appreciation of the degree to which the modern authoritarian state has shaped politics in the contemporary Middle East as well as the possibility that authoritarian governments will loosen their grip on power.

REFERENCES

Abu 'Amr, Ziad. 1995. *al-mujtama' al-madani wa al-tahawal al-dimuqrati fi filastin* *[Civil Society and the Democratic Transformation in Palestine]*. Ramallah: Muwatin, Palestinian Institute for the Study of Democracy.

Anderson, Lisa. 1995. "Democracy in the Arab World: Critique of the Political Culture Approach." In Rex Brynen, Bahgat Korany, and Paul Noble, eds. *Political Liberalization in the Arab World*. Boulder: Lynne Rienner, 77–92.

Bisharah, 'Azmi. 1995. "ay mujtama' madani?" [Which civil society?]. In Ziad Abu 'Amr, *al-mujtama' al-madani wa al-tahawal al-dimuqrati fi filastin*. Ramallah: Muwatin, Palestinian Institute for the Study of Democracy, 133–60.

Brumberg, Daniel. 1992. "The Collapse of the Ruling Bargain and Its Consequences in the Arab World." Paper presented for the Seminar on Prospects for Democratization in the Arab World, SAIS, Washington, 30 January, 1992.

Brynen, Rex, Bahgat Korany, and Paul Noble, eds. 1995. *Political Liberalization in the Arab World: Volume I, Theoretical Perspectives*. Boulder: Lynne Rienner.

Butterworth, Charles E. 1987. "State and Authority in Arabic Political Thought." In Ghassan Salamé, ed. *The Foundations of the Arab State,* London: Croom Helm, pp. 91–111.

Cohen, Jean L., and Andrew Arato. 1992. *Civil Society and Political Theory*. Cambridge: MIT Press.

Eickelman, Dale F., and James Piscatori. 1996. *Muslim Politics*. Princeton: Princeton University Press.

Entelis, John P. 1996. "Civil Society and the Authoritarian State Temptation in the Algerian Politics: Islamic Democracy vs. the Centralized State." In Augustus R. Norton, ed. *Civil Society in the Middle East*. Leiden: Brill, pp. 45–86.

Garnham, David, and Mark Tessler, eds. 1995. *Democracy, War, and Peace in the Middle East*. Bloomington: Indiana University Press.

Gellner, Ernest. 1994. *Conditions of Liberty: Civil Society and its Rivals*. New York: Hamish Hamilton.

———. 1991. "Civil Society in Historical Context." *International Social Science Journal* 129 (August): 495–510.

Goldberg, Ellis. 1993. "Private Goods, Public Wrongs, and Civil Society in Some Medieval Arab Theory and Practice." In Ellis Goldberg, Resat Kasaba, and Joel S. Migdal, eds. *Rules and Rights in the Middle East: Democracy, Law, and Society*. Seattle: University of Washington Press.

Göle, Nilüfer. 1996. "Authoritarian Secularism and Islamist Politics: The Case of Turkey." In Augustus R. Norton, ed. *Civil Society in the Middle East*. Leiden: Brill, pp. 17–43.

Hall, John A., ed. 1995. *Civil Society: Theory, History, Comparison*. Cambridge: Polity.

Hamburg, David. 1996. "Foreword." In Larry Diamond, *Promoting Democracy in the*

1990s: Actors and Instruments, Issues and Imperatives. New York: Carnegie Corporation.

Hudson, Michael C. 1996. "Obstacles to Democratization in the Middle East." *Contention* 5, 2 (Winter): 81–106.

——. 1977. *Arab Politics: The Search for Legitimacy.* New Haven: Yale University Press.

Ibrahim, Saad Eddin. 1995. "Civil Society and Prospects for Democratization in the Arab World." In Augustus R. Norton, ed. *Civil Society in the Middle East, vol. I.* Leiden: Brill, pp. 27–54.

Johnson, James Turner. 1992. "Does Democracy Travel? Some Thoughts on Democracy and Its Cultural Context." *Ethics and International Affairs* 6: 41–55.

Joseph, Suad. 1996. "Democrats and Patriarchs." *Contention* 5, 2 (Winter): 121–30.

Kandil, Amani. 1995. *Civil Society in the Arab World: Private Voluntary Organizations.* Washington: CIVICUS.

Kazemi, Farhad, and Augustus Richard Norton. 1997. "The Rise and Fall of Press Law 93 in Egypt." Unpublished paper.

——. 1996. "Civil Society, Political Reform, and Authoritarianism in the Middle East." *Contention* 5, 2 (Winter): 107–119.

Keane, John. 1988. *Democracy and Civil Society: On the Predicaments of European Socialism, the Prospects for Democracy, and the Problem of Controlling Social and Political Power.* London: Verso.

Kedourie, Elie. 1992. *Democracy and Arab Political Culture.* Washington: Washington Institute for Near East Policy.

Khoury, Philip. 1983. "Islamic Revivalism and the Crisis of the Secular State in the Arab World." In Ibrahim Ibrahim, ed. *Arab Resources: The Transformation of a Society.* London: Croom Helm, pp. 231–236.

Lewis, Peter M. 1992. "Political Transitions and the Dilemma of Civil Society in Africa." *Journal of International Affairs* 42, 1 (Summer): 31–54.

Lustick, Ian. 1996. "Legitimacy and Hegemony in the Post Colonial Middle East." Unpublished paper.

Makiya, Kanan [writing as Samir al-Khalil]. 1989. *Republic of Fear: The Politics of Modern Iraq.* Berkeley: University of California Press.

Mardin, Serif. 1995. "Civil Society and Islam." In John A. Hall, ed. *Civil Society: Theory, History, Comparison.* Cambridge: Polity, pp. 278–300.

Mitchell, Timothy P. 1991. "The Limits of the State: Beyond Statist Approaches and Their Critics." *American Political Science Association* 85, 1 (March): 77–96.

Mosca, Gaetano. 1939. *The Ruling Class: Elementi di Scienza Politica.* Ed. Arthur Livingston. Trans. Hannah D. Kahn. New York: McGraw-Hill.

Moussalli, Ahmad S. 1995. "Modern Islamic Fundamentalist Discourses on Civil Society, Pluralism, and Democracy." In Augustus R. Norton, ed. *Civil Society in the Middle East,* vol. I. Leiden: Brill.

Norton, Augustus R., ed. 1996a. *Civil Society in the Middle East,* vol. II. Leiden: Brill.

——. 1996b. "Political Reform in the Middle East." In Laura Guazzone, ed. *Global Interdependence and the Future of the Middle East.* London: Macmillan.

——, ed. 1995. *Civil Society in the Middle East,* vol. I. Leiden: Brill.

——. 1987. *Amal and the Shi'a: Struggle for the Soul of Lebanon.* Austin: University of Texas Press.

O'Donnell, Guillermo, and Philippe C. Schmitter. 1986. *Transitions from Authoritar-*

ian Rule: Tentative Conclusions about Uncertain Democracies. Baltimore: Johns Hopkins University Press.

Oxhorn, Philip. 1995. "From Controlled Inclusion to Coerced Marginalization: The Struggle for Civil Society in Latin America." In John A. Hall, ed. *Civil Society: Theory, History, Comparison.* Cambridge: Polity, pp. 250–77.

Peréz-Díaz, Victor. 1995. "The Possibility of Civil Society: Traditions, Character and Challenges." In John A. Hall, ed. *Civil Society: Theory, History, Comparison.* Cambridge: Polity, pp. 80–109.

————. 1993. *The Return of Civil Society.* Cambridge: Harvard University Press.

Putnam, Robert D. 1993. *Making Democracy Work: Civic Traditions in Modern Italy.* Princeton: Princeton University Press.

Richards, Alan, and John Waterbury. 1990. *A Political Economy of the Middle East: State, Class and Economic Development.* Boulder: Westview.

Rustow, Dankwart. 1970. "Transitions to Democracy." *Comparative Politics* 2, 3: 337–363.

Salamé, Ghassan, ed. 1994. *Democracy without Democrats? The Renewal of Politics in the Muslim World.* London: Taurus.

————, ed. 1987. *The Foundations of the Arab State.* London: Croom Helm.

————. 1987. *Al-Mujtama' wa al-Dawlah fi al-Mashriq al-'Arabi [Society and State in the Arab East].* Beirut: Center for Arab Unity Studies.

Sartori, Giovanni. 1995. "How Far Can Free Government Travel?" *Journal of Democracy* 6, 3 (July): 101–111.

al-Sayyid, Mustapha Kamel. 1995a. "A Civil Society in Egypt?" In Augustus R. Norton, ed. *Civil Society in the Middle East.* Leiden: Brill, pp. 269–293.

————. 1995b. "The Concept of Civil Society and the Arab World." In Rex Brynen, Bahgat Korany, and Paul Noble, eds. *Political Liberalization in the Arab World: Volume I, Theoretical Perspectives.* Boulder: Lynne Rienner, pp. 131–147.

Schmitter, Philippe C. 1995. "Is It Safe for Transitologists and Consolidologists to Travel to the Middle East and North Africa?" Unpublished paper.

Seligman, Adam. 1992. *The Idea of Civil Society.* New York: Free Press.

Shapiro, Ian. 1993. "Democratic Innovation: South Africa in Comparative Context." *World Politics* 46, 1 (October): 121–150.

Shils, Edward. 1991. "The Idea of Civil Society." *Government and Opposition* 26 (Winter): 3–20.

Singerman, Diane. 1995. *Avenues of Participation: Family, Politics and Networks in Urban Quarters of Cairo.* Princeton: Princeton University Press.

Sullivan, Denis J. 1995. *Non-Governmental Organizations and Freedom of Association: Palestine & Egypt: A Comparative Analysis.* Jerusalem: Palestinian Academic Society for the Study of International Affairs.

Toprak, Binnaz. 1996. "Civil Society in Turkey." In Augustus R. Norton, ed. *Civil Society in the Middle East.* Leiden: Brill, pp. 87–118.

Waltz, Susan. 1996. *Human Rights and Reform: Changing the Face of North African Politics.* Berkeley: University of California Press.

Walzer, Michael. 1991. "The Idea of Civil Society." *Dissent* (Spring): 293–304.

4. Explaining Women's Support for Political Islam
Contributions from Feminist Theory

Jodi Nachtwey and Mark Tessler

INTRODUCTION

Women's support for Islamist movements is perplexing for many Westerners who see Islamist groups as obstacles to women's freedom and independence. Indeed, Islamist discourse has generally aimed at restricting women's public participation by underscoring the value of their roles as mothers and wives. Despite this emphasis on traditional gender roles, however, it appears that women are no less likely than men to endorse the Islamist platform. The basis of such support is frequently explained by economic, political, and cultural factors, with little or no reference to considerations of gender. But do these explanations apply equally to men and women? To understand the basis of popular support for political Islam, it is necessary to examine the circumstances and motivations of women as well as men.

The issue of support for religious activism is not limited to the Middle East. Religious movements thrive in Asia and Latin America, as well as the United States, and some scholars have undertaken cross-national analyses of the origins and growth of such groups (Marty and Appleby 1995). Very little of this research addresses the role of gender, however. When it is considered at all, gender is usually examined in a discursive and legal framework, focusing on the rights and roles of women according to religious tenets. The views of the individual women who actually support religious movements and ideologies are only beginning to be studied (Gerami 1996; Badran 1994). Comparisons of the attitudes toward religious groups held by men and women, both within-

Some of the material in this chapter is based on Mark Tessler and Jolene Jesse, "Gender and Support for Islamist Movements: Evidence from Egypt, Kuwait and Palestine," The Muslim World 86, 2: 200–228.

country and between-countries, will contribute to a fuller understanding of the origins and growth of popular support for religious movements.

The present chapter seeks to make such a contribution. It draws upon both recent developments in the Arab world and theoretical insights from feminist scholarship for conceptual guidance, and it uses public opinion data from Egypt, Kuwait, Palestine, and Morocco to examine the nature and determinants of the attitudes held by ordinary men and women. Presented first is a brief overview of previous research on the growth of Islamist movements. Next, feminist theory is used to identify alternative interpretations of women's support for these movements. Finally, the public opinion data are analyzed in order to compare the views of men and women in the four populations surveyed and to develop and compare profiles of Islamist supporters as a function of both gender and country.

ORIGINS OF ISLAMIST MOVEMENTS

The literature on political Islam identifies several factors contributing to the growing importance of Islamist groups and movements during the last quarter century. These factors can be categorized as political, economic, sociocultural, and external (Moghadam 1994a, p. 8). These categories are not mutually exclusive.

Politically, the countries of the Arab Middle East have undergone vast changes in the last fifty years. The experience of colonialism produced nationalist movements that gained power during the 1950s and 1960s. These movements, and the states they later formed, in almost all cases advocated a model of modernization based on industrialization and development along Western lines. In many instances, there was also an emphasis on secularism in public law and public policy, especially in such areas as education, work, and the status of women. The push toward modernization and secularism was further abetted by the Arab-Israeli war of 1947–1948, in which monarchies and other traditional regimes were discredited by their defeat at the hands of the new Jewish state.

Nationalist leaders made sweeping promises and raised high hopes as they assumed power, and for a decade or so many performed reasonably well. In countries like Egypt, Tunisia, Algeria, Syria, and Iraq, although in different ways, there were important gains in education, industrialization, agriculture, and, in most cases, women's rights. Many nationalist regimes also constructed strong political machines and were effective in carrying out programs of political mobilization.

By the late 1960s and early 1970s, however, the shortcomings of these nationalist governments were more visible than their accomplishments to many of the citizens they ruled. Most of these regimes had turned out to be either corrupt, authoritarian, or both, creating a climate of intolerance in which dissent was suppressed, sometimes brutally, and many ordinary men and women increasingly felt frustrated and marginalized. The result, as expressed by one analyst, was "widespread disillusion with the national liberation model" of government (Moghadam 1994a, p. 8), which in turn, as reported in an important early study, acted "as a trigger to the emergence, appearance, or strengthening of Islamic groups" (Dessouki 1982, p. 25). Another early study, focusing on Tunisia, described how mounting social discontent and political repression during the 1970s contributed to the emergence of a "parallel [Islamist] society with its own laws and rules" (Tessler 1980).

The economic shortcomings of nationalist and secular Arab regimes were as pronounced as their political inadequacies. Despite some early gains, economic growth and development fell far short of expectations in almost all cases, and unemployment and underemployment were particularly serious problems by the 1970s, especially for the young. The latter situation was the result not only of governmental failures but of rapid population growth, which sent increasing numbers of young people into the labor force each year.

Except in the few countries with significant resources from petroleum exports, the combination of poor economic performance and rapid population growth created a situation which contributed to the growth of Islamic political movements. Among the urban poor, legions of young men, unable to find regular employment, spent most days on street corners or in coffee houses, becoming ever more disillusioned and embittered (Tessler 1993). In present-day Algeria, interestingly, they are sometimes called "homeboys" (*houmistes*), boys from the neighborhood, or "wall boys" (*hittistes*), unemployed youth who have nothing to do and so "hang out," leaning against the walls that line many city streets (Brown 1993). In Egypt, Syria, and the Maghrib, these young men joined students and others in antigovernment riots during the late 1970s and early 1980s.

The circumstances of better-educated young people were also increasingly unsatisfactory. Many of those educated after independence could not find jobs in the stagnant private sector and were accordingly dependent on the government for employment. The swelling ranks of the state bureaucracy put further strain on the economy, creating a vicious circle that was antithetical to economic growth. In addition, this situation left many well-educated individuals seriously underemployed, increasing their personal frustration and anger. Better-educated young men and women who are either unemployed or underemployed have thus been another source of support for Islamist movements (Roy 1994, p. 51), which accordingly have found high schools and universities to be fertile fields for recruitment in Egypt (Denoeux 1993), Tunisia (Hermassi 1984), and elsewhere. Indeed, by the late 1970s, Muslim groups were not only active but had in most cases displaced leftist organizations as the primary vehicles for political activity on many high school and university campuses.

Finally, these economic complaints have been reinforced by a large and growing gap between rich and poor, meaning that the burdens of underdevelopment are not shared equitably and that, despite economic difficulties, there are islands of affluence and privilege in most Arab states. A related complaint is that elite membership is determined in most instances not by ability, dedication, or service to society but, rather, by personal and political connections. Resentment of those who benefit from this situation, and of the regimes that are believed to tolerate or even encourage it, is an important additional factor producing support for Islamic movements that present themselves as opponents of the status quo (Tessler 1991, 1997).

These political and economic problems were exacerbated by rapid sociocultural change. Rural-urban migration occurred at a pace far exceeding the absorptive capacity of cities, creating not only shantytowns but anomie and alienation as well (Barakat 1993, p. 170). Many of the new urban residents were exposed to the proliferation of material goods, only to have their desires frustrated by unemployment and the lack of opportunities for advancement (Roy 1994, pp. 3–4).

This situation, as well as rapid social change more generally, created another opportunity for Islamist movements, who appealed to the frustrated social classes by emphasizing familiar religious symbols. Ironically, perhaps, the state itself often gave legitimacy to such activity, seeking to win popular support by proclaiming its own attachment to Islamic values. In addition, in Egypt and a number of other countries, particularly during the 1970s, the regime often encouraged religious movements in order to balance a perceived challenge from the political left. Only later did governments recognize that Islamist movements posed an even greater challenge, but by then it was often too late to control the most radical Muslim groups (Badran 1991, p. 222).

Adding to these domestic considerations was the influence of significant external developments. The Arab-Israeli war of June 1967 was particularly important. With revolutionary regimes in Egypt and Syria defeated even more decisively than had been their feudalistic predecessors in 1948, there was a decline in the influence and prestige of the secular models of development by which these states had been guided. Correspondingly, there was suddenly a new credibility to the Islamist argument that progress could be achieved only if the Arabs were guided by an indigenous political formula, namely that provided by Islam. Calling for governance based on Islamic law, Muslim ideologues proclaimed to the defeated Arabs that Islam "could do what no imported doctrine could hope to do—mobilize the believers, instill discipline, and inspire people to make sacrifices and, if necessary, to die" (Ajami 1981, p. 52).

Another important external factor was the rise of OPEC and the accumulation during the 1970s of huge revenue surpluses by Saudi Arabia and other petroleum-exporting states of the Arab Gulf. These conservative regimes subsequently devoted substantial sums to religious enterprises throughout the Arab world. They provided funds for the construction of religious schools and mosques, and also for Islamic cultural and political organizations (Moghadam 1994a, p. 8).

Finally, the Iranian revolution of 1979 was of critical importance. On the one hand, Iran, too, used some of its considerable wealth from petroleum exports to support Islamic movements in other countries. In addition, however, the Islamic regime in revolutionary Iran supported antigovernment Muslim groups opposed to the status quo in a number of Arab states, providing assistance that sometimes included military equipment and personnel. Moreover, beyond the practical significance of this aid, the Iranian revolution was itself of tremendous symbolic importance. Reversing the experience of the 1967 war, in which the small Jewish state had defeated the many Arab armies ranged against it, the Iranian opposition had, under the banner of Islam, succeeded in ousting a government which possessed enormous military power and was actively supported by the West.

ISLAMIST MOVEMENTS AND WOMEN

Substantial numbers of women support Islamist movements. Such support is an enigma to some Western observers, since it would appear that many of these movements seek to restrict women's political, economic, and social choices. Nevertheless, as will be reported below, women are no less likely than men to support Islamist movements or political orientations, and this, in turn, suggests two interrelated questions. Why does the Islamist message resonate with some Muslim women, and do the same factors explain the Islamist appeal among women and men?

To begin, it must be emphasized that not all Muslim groups have the same views about women. All of these groups are admittedly hostile to Western notions of women's emancipation. For example, almost all strongly advocate Islamic dress for women, oppose any contact between the sexes with the potential to lead to intimacy outside of marriage, and believe that women's roles should be confined to those of wife and mother. At most, a married woman should work outside the home only if this does not interfere with her primary obligation, which is to care for her husband and to bear and raise Muslim children.

At the same time, at least some Islamist groups, including the large and mainstream Muslim Brotherhood, stress the rights as well as the obligations of women. The Brotherhood and many other Muslim groups encourage education for women, for example, even at the highest level. Indeed, the founder of the Brotherhood in Egypt, Hasan al-Banna, favored women's participation in public life and established private schools for the education of women as early as the 1930s. Some Muslim groups also concede that men have neglected women's rights and been excessive in imposing obligations, although they add that this is the result of the overall corruption and spiritual emptiness of the present-day social order (Ibrahim 1982, p. 122).

Reflecting this belief that women should be politically conscious and socially active, female supporters of the Muslim Brotherhood have formed their own organizations in a number of countries. Commonly known as the Muslim Sisters, these groups are particularly active on university campuses in Egypt, Kuwait, and many other Arab and Muslim countries, and they have often been heavily involved in efforts to mobilize student opinion on behalf of the Brotherhood or other Islamist movements. An important model for such Islamist women's organizations is the Society of Muslim Women that was formed in Egypt in the 1950s. The society undertook charitable work in a number of areas. It also carried out underground political work on behalf of the Muslim Brotherhood, especially after the organization was declared illegal (Kepel 1984, p. 29).

These examples make it clear that many associated with the Muslim Brotherhood and other Muslim groups do not believe that Islam desires women to be ignorant or uninvolved in public life. On the contrary, the views of some Western observers notwithstanding, most Islamist movements believe that women should be politically conscious in order to participate in the battle for a just society. At the same time, Islamist leaders defend a patriarchal hierarchy and advocate a traditional model of gender relations centered on the family, making it highly unlikely that women would regard political Islam as a force for the expansion of their roles and choices. Indeed, while Islamist movements appeal to many women, they have threatened others and have been actively opposed by women's organizations in some countries.

The appeal of political Islam to many Muslim women needs to be examined in light of these competing tendencies in the Islamist platform, and both the circumstances of women in the Arab world and theory-oriented feminist scholarship may be consulted for relevant insights. One part of the explanation for this appeal, consistent with one stream of feminist discourse, may be the ability of Islamist movements to promote a model of women that is qualitatively different from that of men. Emphasizing gender differences rather than equality, this perspective gained recognition with the work of Carol Gilligan, who has argued that women have a different form of moral reasoning than do men (Gilligan 1994). Other scholars, sometimes referred to as "mothering theorists," have contributed to this perspective by arguing that women possess particular knowledge, or "maternal thinking," due to their roles as caregivers (Grant 1993; Ruddick 1989). In general, these theorists assert that women have acquired distinctive values through their experiences as mothers, and that these values, such as altruism and caring, are transmitted through the family and enhance social stability and morality (Grant 1993, p. 59).

Accordingly, these theorists assert that encouraging women to play roles similar to those of men only represses unique feminine qualities to the detriment of both individual women and society as a whole. This discourse is popular among many American women of the New Right, who fear that as the role of the homemaker is devalued, society will become "masculinized" and moral authority associated with the home will decline (Klatch 1994).

Mothering theory parallels Islamist discourse in that both regard men and women as being equal yet very different. For example, theorist Muhammad al-Ghazzali stresses that Islam bestows rights and obligations on both men and women, but that these differ according to a natural distinction between the sexes (Talhami 1996, p. 65). According to al-Ghazzali, a women's special nature, including her emotional character and physique, makes her perfectly suited for raising and nurturing children. Moreover, this role is particularly critical since, in the eyes of many Islamists, Western economic and cultural influences promote self-interested individualism and moral laxity in absence of an Islamic state. Women's role in the family is thus essential for preserving a sense of collective responsibility and for instilling emerging generations with Islamic values and ethics. This Islamist message may be especially persuasive to women who believe that social problems result from the neglect of spiritual values.

Considerations of identity may contribute in a similar manner to the appeal of Islamist messages. In countries where traditional values and social institutions are challenged by the spread of foreign cultural forms, women may acquire from their mothering role feelings of both security and pride. With respect to the former, they may take comfort in familiar and clearly defined gender roles during periods of rapid social change. With respect to the latter, and perhaps even more important in light of the struggle to resist Western cultural domination, they may consider it an honor and a privilege to have responsibility for transmitting traditional values and identities to future generations (Moghadam 1994b, p. 19). For these reasons, too, women may find Islamism's emphasis on mothering compelling.

An alternative interpretation of women's support for Islamist movements comes from theorists who have introduced a class dimension into feminist discourse. Attention to the socioeconomic context of women suggests that certain liberal conceptions of women's emancipation may not be universally applicable. In the United States, for example, the call for expanding women's participation in the workplace often does not resonate with lower-class women, who have had no choice but to work and who view domesticity as an escape from the drudgery of low-skill jobs (hooks 1984). Conservatives of the New Right express a similar view. They argue that promoting the economic independence of women discourages men from fulfilling their financial responsibilities to the family and actually, thereby, contributes to women's economic insecurity (Klatch 1994).

These ideas are applicable to the Middle East, where Islamist groups have had success in attracting lower-class women (Badran 1994). For one thing, Islamist movements have gained support among poor women by providing critical assistance through welfare networks and programs. In addition, the economic vision of Islamists is appealing because it promises justice and security. Secular feminism may offer women independence, but it does not call for an improved standard of living. As Ghada Hashem Talhami observes with reference to Egypt, "The [secular] message of individual freedom and independence in the midst of poverty and national humiliation lacked the mobilizational force of the Islamic utopian program" (1996, p. 140). The appeal of the Islamist vision is not limited to individuals of the lower class, however; well-educated women are also attracted by its ideology. Based on equalitarian principles and a belief that societal well-being, rather than the maximization of personal profit, should be the standard of production, the Islamic ideal may also resonate among well-educated individuals with socialist tendencies (Talhami 1996).

Additional insights about women's attraction to Islamist movements come from scholars interested in the relationship between feminism and nationalism. Feminists who study the developing world report that women's political consciousness has frequently taken shape within a framework of nationalism (Heng 1997). They point both to considerations that are relevant for women in particular and to motivations that are shared by women and men. One factor in the former category is the view that colonialism and imperialism reinforce traditional social institutions. Accordingly, the effort to change patriarchal structures requires a struggle against overarching power relationships through movements of national liberation. A related factor, focused on developments at the grassroots level, is that participation in nationalist activities frequently provides women with opportunities to redefine and expand their roles. Both of these considerations enable women to link their quest for progressive gender policies to their participation in the struggle for cultural and national independence (Sinha 1994).

At the same time, women are drawn to nationalist movements for the same overriding reason as men—to combat foreign domination. The motivation in this case is essentially political, even though the protection of cultural integrity may be a related objective. To the extent that the nationalist cause is of paramount importance to some women, or many women, they may give little thought to the possibility that the struggle against foreign domination is also a struggle against patriarchy. Indeed, they may deliberately eschew any concern with issues of gender so as to ensure that men and women are fully united against their common enemy. Further, efforts to mobilize support for the nationalist cause among ordinary citizens may require an emphasis on conservative traditional values. For these reasons, a link between feminism and nationalism may be absent, or even explicitly denounced, by women as well as men, as contrary to the collective good (Moghadam 1994a).

The motivations associated with women's involvement in nationalist movements may also shed light on their support for political Islam. Altering power relationships in order to achieve political freedom and a better life, the primary motivation for women's participation in nationalist movements, is the central objective of Islamist movements as well. These movements believe that domestic governments are dominated by foreign interests and misled by foreign models of development, and hence embodiments of neocolonialism. In pursuit of their objectives, Islamist theoreticians have often reinterpreted religious texts in order to encourage a more traditional view of women's roles, justifying these interpretations not only in terms of fidelity to "true" Islamic principles but also, and even more so, as part of the struggle against an unsatisfactory status quo (Hatem 1993).

Women's support for Islamist movements may reflect their agreement both about the failings of existing governments and about how it may be possible to change the status quo. More specifically, women may believe that an Islamic, non-Western model offers the best chance for breaking free from foreign domination and for improving political, economic, and social conditions. Further, this view may also lead many women to reject contemporary feminism, regarding it as a symbol of patterns of society and culture that contribute to their exploitation and impoverishment and, also, as a source of gender divisions which hinder progress in the struggle for a better life (Badran 1994).

Following these different feminist perspectives, women's support for Islamist movements can be regarded as a consequence of either cultural, economic, or political factors. First it may be hypothesized that women who believe the sexes are naturally different, and who regard these differences as unalterable and appropriate, are more likely to look to Islamist movements for guidance and support. A second proposition is that support for Islamist movements will be pronounced among women who are economically vulnerable or among women who believe that economic justice is more important than individual economic advancement. A third hypothesis is that women who are unhappy with secular governments will support these movements in order to work for the establishment of alternative Islamic political structures and institutions.

All of these hypotheses, however, could also be posited for men. Men are quite likely to share the cultural, economic, and political views identified for women, and past research in the Arab world has shown that Islamist movements have a strong appeal among men who are disillusioned with the political and economic failures of contemporary governments (Tessler 1997). On the other hand, although there is no specific theory to guide expectations, it is at least possible that the relative explanatory power of these factors is different for men and women. For example, insofar as men have traditionally been viewed as the primary household provider and have been more attentive to public affairs, economic and political considerations may be more salient in the case of men. Alternatively, cultural considerations may be more salient for women since some previous research suggests that they have stronger religious attachments than do men (Gallup and Castelli 1989, pp. 50–51).

The possibility of such differences notwithstanding, the preceding analysis leads to the conclusion that women are no less likely than men to support Islamist movements. This is suggested and can be understood through the prism of various feminist discourses, which also help to explain why an Islamist perspective, despite its conservatism, may be more attractive to many women than contemporary Western ideals of gender equality. Practical considerations relating to the life circumstances of Middle Eastern Muslim women may also help to account for their support of political Islam. Islamist movements often provide women with a vehicle by which to assert their autonomy and build social networks outside the home (Arat 1990, p. 21). Moreover, these networks are unlikely to threaten either male family members or a society based on Islam. In this way, women with ties to Islamist movements may actually gain influence within the family and society, to the extent that their religious "credentials" force parents, male siblings, and other men to give greater weight to their views. For at least some women, support for the practice of veiling can also be understood in this context. While more secular women often see the practice as a form of social control, others believe that veiling affords protection and enhances autonomy and is thus both liberating and empowering (Moghadam 1994a, pp. 9–10; Arat 1990, p. 22; Macleod 1991).

Against this background, guided by both theoretical insights drawn from feminist scholarship and information provided by area specialists, two hypotheses may be proposed for an empirical investigation involving the analysis of public opinion data from the Middle East. First, it seems likely that women will be as well represented as men among the supporters of Islamist movements. Second, it seems likely that there will be significant similarities between the men and women who support such movements. To test this first proposition, the attitudes of men and women toward Islamist groups and ideas may be compared. To test the second, the relationship between support for political Islam and selected cultural, economic, and political orientations may be analyzed separately for men and women and the structure of these relationships compared.

DATA BASE AND RESEARCH DESIGN

The data to be presented and analyzed in the present study are from public opinion surveys carried out in Egypt, Kuwait, Palestine, and Morocco. The Egyptian and Kuwaiti data were collected by Dr. Jamal S. Al-Suwaidi, professor of political science at UAE University and director of the Emirates Center for Strategic Studies and Research in Abu Dhabi. The same interview schedule was used in Egypt and Kuwait. The Palestinian data were collected by the Center for Palestine Research and Studies (CPRS) in Nablus, under the supervision of its director, Dr. Khalil Shikaki, and the head of its polling unit, Dr. Nadir Said. The Moroccan data were collected through a collaborative research project sponsored by the American Institute for Maghrib Studies, with Professor Rahma Bourqia of Mohammed V University in Rabat and Professor Mark Tessler of UW-Milwaukee directing the teams of participating Moroccan and American scholars. Surveys in all four countries included questions about support for Islamist movements and/or orientations, as well as questions about the backgrounds and attitudes of respondents.

The Egyptian and Kuwaiti surveys were carried out in mid-1988, based on stratified samples of adults in Cairo and Kuwait City. All respondents are Sunni Muslims; Egyptian Christians and Kuwaiti Shiites were not included. Each sample includes an approximately equal proportion of men and women, and each is also heterogeneous and generally representative with respect to age, education, socioeconomic status, and place of residence. As a result, the 293 respondents interviewed in Egypt and the 300 respondents interviewed in Kuwait are broadly representative of the adult, urban, Sunni Muslim populations from which they are drawn. Information pertaining to sampling and measurement, including the training of research assistants who administered the interview schedule and procedures for assessing measurement validity and reliability, has been reported in detail in previous publications (Tessler and Sanad 1994; Tessler 1997).

The Palestinian survey was conducted in mid-1995. Multistage area probability sampling techniques were employed to select respondents, and the survey instrument was administered by trained interviewers to 1,184 adults residing in the West Bank and Gaza. CPRS has been conducting opinion research in Palestine since 1993 and has earned distinction for the quality of its work with respect to instrument design, interviewer training, and sampling. Some additional information relating to methodology is available elsewhere (Shikaki 1996).

The Moroccan data were collected in 1996–1997. The survey instrument was administered to a representative sample of adults in Rabat, the Moroccan capital, by trained interviewers working under the supervision of scholars from Mohammed V University. The representative sample involved 1,000 households selected through the use of area probability techniques, with one randomly selected member of each household then interviewed about his or her attitudes. The survey instrument was carefully pretested and scaling techniques were employed to establish the validity and reliability of items used to construct the attitudinal measures.

The data from these four samples provide a strong foundation for examining determinants of support for Islamist movements in the Arab world, both in general and with respect to considerations of gender. First, as noted, all four samples are highly representative, at least of the urban population, and all accordingly possess male and female respondents in almost equal proportions.

A second strength of the data base constructed for the present study is the potential to shed light on trends that apply beyond the cases examined. While no single study can be authoritative, a very considerable portion of the variance that exists among Sunni Muslim Arabs is encompassed by the populations from which samples have been drawn. For example, the characteristics and circumstances of the populations of Egypt and Morocco are in at least some respects analogous to those in Tunisia, Algeria, and Jordan. In each of these countries, as well as Egypt, levels of economic development are low and ordinary citizens face serious economic difficulties, including inadequacies of employment, housing, and education. Due to rapid population growth and a continuing exodus from the countryside, these problems are particularly severe among the young and in urban areas. There are also similarities in the political circumstances of these countries. All are (or were) governed by regimes that tolerate a measure of political openness and competition, even as they also tolerate significant corruption and a political class with privileged access to state resources.

Similarly, the situation of Kuwait's population is broadly comparable to that of Arabs in the other states and sheikhdoms of the Persian Gulf. There is a high level of affluence, reflecting the juxtaposition of a small population and great wealth from petroleum exports. There is also a conservative social environment, associated with the historic absence of large and cosmopolitan urban centers. Finally, there is a near-total absence of democratic political forms. Political life is monarchical in character, marked by the dominance of a single family and the corresponding absence of political parties.

Palestinians, being stateless, are probably less typical of other Arab communities. Yet the sample drawn in West Bank and Gaza may shed light on the attitudes of Palestinians elsewhere, and also, perhaps, on the inclinations of occupied and stateless populations more broadly. In addition, the situation in the West Bank and Gaza since the establishment of the Palestine National Authority has in some ways begun to resemble that of Egypt and other Arab republics. There are serious economic problems, and political life is marked by an important degree of openness and competition, even as corruption and authoritarianism are also prominent among patterns of governance.

A third important strength of the present study derives from the comparative analysis that is made possible by the cross-national data base. To the extent that the nature and determinants of attitudes are dissimilar among some or all of the samples, these variations may be attributed, at least in part, to any aggregate, system-level characteristics that differentiate among the populations from which samples have been drawn, such as level of affluence or degree of political openness. In this way, information will be gained about the conditions under which particular attitudes and attitudinal determinants are salient. Alternatively, if identical or similar patterns are found among the four samples, it will be possible to conclude that system-level attributes are irrelevant in these instances, and there will accordingly be greater confidence in their generalizability across different populations within the Arab and Islamic world.

FINDINGS AND ANALYSIS

A number of items in the survey instrument employed in Egypt and Kuwait dealt with attitudes toward Islamist movements. A statistical technique known as factor analysis identified the most reliable and valid of these items (Tessler and Sanad 1994; Tessler 1997), and from these the following item was selected for the present analysis: "Do you support current organized Islamic movements?" In the Palestinian survey, attitudes toward Islamist movements were gauged by an item asking about partisan preferences. Specifically, respondents were asked to identify the political faction they supported, and they were then classified according to whether they chose HAMAS or Islamic Jihad, rather than a party with a nationalist, leftist, or independent orientation.

In the Moroccan survey, no question explicitly solicited respondent attitudes toward Islamist groups. As an approximate indicator, an index was created by combining two survey items. The first asked about the extent to which religion should guide economic and business life in Morocco, and the second asked about the degree to which religion should guide administrative and political matters. While not an exact measure of Islamist support, this index does focus on respondent attitudes toward some of the goals championed by Islamist groups.

These data may be used to test the two hypotheses presented earlier. Findings pertaining to the first proposition, that women are as well represented as men among the supporters of Islamist movements and ideals, are presented in Table 1. The table provides support for this hypothesis, showing that gender-linked differences are of limited magnitude in three of the four cases, and that in the fourth case, that of Palestine, women are actually more likely than men to support Islamist parties. The difference in the Palestinian case is not large, but it is nonetheless sufficient to reach statistical significance.

Contingency table analysis has been employed to test the second hypothesis. This involves examining the relationship between support for Islamist movements and platforms on the one hand and, on the other, both selected cultural, economic, and political orientations and such personal attributes as age and education. These relationships have been examined separately for men and women from each country, permitting comparison across eight respondent categories. The discussion below introduces each orientation and attribute that has been examined, summarizes the way that each has been measured, and then identifies the gender and country categories, if any, for which this measure is related to support for political Islam. A summary of these findings is presented in Table 2.

Cultural Orientations

The cultural variables examined here are personal religiosity and attitudes toward gender equality. The former is measured through indicators of personal piety. For survey instruments containing a large number of items dealing with personal observance and piety, factor analysis was used to identify the most reliable and valid of these items.* The item selected from the Egyptian and Kuwaiti surveys for use in the present study asked respondents, "How often do

---

This procedure was used to select items and to establish measurement reliability and validity throughout the present study. The measures of cultural, economic, or political orientations used in the analysis were selected on the basis of two criteria: high factor loadings and conceptual equivalence.

Table 1. Levels of Support for Islamist Movements and Platforms among Female and Male Respondents from Egypt, Kuwait, Palestine, and Morocco

		Female	Male
Egypt:	Supports	11%	14%
	Somewhat Supports	26%	30%
	Uncertain	9%	7%
	Does Not Support	55%	49%
		101%	100%
Kuwait:	Supports	13%	17%
	Somewhat Supports	33%	38%
	Uncertain	18%	10%
	Does Not Support	37%	34%
		101%	99%
Palestine:	Supports	22%	15%
	Does Not Support	78%	86%
		100%	101%
Morocco:	Religion is Often a Guide	48%	47%
	Sometimes a Guide	17%	17%
	Rarely or Never a Guide	35%	36%
		100%	100%

Note: Figures may not add up to 100% due to rounding

you refer to religious teachings when making important decisions concerning your life?" A similar question was selected in the Moroccan case. It asked respondents, "In case of a personal or family problem, do you consult an *imam* or *fkih*?" For the Palestinian analysis, the survey item selected asked respondents to evaluate their overall level of religiosity.

There are only two instances in which support for Islamist movements and programs is not more pronounced among individuals who are more religious: among male respondents in Egypt and among female respondents in Kuwait. In both instances, there is virtually no difference in the religiosity levels of those who do and do not support political Islam. Among all other categories, there is a statistically significant relationship. Among Palestinians and Moroccans of both sexes, as well as Egyptian women and Kuwaiti men, more religious respondents are more likely to support Islamist groups and the application of religion to political life.

The second cultural orientation concerns gender equality. The item chosen from the Egyptian and Kuwaiti surveys for use in the present study asked respondents whether or not they agreed with the following statement: "Women

Table 2. Attributes and Attitudes Associated with Support for Islamist Movements and Platforms among Female and Male Respondents from Egypt, Kuwait, Palestine, and Morocco

	Female	Male
Egypt:	more religious	younger
	negative view of the government	negative view of the government
Kuwait:	negative view of the government	more religious
		negative view of the government
		better educated
Palestine:	more religious	more religious
	negative view of the government	negative view of the government
	less educated	less supportive of women's rights
		younger
Morocco:	more religious	more religious
		less politically efficacious
		older

Note: Except for two cases, all relationships listed above are statistically significant at the $p < .05$ level. For Palestinian women and Kuwaiti men, the association between government satisfaction and support for Islamist movements is significant at the $p < .10$ level.

should be required to cease work after marriage in order to devote full time to their homes and families." In Morocco, the question asked respondents when women should have the opportunity to work outside the home: always, never, or only before marriage? Palestinian respondents were asked their opinion about the statement: "Women must stay home to serve their husbands and children."

Although Western perceptions lead to an expectation that support for women's rights and opportunities is inversely associated with support for Islamist movements, this is the case for only one of the respondent categories examined: men in Palestine. Otherwise, expectations to the contrary not withstanding, levels of support for Islamist movements are comparable among those who agree and those who disagree that women should have greater rights and opportunities.

Economic Circumstances

To assess the importance of economic factors, two different types of indicators have been included in the analysis. The first involves demographic characteristics. More specifically, education is used as a measure of socioeconomic status and age is used as a measure of the degree to which respondents are personally and professionally established. While neither of these variables is a wholly satisfactory measure of economic circumstances, both are important personal characteristics and both can shed light on the locus and determinants of receptivity to Islamist appeals.

The second type of indicator involves a direct measure of perceived economic security. In Egypt and Kuwait, respondents were asked whether they were satisfied with their financial status. In Palestine, a similar survey item asked whether individuals considered themselves financially secure. Finally, the Moroccan survey included a question which asked respondents, "Over the past five years has your personal standard of living increased, stayed the same, or become worse?"

Neither education nor age possesses consistent or widespread explanatory power. Support for political Islam is associated with higher levels of education among Kuwaiti men and lower levels of education among Palestinian women. In none of the other six respondent categories is there a statistically significant relationship involving education. Relationships involving age are significant in three instances. Support for Islamist movements is associated with younger age among Egyptian men and among Palestinian men, and it is associated with older age among Moroccan men.

These findings suggest that personal economic circumstances may be of little use in accounting for attitudes toward political Islam, and this conclusion is indicated even more clearly by the analysis based on a direct measure of perceived economic security. In none of the eight respondent categories do individuals with a less favorable or secure economic situation have a greater propensity, or a lesser propensity for that matter, to support Islamist movements, parties, or platforms.

Political Judgments

To explore the political aspects of support for Islamist movements and platforms, the analysis includes a measure of respondent satisfaction with government performance. In Egypt and Kuwait, the survey item selected asks respondents whether they agree or disagree that the government usually ignores the needs of ordinary citizens. In Palestine, the question employed assesses the degree to which individuals believe that the Palestinian National Authority "works for the interest of all equally." For the Moroccan case, where only a measure of political efficacy was available, the survey item used asks respondents whether or not they agree that "politics is too complicated to be understood by ordinary citizens."

It is to be expected that respondents with unfavorable evaluations of the government or low levels of political efficacy are more likely than others to support Islamist movements, and this is in fact the case for all respondent categories except for women in Morocco. In two instances, among men in Kuwait and women in Palestine, the relationship is notable and in the anticipated direction but slightly short of statistical significance at the $p<.05$ level of confidence.

Table 2 presents a summary of these findings, identifying the factors that bear a significant relationship with support for Islamist movements or, in the Moroccan case, for guidance from religion in economic and political affairs. It thus provides a listing of the attributes and attitudes that are associated with support for political Islam for men and women in the four countries included in this study.

Not all respondents with a favorable predisposition toward Islamist movements possess these characteristics, of course. Indeed, to the extent that some variables are not related at all to support for political Islam in some respondent categories, those who support Islamist movements in these instances possess attributes and hold attitudes that are similar to those of persons who do not support Muslim political movements. Nevertheless, as shown in Table 2, considerations of gender and nationality define circumstances in which supporters of political Islam *are* drawn to a disproportionate degree from the ranks of individuals with certain identifiable characteristics.

CONCLUSION

The puzzle addressed in this research report is the presumed contradiction, from a Western standpoint, of women's support for Islamist groups whose discourse espouses a conservative model of gender roles. Understanding women's judgments and motivations is important since women are prominently represented among the supporters of these movements.

As the evidence presented here shows, women are as likely as men to support Islamist groups and programs. In fact, in some instances, as illustrated by the Palestinian case, women may actually be more likely than their male counterparts to express Islamist sentiments.

Still, why do women support such groups, and are their reasons different from those of men? Feminist theory was a guide in formulating some responses to these questions. Applying the insights of different streams of feminist scholarship helped to illuminate the cultural, economic, and political factors that may account for women's attitudes and behavior. By empirically testing the explanatory power of these factors, for women as well as men, some conclusions can be drawn about the individual attitudes and attributes that are associated with Islamist support. Three conclusions stand out: (1) cultural and political factors are more important than economic considerations; (2) relationships vary as a function of social context; and (3) generally speaking, the factors that are most useful in explaining women's behavior also have the greatest explanatory power among men.

In almost all cases, individuals exhibiting greater religiosity in their personal lives are more likely to support Islamist movements or the application of religion in public affairs. Only among Kuwaiti women and Egyptian men was this not the case. By contrast, attitudes toward gender equality, the other variable measuring cultural orientations, have little explanatory power. Only among Palestinian men, and to a lesser extent among Palestinian women, were more traditional notions of women's roles associated with support for Islamist parties.

The significance of religiosity but not attitudes toward gender may seem like a contradiction, but several explanations of these results are plausible. One, suggested by previous research among Muslim women activists in Egypt, is that Islamists and feminists agree, albeit for different reasons, that women should be allowed and even encouraged to participate actively in the public sphere (Badran 1994). The main difference between these two categories of women lies in their views about private gender relations and their attitudes toward the establishment of an Islamic state (Badran 1994; Hatem 1993). Had additional survey measures been available, it might have been possible to examine some of these other dimensions.

A second possible explanation, which may be more pertinent in assessing the views of ordinary citizens, is that support for political Islam does not reflect a desire for traditional cultural forms and behavioral models but rather for Islamic values associated with the construction of a just and harmonious society. These values include equality, fairness, the rule of law, and protection of the weak. While additional survey items would also be needed to investigate this possibility, it is consistent with the present study's findings related to political attitudes, which are summarized below.

As reported, political factors, and regime evaluations in particular, are generally associated with attitudes toward political Islam. Among women in Egypt and Kuwait and among men in Egypt, Palestine, and Morocco, dissatisfaction with government performance and responsiveness to ordinary citizens is associated with greater support for Islamist movements and platforms. If cases of borderline statistical significance are included, this relationship also exists among Palestinian women and Kuwaiti men. This finding provides support for past research which has emphasized the political factors fueling Islamist movements (Tessler 1997). The inability of regimes to solve critical social problems has led to the erosion of their legitimacy and has increased the credibility of Islamist solutions.

The economic explanation of Islamist support appears to be weak. Neither education nor age, which were used as proxy measures of socioeconomic status and security, displayed consistent or widespread explanatory power. Even more significant, direct measures of perceived economic security are not related to attitudes toward political Islam among respondents in any of the categories based on gender and country. A few of the statistically significant relationships involving education or age might be interpreted in light of the concerns of the present study. For example, the fact that younger men in Egypt and Palestine are more supportive of political Islam might indicate that, for these respondent categories, economic vulnerability increases receptivity to Islamist appeals. For the most part, however, the few significant relationships involving indirect economic measures are peripheral to the present inquiry and do not challenge the overall conclusion that economic circumstances do not account for the variance in support for Islamist movements and platforms.

Given that high levels of personal religiosity and unfavorable evaluations of the government clearly emerge as the most important factors contributing to support for Islamist movements, the underlying values linking these cultural and political orientations suggest what may be the best way to understand support for political Islam. As noted earlier, this involves justice, the rule of law, equity, and protection of the weak.

In the countries included in the present study, and perhaps in other Muslim societies as well, political Islam appears to be seen, first and foremost, as a vehicle for protesting the perceived ethical and moral deficiencies of governments that are in power. If this interpretation is correct, it is among those who are most concerned about such deficiencies, those who feel most strongly the need for greater justice, fairness, and respect for the rule of law, that support for Islamist movements is disproportionately high. Also, in general, this is the case regardless of the personal economic circumstances within which individuals reside, and it is notable as well that a desire for greater morality in public affairs does not carry with it a preference for traditional gender roles.

Finally, with respect to this study's interest in gender, it is significant not only that attitudes toward gender roles are generally unrelated to attitudes toward Islamist movements, but, more broadly, that similarities between men and women are more striking than differences in the profiles of respondents who are more supportive of political Islam. Despite some variation of potential interest, the combined salience of personal religiosity and negative evaluations of the government, as noted above, is for the most part associated with favorable attitudes toward Islamist movements and messages among both men and women.

While these findings may contribute to a fuller understanding of support for Islamist movements among men and women in the Muslim world, the central purpose of this study has been to illustrate how social science theory can inform research on topics that are usually associated with area studies scholarship. Toward this end, feminist theory has helped to explicate support for Islamist movements by highlighting the neglect of women's motivations in past studies and, more particularly, by suggesting how their circumstances and calculations may actually lead many women to take a favorable view of political Islam. At the same time, although feminist theory provided valuable insights involving cultural, economic, and political considerations, these insights could not be translated into plausible explanations of women's behavior unless grounded in specific real-world situations. Further, these insights gave rise to different and to some extent competing explanations, which could only be assessed through the kind of in-depth fieldwork that is impossible without area expertise. Thus, in summary, this study illustrates both the relevance of disciplinary theory, feminist theory in this case, and the value of research in which both theory and area studies perspectives make a contribution.

The findings from this investigation also make an analytical contribution to feminist scholarship, demonstrating that scholarly influence can flow in both directions in the relationship between theory and area studies research. More specifically, these findings indicate that the orientations of women are shaped by the same considerations as the orientations of men, by personal religiosity and political judgments in the present study, and that factors which might be expected to have more salience for women than men are in fact less important. This, in turn, suggests that those streams of feminist theory which are grounded in the experience of Western women may need to broaden their conceptual scope and pay more attention to overarching contextual considerations in the formation of women's attitudes. Indeed, this has been the focus of a growing body of writing by Third World women (Mohanty 1991). It appears in this connection that the gender-specific issues emphasized by some Western feminists are of only limited relevance to many Middle East Muslim women, and perhaps to other Third World women as well, and that feminist priorities, as well as gender itself, are less important than religious and political factors in shaping attitudes and behavior. This observation, which helps to explain why Western feminism has not always found a receptive audience in the Arab world, deserves attention from all who seek to understand the orientations of women in the Middle East.

REFERENCES

Abu-Amr, Ziad. 1994. *Islamic Fundamentalism in the West Bank and Gaza: Muslim Brotherhood and Islamic Jihad.* Bloomington: Indiana University Press.

Ajami, Fouad. 1981. *The Arab Predicament: Arab Political Thought and Practice since 1967.* Cambridge: Cambridge University Press.

Arat, Yesim. 1990. "Islamic Fundamentalism and Women in Turkey." *Muslim World* 80: 17–23.

Badran, Margot. 1995. *Feminists, Islam, and Nation: Gender and the Making of Modern Egypt.* Princeton: Princeton University Press.

———. 1994. "Gender Activism: Feminists and Islamists in Egypt." In *Identity Politics and Women: Cultural Reassertion and Feminism in International Perspective.* Ed. Valentine M. Moghadam. Boulder: Westview.

———. 1991. "Competing Agenda: Feminists, Islam, and the State in Nineteenth- and Twentieth-Century Egypt." In *Women, Islam, and the State.* Ed. Deniz Kandiyoti. London: Macmillan, pp. 201–236.

Barakat, Halim. 1993. *The Arab World: Society, Culture, and State.* Berkeley: University of California Press.

Brown, Kenneth. 1993. "Lost in Algiers." *Mediterraneans* 4 (Summer): 8–18.

Denoeux, Guilain. 1993. "Religious Networks and Urban Unrest: Lessons from Iranian and Egyptian Experiences." In *The Violence Within: Cultural and Political Opposition in Divided Nations*. Ed. Kay B. Warren. Boulder: Westview.

Dessouki, Ali E. Hillal. 1982. "The Islamic Resurgence: Sources, Dynamics, and Implications." In *Islamic Resurgence in the Arab World*. Ed. Ali E. Hillal Dessouki. New York: Praeger, pp. 3–31.

Gallup, George, Jr., and Jim Castelli. 1989. *The People's Religion: American Faith in the 90's*. New York: Macmillan.

Gerami, Shahin. 1996. *Women and Fundamentalism: Islam and Christianity*. New York: Garland.

Gilligan, Carol. 1994. "In a Different Voice." In *Feminism in Our Time: The Essential Writings, World War II to the Present*. Ed. Miriam Schneir. New York: Vintage.

Grant, Judith. 1993. *Fundamental Feminism: Contesting the Core Concepts of Feminist Theory*. New York: Routledge.

Hatem, Mervat. 1993. "Toward the Development of Post-Islamist and Post-Nationalist Feminist Discourses in the Middle East." In *Arab Women: Old Boundaries, New Frontiers*. Ed. Judith Tucker. Bloomington: Indiana University Press.

Heng, Geraldine. 1997. "'A Great Way to Fly': Nationalism, the State, and the Varieties of Third-World Feminism." In *Feminist Genealogies, Colonial Legacies, and Democratic Futures*. Ed. M. Jacqui Alexander and Chandra Talpade Mohanty. New York: Routledge.

Hermassi, Elbaki. 1984. "La société tunisienne au miroir islamiste." *Maghreb-Machrek* 103: 39–56.

hooks, bell. 1984. *Feminist Theory: From Margin to Center*. Boston: South End.

Ibrahim, Saad Eddin. 1982. "Islamic Militancy as Social Movement: The Case of Two Groups in Egypt." In *Islamic Resurgence in the Arab World*. Ed. Ali E. Hillal Dessouki. New York: Praeger, pp. 117–137.

Kandiyoti, Deniz. 1991. "Introduction." In *Women, Islam, and the State*. Ed. Deniz Kandiyoti. London: Macmillan, pp. 1–21.

Kepel, Gilles. 1984. *Muslim Extremism in Egypt*. Berkeley: University of California Press.

Klatch, Rebecca E. 1994. "Women of the New Right in the United States: Family, Feminism, and Politics." In *Identity Politics and Women: Cultural Reassertion and Feminism in International Perspective*. Ed. Valentine M. Moghadam. Boulder: Westview.

Macleod, Arlene Elowe. 1991. *Accommodating Protest: Working Women, the New Veiling, and Change in Cairo*. New York: Columbia University Press.

Marty, Martin E., and R. Scott Appleby. 1995. *Fundamentalisms Comprehended*. Chicago: University of Chicago Press.

Moghadam, Valentine M. 1994a. "Introduction and Overview: Gender Dynamics of Nationalism, Revolution, and Islamization." In *Gender and National Identity: Women and Politics in Muslim Societies*. Ed. Valentine M. Moghadam. London: Zed, pp. 1–17.

———. 1994b. "Introduction: Women and Identity Politics in Theoretical and Comparative Perspective." In *Identity Politics and Women: Cultural Reassertion and Feminism in International Perspective*. Boulder: Westview.

Mohanty, Chandra Talpade. 1991. "Under Western Eyes: Feminist Scholarship and

Colonial Discourses." In *Third World Women and the Politics of Feminism*. Ed. Chandra Talpade Mohanty, Ann Russo, and Lourde Torres. Bloomington: Indiana University Press.

Roy, Olivier. 1994. *The Failure of Political Islam*. Cambridge: Harvard University.

Ruddick, Sara. 1989. *Maternal Thinking: Toward a Politics of Peace*. Boston: Beacon.

Sanad, Jamal, and Mark Tessler. 1990. "Women and Religion in a Modern Islamic Society: The Case of Kuwait." In *Religious Resurgences and Politics in the Contemporary World*. Ed. Emile Sahliyeh. Albany: State University of New York Press.

Sinha, Mrinalini. 1994. "Gender in the Critiques of Colonialism and Nationalism: Locating the 'Indian Woman.'" In *Feminists Revision History*. Ed. Louise Shapiro. New Brunswick: Rutgers University Press.

Shikaki, Khalil. 1996. "The Transition to Democracy in Palestine." *Journal of Palestine Studies* 98 (Winter): 12.

———. 1994. "Reports of Public Opinion Surveys Conducted in the West Bank and Gaza." Nablus, West Bank: Center for Palestine Research and Studies.

Talhami, Ghada Hashem. 1996. *The Mobilization of Muslim Women in Egypt*. Gainesville: University Press of Florida.

Tessler, Mark. 1997. "The Origins of Popular Support for Islamist Movements: A Political Economy Analysis." In *Islam, Democracy, and the State in North Africa*. Ed. John P. Entelis. Bloomington: Indiana University Press.

———. 1993. "The Alienation of Urban Youth." In *State and Society in Contemporary North Africa*. Ed. I. William Zartman and Mark Habeeb. Boulder: Westview.

———. 1991. "Anger and Governance in the Arab World: Lessons from the Maghrib and Implications for the West." *The Jerusalem Journal of International Relations* 13: 7–33.

———. 1980. "Political Change and the Islamic Revival in Tunisia." *The Maghreb Review* 5: 8–19.

———, and Jamal Sanad. 1994. "Will the Arab Public Accept Peace with Israel? Evidence from Surveys in Three Arab Societies." In *Israel at the Crossroads*. Ed. Gregory Mahler and Efriam Karsh. London: Tauris.

5. Influencing Public Policy
Banking and the Political Economy of Collective Action

Clement M. Henry

Inspired by the breakup of a number of authoritarian regimes first in Latin America, then in Eastern Europe, and finally in the Soviet Union, many political scientists have become engaged over the past decade in studies of transitions to democracy and the subsequent problems of democratic consolidation. In this context civil society became a major focus of comparative politics. Although democracy eluded most Middle Eastern countries, area specialists followed prevailing global trends and investigated the development of civil society in the Middle East and North Africa (MENA) as a prelude to democracy. Civil society, a concept articulated originally in Western political theory, became a global concept.

Traveling so far and so fast over the past decade, the concept of civil society was stretched to fit a variety of non-Western societies (Sartori 1970). As Jillian Schwedler points out, "Much of the recent theoretical work on civil society has replaced the idea of civil society as a result of capitalist expansion with the idea that it is a sphere of democratic interaction" (Schwedler 1995, p. 5). Augustus Richard Norton, who headed the massive project on civil society in the MENA, wisely refused to bind the many collaborators to strict definitions of the concept. His goal was "to provide an outline image of Middle East civil society without getting bogged down, unnecessarily, in post-modernist obfuscation or ideal-typical fixations" (Norton 1995, p. 11). The value of his project lay in its broad scope, enlisting numerous descriptions of relationships between regimes and their oppositions, or between state and civil society, and encouraging scholars to debate the concept of civil society "existentially, theoretically, conceptually, normatively, and ontologically" (1995, p. 25). Yet, given the elusive nature of the concept, and the incredible amount written about civil society, not only in the MENA but in many other parts of the world, it remains difficult to engage in any systematic comparisons.

At the risk of adding to the confusion, I shall try in this essay to present an approach which offers a way of engaging in systematic comparisons of civil society in different parts of the world. Employing a political economy perspective, I shall first report on research that examines the commercial banking system in the MENA as a way to locate an emerging bourgeoisie and to assess its potential for participating in civil society. Next, by focusing on historical and contextual factors, as well as social science theory, I shall attempt to provide a more accurate assessment of the strength of civil society in the MENA relative to that of the state. Finally, I shall turn to other region-specific considerations in order to argue that the genesis of civil society may more closely resemble paradigmatic Western experience in the MENA than in other non-Islamic and non-Christian parts of the developing world.

THE POLITICAL ECONOMY APPROACH

In haste to extend the concept of civil society to embrace the "Third Wave" of democratic transitions which crested in the early 1990s (Huntington 1991), many writers lost sight of its Western bourgeois origins. Particularly in Middle Eastern studies, chastened by Edward Said's trenchant attacks on Orientalism, many area experts have tried to purge their intellectual baggage of exclusively Western concepts lest they distort and possibly denigrate the MENA's social and cultural realities. Hegel, for instance, was a supreme Orientalist (Hentsch 1992, pp. 139–145), but he also developed a concept of civil society that purports to be universal. As elaborated by Jürgen Habermas, Hegel's concept offers a useful starting point for comparing civil society across cultures wherever international capitalism has penetrated. In his brilliant *Habilitationschrift: An Inquiry into a Category of Bourgeois Society* (second doctoral dissertation), Habermas traces the emergence of a "public sphere" and public opinion in late-seventeenth-century England and subsequently in other European countries. In England in the late seventeenth century, the articulation of public opinion through the coffee houses, commercial newsletters, and educated salons is associated with "a new conflict of interest between the restrictive interests of commercial and finance capital on the one side and the expansive interests of manufacturing and industrial capital on the other" (Habermas 1994, pp. 57–58). It was hardly coincidental that the Bank of England was also founded at this time.

While history never exactly repeats itself from one country to the next, it is still possible to locate emerging bourgeoisies in non-Western societies. The experience of a late developing Western country offers a clue for identifying these bourgeoisies. Writing in 1910 from a democratic Marxist standpoint, Rudolph Hilferding analyzed Imperial Germany's concentrated universal banking system and the oligopolistic power it had acquired from deploying Germany's scarce finance capital. Capital concentration was the banks' defense against the heavy capital requirements of Germany's efforts to industrialize. A small number of huge commercial banks acquired control over much of German industry, as Lenin, following Hilferding, subsequently pointed out. Whether or not the state is the executive committee of the bourgeoisie, the German model offers an interesting comparative benchmark for latecomers to international capitalism. It illustrates effective collective action among bankers, even if the Reich's imperialist policies could not be fully explained by the decisions of a bourgeoisie centered on the boards of a small number of universal banks. To what extent was this model of the commanding heights of a political economy diffused to the late latecomers on the other side of the Mediterranean and in other parts of the non-Western world?

BANKING IN THE MENA

The MENA offers an especially fertile field for comparisons because its economies are heavily indebted not only to external Western, international, and Japanese lenders but also to domestic creditors. Ratios of total domestic credit to gross domestic product (published monthly in the IMF's *International Financial Statistics*) tend to be significantly higher in the MENA countries than elsewhere in the developing world. Commercial banking displays similar patterns throughout the world penetrated by international capitalism, but in the MENA, commercial banks are especially revealing mirrors of the respective domestic economies simply because economic enterprises are so highly leveraged, dependent on credit from the commercial banks. Alternative sources of financing, such as stock markets, remain marginal and largely subordinated to the commercial banks—as in Imperial Germany in Hilferding's day. Examining the commercial banks can therefore offer a way of identifying and comparing bourgeoisies in different countries.

Money speaks a universal language, and financial relationships can be compared and analyzed across cultures, outside the MENA as well as between countries within the region. The only condition, to ensure comparability, is that commercial banks, rather than stock markets, be the principal source of business finance. Well understood Western commercial banking models have long since subordinated or displaced any "traditional" financial practices, even if those famous modern *lettres de change* that had so fascinated Montesquieu in the eighteenth century probably originated in Muslim countries or further east. Indeed, one prelude to the comparative analysis of commercial banking systems is to contrast the patterns of colonial financial penetration, so as to identify their metropolitan models. In my own research on Algeria, Egypt, Morocco, Tunisia, and Turkey, Hilferding proved to be the pivotal Western theorist who could inform the narrative, but there were contending models of commercial banking (Henry 1996).

The principal competitor was an Anglo-Saxon model featuring multiple centers of financial power and sharp structural distinctions between retail and investment banking that are only very recently becoming undone. French banking more closely came to approximate the German model as the nineteenth century drew to a close. French colonies did not keep up, however, with the Metropole's financial progress. Like the "fragments" of European thought discussed by Louis Hartz (1964) in a variety of settler states, Algerian and Tunisian banking remained frozen in earlier preindustrial French patterns. Colonized after Tunisia, however, Morocco as well as Turkey inherited the German legacy. In Egypt, by contrast, an Anglo-Saxon hybrid of competing models flourished because the "veiled" British protectorate remained financially more open than France's North African possessions. The independent successor states in turn reshaped their respective banking systems, but the most thoroughly nationalized and rationalized of them, in Algeria and Egypt, retained their colonial differences. A bare decade of Nasserism could not stamp out Egypt's rich financial heritage. Algeria had lost its Mediterranean trading heritage in 1830, the year French colonialism began in that country.

All five of these countries, like so many other internationally indebted countries, then fell under the spell of the IMF and the World Bank—Algeria finally following the others, conveniently completing my comparative design in 1989 after the research was already well under way—and experienced comparable stimuli to reform their respective commercial banking systems along Anglo-Saxon lines. The politics of financial adjustment could then be followed in each country, and any gaps in my research concerning the details of one country's experience could usually be filled in with clues from a neighbor's experiences. I supplemented traditional interviewing of political and financial elites both by World Bank documents (usually accessible through U.S. embassies if they were deemed confidential and therefore unavailable at the Bank) and by the published financial statements of the two hundred or so commercial banks in the region (collected wherever possible over at least a ten-year period). Similar studies of financial adjustment could be replicated in scores of other developing countries that have undergone similar adjustments in the wake of the international debt crisis of the 1980s. As an Egyptian minister commented, the IMF medicine is like that of a military hospital: "iron and arsenic to all" (Hilal 1987, p. 171).

I was looking for redistributions of financial power along the lines suggested by the Hilferding model of universal banking. Despite reformers' efforts to develop local stock exchanges—even in Algeria—they remain relatively weak, as in Imperial Germany at the turn of the century, and commercial banks remain the principal sources of finance capital, servicing heavily indebted enterprises. To be sure, the World Bank's structural adjustment programs in the financial sector called for more competitive, market-oriented commercial banking, as well as new capital markets structured on Anglo-American lines. Yet the main effect of cleaning up the mountains of nonperforming loans was to strengthen some "good" privately owned oligopolists at the expense of indifferently managed banks in the public sector. Ongoing processes of financial reform raise two basic research questions. 1) Might some of the private sector banks not only be revitalized by financial reform but become capable of engaging in the silent sort of collective action discussed earlier, standing up to their respective regimes by allocating their commercial loans (finance capital, in effect) independently of the government to projects of their own choosing? 2) If they were to acquire real financial autonomy, how, if at all, would their ability to engage in collective action affect the respective political regimes?

THE PROSPECTS FOR COLLECTIVE ACTION AND AUTONOMY

The capacity to engage in collective action is not directly observable, but it can be inferred from the structure of a commercial banking system. The Berlin banking system observed by Hilferding was heavily concentrated in the hands of a few large commercial banks that could dictate its conditions to much of Germany's heavy industry. Were comparable structures emerging in any of the Debt Crescent countries? It was possible to map out the market shares of the various commercial banks in each country, to evaluate their financial perform-ance, and to identify their ownership. A substantial private sector was emerg-ing everywhere except in Algeria, and the degree of its concentration and the financial performance of its individual banks could be ascertained from their respective annual reports. Since international financial institutions insist on standard disclosure rules, ratios can be constructed from publicly available records to measure the financial performance and market share of each bank.

In Turkey, the Crescent's most hospitable historic home to Hilferding, a strong nucleus of private oligopolists could be identified, paralleling the indus-trial groups that had emerged in the 1960s and 1970s. In Morocco, too, a strong nucleus was visible, but the king dominated the private sector as well as the government. In fact, before deregulating the system in 1991, the Moroccan *makhzan* reinforced its presence in the banking sector by acquiring a dominant position in the strongest of its commercial banks and minority shareholdings in other banks as well. In Algeria, Egypt, and Tunisia, by contrast, the public sector retained most of the financial assets. Tunisia displayed a stronger nucleus of private oligopolists than Algeria or Egypt. Egypt had a large number of private sector banks opened as a result of Sadat's *infitah*, but a close inspection of their capital structure showed that private Egyptian investors owned much less of their capital than state-owned enterprises or parastatals, public sector banks, and foreign banks. Private Egyptian capital, moreover, tended to be dispersed in a number of banks. Outside the Islamic sector, only one commer-cial bank was fully owned by private investors and it controlled less than 1 percent of the commercial banking system's deposits.

From these data only Turkey and Morocco revealed private sectors capable of collective action. In Turkey, big business supported Prime Minister Turgut Özal's economic reform program until about 1987, and the prime minister relied upon the private banking oligopoly, as well as upon his appointees to the big public sector banks, to discipline any major political adversaries in the business community by calling in loans. In Turkey, however, the capacity of the banks to engage in collective action did not have the same political implications as in the other countries. Turkey enjoyed a significant degree of political pluralism, even in the wake of the military intervention of 1980, whereas independent power centers were not tolerated elsewhere in the Debt Crescent. In Morocco, the king had astutely preempted any possible political impact of a deregulated financial oligopoly by acquiring a controlling interest in the key players. King Hassan could afford to liberalize Morocco's economy because liberalization merely meant substituting his makhzan's oligopolistic control of markets for the traditional administrative controls.

In Tunisia, a privately owned banking oligopoly was far less developed than in Morocco, but it was growing more in the late 1980s and early 1990s than the state-owned sector and was beginning to show some signs of independence. One bank in particular, founded by Habib Bourguiba Jr. and Mansour Moallah, a former government technocrat, came to be perceived as a challenge to the regime. Moallah had assembled private capital mainly from the business community of Sfax, the country's second largest city, and supplemented this with some funds from the Arab Gulf states. His bank grew rapidly and challenged the state's monopoly over credit allocation, thereby threatening one of the regime's principal channels for distributing political patronage. President Ben Ali's orders to parastatals in May 1993 to punish Moallah by withdrawing deposits from his bank seems less a story about eliminating a potential rival in the 1994 presidential elections than a preemptive move against a critical nucleus of private sector investors. Ultimately, however, perhaps in a decade or so, Tunisia's private sector is bound to acquire more autonomy. It is hypothesized that capitalist pressures will then oblige the regime to become more accountable to the business community, and possibly to the general public as well.

Commercial banking systems are interesting to study in the Debt Crescent and in other middle-income countries that may be undergoing political transitions toward more pluralism and democracy. As targets of internationally sponsored reforms, these financial systems are bound to acquire greater autonomy, which in turn is likely to curtail the patronage currently being laundered through the respective banking systems. Since each of the regimes seems very dependent upon patronage, given its lack of legitimacy, bankers may become the unintentional midwives of political change. Patrimonial regimes will be required to change, either to become really tough bureaucratic-authoritarian regimes or to practice what they are currently preaching—that they are preparing the way for "democracy." Rationalizing their finance will break the umbilical cord of patronage.

Under either scenario, however, civil society will have acquired an economic base. Moreover, its progress is measurable, documented by the annual statistics of commercial banking systems in the region, together with independent analyses of their ownership and financial performance (Henry 1996).

If these regimes are to evolve in a bureaucratic-authoritarian direction, they will require a tougher political formula which legitimizes the need to purify their respective societies before practicing democracy. The line of argument that an Arab hardliner might make in this connection is that society must be cured of religious fanaticism before any substantial political liberalization, much less democratization, can occur. Indeed, political Islam is already the bogey man manipulated by incumbent regimes to rally the support of their Westernized elites, although it seems unlikely that anti-Islamism can offer them any durable support, even among the middle classes. Political Islam presents the other driving force, sometimes complementing and sometimes clashing with privately owned finance capital, that is deepening contemporary civil society in the MENA. Its rise may also be reflected in the development of a particular form of commercial banking, the "Islamic" banks.

UNIVERSALIZING CIVIL SOCIETY

The trouble with much of the recent literature about civil society is that it relies too heavily on a misreading of Tocqueville and reifies civil society as sets of modern, "secular," voluntary associations juxtaposed to atavistic communal or religious ones. This interpretation has powerful support in the American political science discipline. Robert Putnam's work (1993) contrasting northern and southern Italy, for instance, is a technical masterpiece of comparative politics and an orientalist classic (though this was not quite his intention). It eulogizes the civility of the northerners, whose historical roots in the arts of urban association (mainly football clubs, it turns out on a closer reading, p. 92) enable them to "make democracy work." Their poor southern compatriots, by contrast, wallow in an oriental culture of amoral familism, clientelism, and authoritarian religion. Putnam's study has elicited tremendous interest and worry in America about our own declining art of association. In this sense, too, his work reflects the grand orientalist tradition of imputing the subject's darker side or limitations to the other, the object of investigation.

Civil society in the sense of autonomous football associations, Rotary clubs, and the like remains weak and largely useless to those in the MENA who want to make democracy work. Strengthening or establishing more "secular" NGOs in Egypt, for instance, would be like trying to build up that nebulous third force in the Vietnamese politics of the 1960s. On the straitened peripheries of Egypt's stagnant political landscape, the Islamists are virtually the only political forces (and I emphasize the plural) with mass followings. Does this mean that Egyptian society cannot be civil or does it indicate that civil society needs to be redefined?

In my opinion, civil society needs to be redefined in a way that negates Hegel in a double sense and deepens his original meaning. It is no longer possible to order recalcitrant regional realities with a conceptual toolbox derived exclusively from Western experiences with modernization. Neither is it useful or appropriate, like Hegel's stubborn slave in a colonial situation, to reify traditional values, whether Islamic or Western, as exemplified in Huntington's "clash of civilizations" (1993). Methodological liberation instead requires relativizing Western experience and searching for a more universal concept of modernization and its civil society correlates. As I have learned from recent revisits to the Egyptian Engineers Syndicate, a citadel of Egyptian modernity taken over by Islamists, they are no longer interested in modernizing Islam but rather in Islamizing modernity (Moore 1994, pp. 211–234). François Burgat's advice to the North, i.e. to a hypothetical Western colleague, is appropriate:

> He is not required to negate or even to minimize his relation to history in general or to political thought in particular but rather to historicize it and renounce his arrogant pretension to hegemony in the matter of producing legitimacy. It is demanded of him to admit that the history of ideas is not reducible to the itinerary of "subcultures" of his colonial periphery nourished by his science and rationality and to put an end to "conflating the civilized being with western being." It is demanded of him to recognize the right of a Southern [non-western] culture to articulate its production of values in light of its own historic legacy and to express these values in bringing forth an ensemble of referents specific to its culture. It is demanded of him to understand that he never had nor will ever enjoy a monopoly of access to universal truths (1995, p. 236).

To historicize Western civil society is to relate it not to secular voluntary associations but rather to its original progenitors, the Puritans of Marian England and Holland and their mass parties that took shape in the seventeenth century (Walzer 1965). In the spirit of the late Ernest Gellner, who unfortunately deviated in his recent work on civil society (1994) from his original comparisons between Puritanism and Sunni Islam (1981, pp. 42–62), Western and Islamic versions of civil society are comparable in that each was equally driven by stern literalist monotheism. Alexis de Tocqueville made parallel observations of American civil society, which most of his contemporary admirers, imbued with a "secular" conception of civil society, seem to forget. Associations were indeed a bulwark against tyranny of the majority, but nowhere else in Western civilization was freedom of thought more constrained than in America (Tocqueville I, pp. 273, 275) by the hypocrisy of that very same self-righteous religiosity which fostered the American art of association.

Political Islam does indeed seem to be the driving force behind civil society in most of the MENA countries. And just as civil society progressed with the accumulation of private finance capital in Western contexts, so its progress in the MENA may be reflected in an accumulation of capital associated with Islamic commercial banking. Islamic capital already accounts for a substantial share of the privately held resources in Egypt, Jordan, and a number of other

Arab countries. It bears special examination for its new discourses and its potential for disciplining and moderating some of the self-righteous excesses of a vibrant civil society. Just as there was some "affinity" between Protestantism and the spirit of capitalism (Weber 1930), Islamism is certainly compatible with certain forms of capitalism, as the Algerian FIS demonstrated by its tacit support for the devaluation of the dinar in 1989.

An official Islamic banking sector survives in Egypt and Turkey. Egypt's informal sector, fueled by remittances from Gulf countries, temporarily dwarfed all other forms of private capital accumulation only to fail, ultimately, for a variety of reasons, not least because it threatened the state's financial hegemony. In any event, the private Islamic banking sector is bound to grow, and other commercial banks have established Islamic branches to attract some of the available business. Even under hardline military rule, Algeria has permitted Islamic banks to be established. Whether they compete or cooperate with one another, the Islamic and non-Islamic private banking sectors are bound to accumulate substantial capital and acquire the capacity to engage in collective action. This will certainly occur so long as the countries in which they are located follow those prescriptions of the IMF and World Bank that promote integration into the world capitalist order.

CONCLUSION

The research summarized in this paper illustrates the importance of drawing upon both general theoretical insights and area-specific knowledge in seeking to understand many aspects of politics and society in the Middle East and North Africa. Against this background, the noticeable absence of democracy in the MENA countries makes the study of civil society important and intriguing. But while civil society is receiving increased attention in research on democratic transition and consolidation, in studies undertaken in response to the recent demise of authoritarian regimes in many parts of the globe, the concept cannot be applied in the MENA without attention to contextual considerations. Furthermore, its application will be of limited value unless it is utilized in a way that promotes systematic, comparative analysis.

Mindful of these considerations and constraints, the present study has approached the Middle East and North Africa in a manner informed by social science theory, while at the same time seeking to universalize the concept of civil society to make it more applicable to non-Western societies. Utilizing a political economy perspective and the German historical experience as a model, it examines commercial banking systems of the MENA in order to locate emerging bourgeoisies and to evaluate the political significance of this very critical sector of society. This has provided a useful comparative framework, since commercial banks are the primary source of financial capital in the MENA and their strength can be assessed through international financial statistics.

While the strength of commercial banking systems varies cross-nationally, it is generally limited by state authority. Due to internationally sponsored economic reforms, however, private banking is likely both to grow and to gain more autonomy vis-à-vis the state in the coming years. In addition, the growing number of Islamic banks may also contribute to the potential power of these financial systems. While religious organizations have often fallen outside traditional meanings of civil society in the Western context, a closer look shows that viewing civil society only in terms of secular organizations is inadequate and ignores important similarities with Western history.

Using social science theory as a guide, this study thus provides a way to track developments of civil society in the MENA and to anticipate political change in a way that is more coherent and comparative. Acknowledging historical and regional differences also contributes to a better formulation of theoretical concepts, in this case that of civil society. With these considerations in mind, scholars can better consider the future possibilities for democracy in the Middle East and North Africa.

Whether capital accumulation will render political Islamist voices more "civil" and Westernized elites less distrustful of Islamists remains to be seen. Nevertheless, analyzing MENA banking systems through the prism of civil society enhances our understanding of the region's political economy and prospects for democratization. Also, and equally important, attention to the Islamic component, which is prominent in the MENA countries and which strikingly parallels Western "Protestant" experiences, enables the notion of civil society to acquire greater universality. With the Hegelian concept now seeming to embrace the cultural particularities of both the MENA and the West without any significant loss of meaning, the approach guiding the present study would appear to offer theoretical and conceptual enrichment, as well as insights about the Middle East and North Africa. The task does not end here, however, but must rather be carried out with respect to other cultures, including that of China, which is expected to become increasingly important in the twenty-first century. In these instances, too, there is likely to emerge a capitalism that is truly global and which will reshape states, private property, and bourgeoisies through, in part, a financial system of commercial banks.

REFERENCES

Burgat, François. 1995. L'islamisme en face. Paris: La Découverte.
Gellner, Ernest. 1994. Conditions of Liberty: Civil Society and its Rivals. London: Hamish Hamilton.
———. 1981. Muslim Society. London: Cambridge University Press.
Habermas, Jürgen. 1994. The Structural Transformation of the Public Sphere: An Inquiry into a Category of Bourgeois Society. Cambridge: MIT Press.
Hartz, Louis B. 1964. The Founding of New Societies. New York: Harcourt Brace.
Henry, Clement M. 1996. The Mediterranean Debt Crescent: Money and Power in Algeria, Egypt, Morocco, Tunisia, and Turkey. Gainesville: University Press of Florida.

Hentsch, Thierry. 1992. *Imagining the Middle East.* Montreal: Black Rose Books.

Hilal, Rida. 1987. *The Construction of Dependency.* (In Arabic). Cairo: Dar Al-Mustaqbal Al-Tarabi.

Hilferding, Rudolph. 1981, 1910. *Finance Capital: A Study of the Latest Phase of Capitalist Development.* London: Routledge.

Huntington, Samuel P. 1991. *The Third Wave: Democratization in the Late Twentieth Century.* Norman: Oklahoma University Press.

———. "The Clash of Civilizations?" 1993. *Foreign Affairs* 72, 3 (Summer): 22–49.

Moore, Clement Henry. 1994. *Images of Development: Egyptian Engineers in Search of Industry.* 2nd ed. Cairo: American University in Cairo Press.

Norton, Augustus Richard. 1993. "The Future of Civil Society in the Middle East." *The Middle East Journal* (Spring): 205–216.

———, ed. 1995. *Civil Society in the Middle East, I.* Leiden: Brill.

———, ed. 1996. *Civil Society in the Middle East, II.* Leiden: Brill.

Putnam, Robert. 1993. *Making Democracy Work: Civic Tradition in Modern Italy.* Princeton: Princeton University Press.

Sartori, Giovanni. 1970. "Concept Misinformation in Comparative Politics." *American Political Science Review* 64, 4 (December): 1033–1053.

Schwedler, Jillian, ed. 1995. *Toward Civil Society in the Middle East? A Primer.* Boulder: Lynne Rienner.

Tocqueville, Alexis de. 1959. *Democracy in America.* 2 vols. New York: Vintage.

Walzer, Michael. 1965. *Revolution of the Saints: A Study in the Origins of Radical Politics.* Cambridge: Harvard University Press.

Weber, Max. 1930. *The Protestant Ethic and the Spirit of Capitalism.* London.

6. Toward a Theory of International Labor Migration
Evidence from Egypt

Magda Kandil

INTRODUCTION

The study of labor migration in Egypt offers an excellent illustration of the way that theories and methods from the discipline of economics can be utilized to increase our understanding of critical issues facing developing countries in the Middle East and elsewhere. On the one hand, theoretically oriented empirical analyses can shed light on the determinants and implications of Egyptian labor migration, producing practical as well as scientific insights about this important dimension of Egyptian economic life. On the other, by examining important cause-and-effect variable relationships under particular conditions, such studies can also contribute to the refinement of relevant bodies of economic theory, and thereby play a role in the development of analytical insights of more general applicability.

Over the last three decades, there has been a massive outflow of Egyptians going to work in neighboring Arab oil-producing countries. Although Egyptian labor migration has increased steadily since the early 1950s, there has been a profound change in the magnitude and nature of this migration since 1973. This is partly because Egypt, a highly populated country, has suffered from severe economic problems as a result of its participation in several wars in the Arab-Israeli conflict. The cost of war depleted the country's limited productive resources, the result being severe economic shortages that accelerated price inflation in the face of the increased demand by the growing population. In addition, given the limited growth of real job opportunities and investment capabilities, Egypt has been unable to efficiently absorb the increasing supply of its growing population. Egyptians' desire to migrate has, therefore, been stimulated by pressure on inhabited areas, deterioration in general living conditions, housing and transportation crises, and lower-quality health services, education services, and infrastructure.

Deterioration in domestic conditions is not enough, however, for migration to take place. Sources of attraction have to exist and be evaluated by potential migrants. Better conditions in the destination countries represent pull factors that encourage people to migrate. The Arab oil-producing countries have enjoyed a significant increase in their wealth as a result of a sharp increase in energy prices following the world energy crises in 1973 and 1979, and these countries subsequently engaged in large-scale restructuring and development programs that created chronic labor shortages. The sharp contrast in wealth and size of the labor force has created a pronounced difference in rewards for employment in Egypt and the Arab oil-producing countries, which in turn has attracted a large number of Egyptian workers to neighboring Arab oil-producing countries such as Kuwait, Saudi Arabia, the Gulf States, and Libya.

This phenomenon is worth studying from several aspects. First, a thorough investigation of factors determining this migration ought to be considered. Second, research should analyze the consequences of this migration on three groups: (1) the labor-exporting countries, (2) the labor-importing countries and their citizens, and (3) the migrants themselves.

In Kandil and Metwally (1992), we focused on the first issue, determinants of the Egyptian labor migration to Arab oil-producing countries. Push and pull factors are considered in this regard. Push factors include low wages, high inflation rate, and high density of population in Egypt. Pull factors are primarily higher wages offered to workers in neighboring Arab oil-producing countries. The results are consistent with theory's prediction: an increase in income in the destination countries relative to its counterpart in Egypt has a significant positive impact on the migration rate from Egypt to these countries. Similarly, an increase in the density of Egypt's population stimulates the desire of Egyptians to migrate, as does an increase in the inflation rate in Egypt. These results suggest that migration is the outcome of optimizing behavior in which migrants have responded positively to push and pull factors.

There are positive and negative aspects of migration in labor exporting countries. On the positive side, remittances sent home by Egyptian migrants have become a valuable source of foreign exchange for this country. In addition, the departure of migrants can be seen as an effective way of reducing the unemployment rate, the most pressing problem facing Egypt. On the negative side, one needs to consider such factors as the labor supply shortages that have resulted in some areas of the Egyptian labor market. In addition, the accumulation of savings by migrants has affected the level of aggregate spending in the Egyptian economy. There has been an increase in consumption spending, particularly for luxury goods. This increased spending has created severe inflationary pressures in an economy in which productive resources are very limited.

In Kandil and Metwally (1990), we address the issue of the impact of workers' remittances on the Egyptian economy in some detail. One of the major effects of massive Egyptian worker migration has been the dependency of the Egyptian economy on remittances as a source of foreign exchange. We thus analyze the impact of remittances on Gross National Product (GNP), finding a large positive impact of remittances on GNP and its major components in Egypt. The investigation also offers some policy recommendations designed to maximize the positive impact of migrants' remittances on the Egyptian economy.

EGYPT'S EXPERIENCE WITH LABOR MIGRATION

Egypt has long been a land of immigrants not emigrants (Choucri and El-Din 1977). Egyptians have a reputation for preferring their own soil. The history of labor migration in Egypt can thus be divided into two episodes: the pre- and post-oil boom (1973) periods.

Historically, systematic migration began in the 1930s when Egypt sponsored a program transferring school teachers to Iraq. This was extended to include other Arab countries after the 1952 revolution. During that period, Egyptian labor migration was tightly controlled by the government and took two forms: temporary migration to work in Arab and African states and permanent migration to West Europe, North America, and Australia. The majority of migrants were professionals or high-ranking administrators (Amin and Awny 1985). The government attempted to regulate both forms of migration according to what were perceived as Egypt's interests abroad, as well as its manpower needs at home. In general, Egyptian labor migration during the pre-oil boom period was closely tied to the political relationships between Egypt and neighboring Arab countries.

After the October 1973 war, there was a shift in Egypt's economic policy towards greater liberalization. As a result, the Egyptian government adopted procedures that facilitated the migration of Egyptian labor. Traditionally, Egyptian workers migrated primarily to Libya and Sudan. However, the world energy crisis beginning in 1973 led to an accumulation of massive petro-dollar surpluses in sparsely populated Arab oil-producing countries, which in turn led to an increase in the demand for skilled and unskilled Egyptian workers in these countries.

As a result, there has been an increase in the number of migrants from Egypt to Saudi Arabia, Kuwait, the United Arab Emirates, Qatar, and Iraq. This migration has been temporary since the legal structure in most Arab countries discourages the permanent residence of migrants, and since many Egyptians have an intrinsic desire to return home after satisfying their financial objectives.

Political relationships have also affected the Egyptian labor migration to

Table 1: Annual Flow of Egyptian Workers to Arab Countries

Year	Number of Workers
1966	2,923
1967	3,942
1968	5,829
1969	3,160
1970	6,427
1971	6,427
1972	26,361
1973	30,572
1974	29,048
1975	34,440
1976	53,429
1977	81,159
1978	93,445
1979	111,364
1980	108,950
1981	76,675
1982	74,489
1983	90,207
1984	91,730
1985	94,688
1986	86,935

Note: Data include major oil-producing countries: Saudi Arabia, Libya, Kuwait, Oman, Qatar, U.A.E., and Iraq.

Source: CAPMAS, different issues.

neighboring Arab countries. President Sadat's peace initiative and the subsequent signing of the Camp David Accords in 1978 increased the level of political tension between Egypt and neighboring Arab countries. All Arab oil-producing countries suspended their political relationships with Egypt. Accordingly, the deterioration of relations between Egypt and its neighboring countries impacted negatively on migration from Egypt to these countries after 1979.

In the absence of accurate data on the number of Egyptian workers abroad, two different estimates are proposed. The first is provided by the Central Agency for Public Mobilization and Statistics (CAPMAS).[1] It illustrates the annual flow of Egyptian workers to Arab countries. Table 1, which covers the period 1966 to 1986, suggests that there was a steady increase in the number of Egyptian migrants to Arab oil-producing countries between 1969 and 1979. However, the rate of increase was greatest between 1971 and 1973, after which

Table 2: Number of Egyptian Workers Abroad across Major Host Countries in 1975

Country	Number of Workers	Percentage
Libya	229,500	57.7
Saudi Arabia	95,000	23.9
Kuwait	37,558	9.4
United Arab Emirates	12,500	3.1
Iraq	7,000	1.8
Oman	4,600	1.2
Jordan	5,300	1.3
Yemen	2,000	0.5
Qatar	2,800	0.7
Bahrain	1,237	0.3
Total	397,545	

Source: Birks, J. S., and C. A. Sinclair, International Migration and Development in the Arab Region, ILO, Geneva (1980).

growth continued at a more moderate rate. The only exception to this growth was a slight reduction in the number of migrants between 1973 and 1974. In the wake of the Camp David Accords, as noted, there was a significant reduction in the number of Egyptian migrants to these countries. Labor migration again increased after 1982, but the numbers remained below the record high reached in 1979.

An alternative estimate was prepared by the Department of Economics at the University of Durham, as part of the "International Migration Project" sponsored by the International Labor Organization. Unlike the previous estimate, this estimate approximates the number of Egyptian workers in major destination countries in 1975. Table 2 shows that in 1975 there were 397,545 Egyptian nationals employed abroad, mainly in Arab oil-producing countries such as Libya and Saudi Arabia.

The figures in Tables 1 and 2 provide evidence suggesting that the Egyptian government has encouraged migration, in particular since the adoption of the open-door policy in 1973. This is supported by the fact that the government established a Ministry of Migration in February of that year (Dessouki 1982). Migration policies in Egypt have been confusing, however, reflecting a lack of consensus concerning goals and means. Policies have fluctuated from prohibition to regulation to encouragement, with two competing views predominating: one advocating migration as a solution to the problem of manpower surplus, and the other emphasizing the negative consequences of migration.

Table 3: Millions of Egyptian Pounds Remitted by Migrants to Their Home Country

Year	Remittances to Egypt
1970	2.5
1971	2.8
1972	35.4
1973	34.1
1974	153.3
1975	240.9
1976	393.8
1977	623.4
1978	1,248.8
1979	2,208.4
1980	2,856.6
1981	1,731.1
1982	2,632.3
1983	3,268.5
1984	2,907.4
1985	2,472.0
1986	3,200.0
1987	4,142.4
1988	5,362.3

Note: Compiled from the Central Bank of Egypt, *Annual Report*, several issues.

Egypt's actual experience nevertheless suggests that the first view has had more impact on the design of migration policy.

Following the death of President Nasser in September 1970, President Sadat adopted a liberal migration policy. In 1971, the Egyptian Constitution established emigration, permanent or temporary, as a right (Article 52). In 1975, the Egyptian parliament ratified the treaty for manpower movement between Arab countries. In addition, the Egyptian government played a specific role in the encouragement of labor migration. First, the government has undertaken a responsibility to assist nationals in finding employment opportunities abroad by studying foreign as well as Arab labor markets to identify their requirements and conditions of employment. Second, the Egyptian government has taken measures to assist its nationals in preparing for migration and travel. These measures include the provision of training for jobs that are not available in Egypt and then channeling trainees to foreign labor markets in their respective fields of specialization. In addition, the Egyptian government has also made

Table 4: Components of Egyptian Migrants' Remittances, in Millions of Egyptian Pounds

Year	Financial Transfers	Increase in Foreign Currency Deposits within Egypt	Imports Financed by Own-Exchange Import System	Undeclared Goods
1975	167.9	53.6	92.7	116.7
1976	198	90.1	167.5	170.7
1977	284	147.4	265.2	242.6
1978	558.8	201.0	587.2	319.4
1979	490.5	301.6	883.3	357.3
1980	642.7	536.1	1,070.0	432.0
1981	444.8	502.8	935.7	457.4

Source: National Specialized Councils: *The Economics of Egyptian Migrants' Savings*, Arab Center for Research and Publishing, Cairo (1983), p. 103.

efforts to look after the interests of migrants in countries of destination and to link them to their homeland.

The Egyptian government's policies towards encouraging migration are highly dependent on the economic benefits of labor migration. Remittances are among the major economic results of the Egyptian labor migration. These are savings of migrants on income earned abroad that are remitted to their home country. In 1970 these remittances were estimated to be 2.5 million Egyptian pounds. This number increased dramatically over the seventies and early eighties, as shown in Table 3. In 1973, the amount of remittances was almost fourteen times its 1970 value, and it has continued to grow since then.[2]

In 1983, an attempt was made by the National Specialized Councils to break down the total remittances figure into four categories: financial transfers converted into Egyptian pounds; the increase in foreign currency deposits in Egyptian or foreign banks operating in Egypt; imports financed by the Own-Exchange Import System; and undeclared goods brought into Egypt by returning migrants. Table 4 shows the estimates for these different components of Egyptian migrants' remittances. The breakdown suggests that the largest component of migrants' savings is spent on the purchase of foreign products through the Own-Exchange Import System. In addition, the various components of remittances have grown over time. The largest growth is in imports financed by the Own-Exchange Import System and in foreign currency deposits in financial institutions in Egypt.

Remittances have become an important source of foreign exchange to Egypt. The impact of these remittances on Egypt's balance of payments is probably the

Table 5: Major Sources of Foreign Exchange in Egypt, in Millions of Egyptian Pounds

Year	Remittances	Suez Canal	Petroleum	Tourism
1976	393.8	121.7	149.1	263.2
1977	623.4	167.4	160.8	430.3
1978	1,248.8	201.1	188.5	395.7
1979	2,208.4	412.1	534.3	319.8
1980	2,856.6	464.3	1,369.3	413.5
1981	1,731.1	621.8	1,454.3	317.5
1982	2,632.3	657.8	1,444.7	245.0
1983	3,268.5	678.8	1,399.3	231.2
1984	2,907.4	665.4	1,263.6	332.2
1985	2,472.0	654.2	1,764.6	477.3
1986	3,200.0	769.0	1,040.7	685.8
1987	4,142.4	844.5	1,078.1	985.4
1988	5,362.3	904.6	1,276.9	1,415.9

Note: Tourism figures are from the Central Bank of Egypt (1990); Suez Canal and Petroleum are from *International Financial Statistics Yearbook* (1990).

most favorable aspect of the phenomenon of labor migration. Table 5 contrasts the magnitudes of these remittances to other major sources of foreign exchange in the Egyptian economy, such as petroleum, the Suez Canal, and tourism. Over a period of time that extends from 1976 to 1988, remittances are indeed the most important single source of foreign exchange to the Egyptian economy, surpassing even petroleum. These remittances have, therefore, a variety of consequences on aggregate demand in Egypt, depending on how they are spent and by whom. In addition, the flexibility by which domestic supply reacts to the increased demand determines whether the increased remittances will have positive employment effects or adverse inflation effects.

Egypt's experience also suggests that the growth of remittances has not been without some negative aspects. The most important among these negative aspects is the impact of increased income in the form of savings that migrants have accumulated on consumption spending in Egypt. It has been noted that the increased spending resulting from higher income for Egyptian migrants has caused a change in the domestic consumption behavior in Egypt in favor of imports. This has resulted as migrants returned or visited their home country, bringing with them a large amount of savings to spend. This expenditure has been directed, in most cases, towards luxurious imported goods. Consequently, new consumption patterns have spread in the Egyptian economy as other Egyptians tried to copy these spending patterns.[3] This has led to a growing concern that the largest share of remittances is spent on luxurious and flagrant consumption that has an adverse impact on the economy of a developing country with limited resources, such as Egypt.

One might have expected that the increased demand resulting from remittances has been directed, at least in part, towards private investment projects. Such projects would contribute to the future productive ability of the economy and, accordingly, ought to be encouraged. Unfortunately, the evidence suggests that investment spending that has resulted from remittances has been directed towards the more secure and quick-profit channels that are considered to be unproductive in nature and, in turn, contribute very little to development. Examples of this investment spending include building, buying living accommodations, and trading in imported goods.[4]

The above discussion suggests that remittances have generated demand without contributing to the productive capacity of the Egyptian economy.[5] Inflation has been aggravated as a result. In addition, the migration of Egyptian workers has affected the supply side of the economy in a way that is considered to be inflationary. As Egyptian workers migrated to the Arab oil-producing countries, they left behind them a market with excess demand for their skills. This market has been forced to meet this excess demand by relying on young and inexperienced workers. The results are low-quality and highly priced products and services that have created further inflationary pressures in the Egyptian economy.

DETERMINANTS OF THE EGYPTIAN LABOR MIGRATION

The study of labor migration in Egypt offers an apt illustration of the way economic theory can be utilized to understand factors underlying this important dimension of Egyptian economic life. Theoretical explanations for labor mobility between countries produce scientific insights about the determinants of the Egyptian labor migration to the Arab Oil Producing Countries (AOPC).

Theoretical Background

The theoretical analysis of labor migration is based mostly on the economic theory of factor mobility. A thorough treatment of this discussion is found in Meade's theory of international economic policy (1955). Under the assumption of zero migration cost and perfect mobility, this theory predicts that in a situation characterized by international differentials in real wages, labor will migrate from the low wage to the high wage region, until real wages are equalized. In this view, differentials in real wages are considered as a central determinant factor of labor migration.

In other theoretical developments, labor migration among nations is to be explained as the result of demand and supply conditions in the labor market (Fabricant 1970 and Willis 1974). A shortage of labor in one sector or area will cause a rise in its price relative to that of labor elsewhere, and labor will move in response until demand and supply are equalized.

Lee (1966) contributed to the literature by developing a general scheme explaining labor migration. He divided forces contributing to the decision to migrate into "pluses" and "minuses." The former pull individuals towards them and the latter tend to push them away. According to this theory, every act of migration involves an origin, a destination, and an intervening set of obstacles. The decision to migrate and the migration process depend on the following factors: (1) factors associated with the area of origin, (2) factors associated with the area of destination, (3) intervening obstacles, and (4) personal factors. Factors of origin and destination can be either positive or negative. Positive factors at destination and negative factors at origin tend to attract migrants away from the origin to the destination. The larger the differences between conditions at origin and destination, the higher is the probability of migration. Intervening obstacles can be physical or legal barriers to migration or simply the cost and burden of moving. Personal factors relate to the individual's characteristics, such as age, health, marital status, and family ties at home.

Another important theoretical contribution explaining migration has been developed by Sjaastad (1962). An individual migrates in the expectation of being better off. In this process, the migrant recognizes that immediate costs are balanced against future expected return and moves if he believes that benefits will exceed costs.

To summarize, factors emphasized in theory as important determinants of the decision to migrate include differences in the availability of labor force and, in turn, labor rewards between destination and origin, differences in the economic and general conditions of the two countries, and the cost of migration. Differentials in real wages as well as demand and supply conditions are relevant to the analysis of labor migration from Egypt to the AOPC. As indicated above, Egypt's participation in the Arab-Israeli conflict depleted the country's limited productive resources and accelerated price inflation. This is in contrast to the fast growth of petro-dollars in the Arab oil-producing countries. Subsequently, the AOPC have engaged in massive development programs, creating severe labor shortages in sparsely populated economies. The severe shortages have in turn increased labor rewards and thereby provided incentives for poorly paid Egyptian workers to migrate to neighboring countries. Furthermore, the Egyptian government's policies towards migration have aimed at eliminating bureaucratic constraints, which has made it easier for migration to take place. The decision to migrate is temporary, however, which reduces the cost of migration involving long-term adjustments by migrants and their families.

Empirical Analysis

An empirical model is formulated using push and pull factors to explain the migration rate from Egypt to the AOPC. Push factors represent a deterioration

Table 6: Some Evidence on the Inflation Rate and Per Capita Real Income in Egypt

Year	Consumer Price Index	Inflation Rate	Per Capita Real Income
1968	76.5	0.013	2.37
1969	79.1	0.034	2.38
1970	82.1	0.038	2.46
1971	84.7	0.032	2.45
1972	86.5	0.021	2.60
1973	90.2	0.042	2.86
1974	100.0	0.11	2.87
1975	109.6	0.096	2.96
1976	120.9	0.10	3.58
1977	136.3	0.13	4.17
1978	151.4	0.11	4.56
1979	166.5	0.10	2.80
1980	200.8	0.21	2.82
1981	220.9	0.10	2.75
1982	254.6	0.15	2.87
1983	292.6	0.15	2.85
1984	345.9	0.18	2.57
1985	418.4	0.21	2.35
1986	518.40	0.24	3.11
1987	620.49	0.20	3.22
1988	729.69	0.18	3.33

Notes:
The consumer price index is obtained from the *International Financial Statistics*, 1990 Year Book, International Monetary Fund.

The inflation rate is defined as: $\frac{P_t - P(t-1)}{P_t}$ where P_t is the aggregate price level, as measured by the consumer price index.

Per capita real income is measured by dividing per capita nominal income in Egypt by the corresponding consumer price index. Data for the nominal per capita income in Egypt are obtained from the *International Financial Statistics*.

in domestic conditions pushing Egyptians to migrate. These factors are approximated by population density and the inflation rate in Egypt. A description of recent movements in these variables is designed to explain their roles as push factors in Egyptian migration.

One of the most crucial problems facing Egypt is the rapid rate of population growth: 2.8 percent, which adds nearly one and a half million people to the population each year. In November 1986, the population reached 50 million people (CAPMAS 1987); currently it is estimated at approximately 60 million. Population is concentrated in less than 4 percent of the total geographic area (Ikram 1980), the Nile Valley and the Delta being among the most densely populated areas in the world. Moreover, there were 719 people per square kilometer in 1968 and 1,101 in 1985. One of the most striking effects of this situation has been increasing pressure on cultivated land and a decline in the number of *feddans* per capita. This has led to a decrease in land productivity, a subsequent increase in wheat imports, and a steady decline in the export of traditional agricultural crops. In addition, increasing population has led to a rapid increase in enrollment in learning institutions, which lack adequate facilities and qualified teachers. Given the number of graduates in almost all fields compared with real job opportunities and investment capabilities, Egypt has been unable to efficiently absorb the increasing supply of its university graduates. Egyptians' desire to migrate has, therefore, been stimulated by pressure on inhabited areas, deterioration in general living conditions, housing and transportation crises, and lower-quality health services, education services, and infrastructure.

The second push factor included in the empirical model is the inflation rate in Egypt, which approximates the cost of living. The inflation rate has been rising steadily. Table 6 presents data for the consumer price index in Egypt and the corresponding inflation rate, as well as the per capita real income in Egypt over the same period. The inflation rate of the consumer price index rose from 1 percent in 1968 to about 21 percent in 1985 and has remained high since that time. This was not matched by an equivalent rise in nominal personal income. As a result, the deterioration in real income, especially in the late seventies and in the eighties, stimulated Egyptians' desire to emigrate.

Deterioration in domestic conditions is not enough, however, for migration to take place. Sources of attraction have to exist and be evaluated by potential emigrants. Better conditions in the destination countries represent pull factors that attract people to migrate. These factors are approximated by per capita income in destination countries compared to Egypt. A rise in this ratio is expected to attract more Egyptians to migrate.

Towards a formal investigation of the determinants of Egyptian labor migration, a time-series regression is estimated. Based on data availability, all data are annual over the sample period 1968–1986. The dependent variable measures the migration rate from Egypt to the AOPC. It is measured by the total number of female and male workers who migrated from Egypt to seven major Arab oil-producing countries (Saudi Arabia, the United Arab Emirates, Kuwait, Oman, Qatar, Libya, and Iraq) divided by the population of Egypt. Variance in this rate is explained by the population density in Egypt, the inflation rate in Egypt, and the ratio of per capita income in the AOPC relative to its counterpart in Egypt.

The estimation of the empirical model identifies how the migration rate varies in relation to the explanatory variables that are likely to serve as important determinants of migration. All explanatory variables were found to have a statistically significant impact on the migration rate from Egypt to the AOPC. In general, domestic inflation and population density have the expected "push" effects on migration from Egypt to the Arab oil-producing countries. Further, the differential in the per capita income between the destination countries and Egypt has the expected "pull" effect on migration from Egypt to these countries. Estimation results indicate that a ten percent increase in population density in Egypt increases the Egyptian migration rate by 25 percent. By contrast, an increase of the same magnitude in the inflation rate in Egypt increases the migration rate in Egypt by approximately two percent. Furthermore, an increase of ten percent in the ratio of per capita income in the Arab oil-producing countries to its counterpart in Egypt increases the Egyptian migration rate by six percent. These magnitudes suggest that changes in the domestic population density appear particularly important in determining the Egyptian migration rate to neighboring Arab oil-producing countries.

THE IMPACT OF MIGRANTS' REMITTANCES ON THE EGYPTIAN ECONOMY

Remittances are among the major economic results of the Egyptian labor migration. Economic theory again calls attention to the factors which determine the impact of remittances on the Egyptian economy.

Theoretical Background

Towards a formal theoretical evaluation of the impact of remittances on the Egyptian economy, remittances are included in a structural model describing components of aggregate spending in Egypt. The value of income generated in the economy equals the sum of private spending on consumption and investment; government spending; exports and remittances; minus imports. Private consumption, private investment, and imports all increase with income, with parameters that measure the rates to consume, invest, and import.

The model's solution establishes that the value of remittances increases income with a magnitude that equals the remittances' multiplier. The value of the multiplier indicates that an increase in remittances of one Egyptian pound generates more than one pound of increase in income. The remittances' multiplier increases with the rates of domestic spending on private consumption and investment. In contrast, imports represent leakage out of domestic income and thereby decrease the remittances' multiplier.

Empirical Analysis

Towards a formal theoretical evaluation of the impact of remittances, an empirical model that approximates structural relationships characterizing the

Table 7: Ratio of Remittances to GNP and Its Major Components In Egypt

Year	% of R to GNP	% of R to C	% of R to I	% of R to N	% of R to X
1970	0.09	0.12	0.59	0.44	0.57
1971	0.09	0.13	0.60	0.43	0.61
1972	1.04	1.51	7.05	4.86	6.67
1973	0.94	1.43	6.82	4.68	6.41
1974	3.75	5.34	21.20	10.99	17.22
1975	5.08	6.89	16.79	12.54	25.41
1976	6.14	9.46	23.77	22.22	38.09
1977	9.53	12.68	25.99	24.21	35.16
1978	11.60	19.94	40.89	37.66	64.21
1979	16.49	26.49	51.36	40.74	65.94
1980	17.14	25.91	66.00	44.56	66.09
1981	9.38	15.52	33.24	23.52	32.62
1982	12.34	18.25	47.27	32.25	72.62
1983	12.55	20.04	49.53	38.98	53.07
1984	9.49	14.47	42.08	29.88	45.63
1985	6.89	10.98	34.53	26.01	38.37
1986	8.12	12.61	44.39	35.41	53.79
1987	8.85	11.52	51.46	31.42	51.74
1988	9.83	12.55	41.13	24.73	41.43

Note: R=remittances by Egyptian migrants to their home country; C=private consumption spending; I=private investment spending; N=Egypt's imports; X=Egypt's exports.

Egyptian economy is estimated. The parameters describing these relationships are used to determine the remittances' multiplier, i.e., the impact of a change in remittances on Gross National Product (GNP) in Egypt.

Substituting the relevant parameters from estimation into the formula for the multiplier indicates that an increase of one million Egyptian pounds in remittances results in an increase in GNP of 2.2 million Egyptian pounds. Further, the remittances' multiplier depends positively on the rates to consume and invest out of income. In contrast, the rate to import out of income decreases the multiplier. Accordingly, in order to maximize the positive impact of remittances on GNP in Egypt, policies should aim at increasing the desire to spend on domestic products and discouraging expenditures on imported products.

Table 7 summarizes the ratio of remittances to GNP and its major components: consumption, investment, imports, and exports. Except for 1973, the ratio of remittances to GNP and its major components increased steadily in the seventies and reached a record high in 1979. A reduction in the number of

Table 8: The Multiple Effect of Remittances on Consumption

Year	Remittances	Actual Consumption	Consumption Induced by Remittances	% of Induced to Actual Consumption
1970	2.5	2,011	3.5	0.17
1971	2.8	2,237	3.9	0.17
1972	35.4	2,339	49.9	2.13
1973	34.1	2,377	48.1	2.02
1974	153.3	2,871	216.2	7.53
1975	240.9	3,493	339.7	9.73
1976	393.8	4,163	555.3	13.34
1977	623.4	4,916	978.9	17.88
1978	1,245.8	6,264	1,756.6	28.04
1979	2,208.4	8,338	3,113.8	37.34
1980	2,856.6	11,023	4,027.8	36.54
1981	1,731.1	11,155	2,440.9	21.88
1982	2,632.3	14,427	3,711.5	25.73
1983	3,268.5	16,307	4,608.6	28.26
1984	2,907.4	20,093	4,099.4	20.40
1985	2,472.0	22,509	3,485.5	15.48
1986	3,200.0	25,379	4,512.0	17.78
1987	4,142.4	35,947	5,840.8	16.25
1988	5,362.3	42,729	7,560.8	17.69

migrants after the Camp David Accord affected the magnitude of remittances and, in turn, their ratios to GNP and its major components in Egypt. Nonetheless, the figures of Table 7 suggest that remittances have increased at a remarkably higher rate compared to any of the other components of GNP in Egypt. The growth in remittances is likely, however, to have impacted on the growth of these components. The estimate of the remittances' multiplier is used to measure the exact contribution of remittances to the growth in each of the components of GNP in Egypt.

First, consider the effect of remittances on consumption, the largest component of domestic spending in Egypt. This effect is approximated by the product of the rate to consume out of income and the remittances' multiplier. An increase of one million Egyptian pounds in remittances results in an increase in private consumption of 1.41 million Egyptian pounds. The proportion of private consumption induced by remittances is calculated by multiplying the actual value of remittances by 1.41. The ratio of this induced component to the actual value of consumption between 1970–1988 is shown in Table 8. The results indicate that while remittances induced .17 percent of private con-

Table 9: The Multiple Effect of Remittances on Investment

Year	Remittances	Actual Investment	Investment Induced by Remittances	% of Induced to Actual Investment
1970	2.5	427	1.43	0.33
1971	2.8	467	1.60	0.34
1972	35.4	502	20.18	4.02
1973	34.1	500	19.44	3.89
1974	153.3	723	87.38	12.09
1975	240.9	1435	137.31	9.57
1976	393.8	1657	224.47	13.55
1977	623.4	2399	355.34	14.81
1978	1248.8	4300	1258.79	29.27
1979	2208.4	4300	1258.79	29.27
1980	2856.6	4328	1628.26	37.62
1981	1731.1	5208	986.73	18.95
1982	2632.3	5569	1500.41	26.49
1983	3268.5	6599	1863.05	28.23
1984	2907.4	6910	1657.22	23.98
1985	2472.0	7158	1409.04	19.68
1986	3200.0	7209	1824.00	25.30
1987	4142.4	8050	2361.17	29.33
1988	5362.3	13037	3056.51	23.44

sumption in 1970, this ratio increased to 37.34 percent in 1979. Subsequently, the ratio dropped to 17.69 percent in 1988.

Second, consider the effect of remittances on the second component of private spending—investment. This effect is approximated by the product of the rate to invest out of income and the remittances' multiplier. An increase of one million Egyptian pounds in remittances results in an increase in private investment of 0.57 million Egyptian pounds. The proportion of private investment induced by remittances is measured by the actual values of remittances multiplied by 0.57. Table 9 contrasts the values of the induced component of investment to the actual values over time. The numbers suggest that while remittances induced only 0.33 percent of private investment spending in Egypt in 1970, remittances induced a share that equals approximately one-fourth, 23.44 percent, of private investment spending in 1988.

Finally, consider the effect of remittances on the amount of leakage out of domestic income, i.e., imports. This effect is approximated by the product of the rate to import out of income and the remittances' multiplier. An increase of one million Egyptian pounds in remittances results in an increase in imports

Table 10: The Multiple Effect of Remittances on Imports

Year	Remittances	Actual Imports	Imports Induced by Remittances	% of Induced to Actual Imports
1970	2.5	574	1.93	0.34
1971	2.8	649	2.16	0.33
1972	35.4	729	27.26	3.74
1973	34.1	729	26.26	3.60
1974	153.3	1395	118.04	8.46
1975	240.9	1921	185.49	9.66
1976	393.8	1772	303.23	17.11
1977	623.4	2575	480.02	18.64
1978	1248.8	3316	961.58	28.99
1979	2208.4	5421	1700.47	31.37
1980	2856.6	6410	2199.58	34.31
1981	1731.1	7361	1332.95	18.11
1982	2632.3	8163	2026.87	24.83
1983	3268.5	8385	2516.75	30.01
1984	2907.4	9731	2238.70	23.01
1985	2472.0	9505	1903.44	20.03
1986	3200.0	9038	2464.00	27.26
1987	4142.4	13184	3189.65	24.19
1988	5362.3	21680	4128.97	19.05

of 0.77 million Egyptian pounds. The proportion of imports induced by re-mittances is measured by the actual value of remittances multiplied by 0.77. Table 10 contrasts the actual magnitudes of imports to their induced values by remittances. While the ratio of the induced component to the actual value of imports was only 0.34 percent in 1970, this ratio reached 19.05 percent in 1988.

SUMMARY AND CONCLUSION

By analyzing the determinants and implications of the Egyptian labor migra-tion to neighboring Arab oil-producing countries, this study illustrates the way that empirical analyses of economic theory can be used to analyze critical issues facing economic development. Egypt's experience with labor migration is cer-tainly not unique among countries of the Middle East. Across many countries of the region, labor is attracted to better working conditions and higher wages in neighboring, more endowed countries. By analyzing Egypt's experience with labor migration and by reviewing the theoretical literature identifying its determinants and implications, the present paper demonstrates the value of extending the research on migration to other similar experiences in the Middle East and elsewhere.

Focusing on important cause-and-effect variable relationships, the present study illustrates important determinants of the Egyptian labor migration. Factors determining an individual's decision to migrate include age, the unemployment rate, density of population, the level of income, the educational level, distance, the growth rate of income, the expected real wage, and the inflation rate. Due to data limitations, the empirical investigation accounts for only three of these variables: the ratio of per capita income between destination countries and Egypt, the inflation rate in Egypt, and the population density in Egypt. The first factor is representative of pull factors in destination countries and the latter two factors are representatives of push factors in Egypt.

Egyptian labor migration increases as a function of rises in the ratio of per capita income in the Arab oil-producing countries to per capita income in Egypt. In addition, population density and price inflation in Egypt impact positively on labor migration to the Arab oil-producing countries. The results also indicate a significant decrease in the number of Egyptian migrants following the rise of political tension between Egypt and its neighboring countries in the wake of the Camp David Accords.

These findings are consistent with the economic theory of factor mobility. Migration from Egypt to Arab oil-producing countries constitutes an efficient process of labor transfer from low income to high income countries. As for the implications of labor migration, the empirical analysis quantifies the importance of this factor for income and major components of aggregate spending in Egypt. The results suggest that migrants' remittances have a strong positive impact on GNP in Egypt. An increase of 10 million Egyptian pounds in remittances has increased GNP in Egypt by approximately 22 million Egyptian pounds. In addition, remittances have had positive, although not equal, impacts on major components of aggregate spending in Egypt: private consumption, private investment, and imports. The largest impact is on private consumption spending and the smallest impact is on private investment spending.

Clearly, remittances are among the major benefits resulting from migration. To maximize the inflow of these remittances, the Egyptian government needs to consider such measures as the establishment of a suitable banking system and desirable channels of investment. Furthermore, policies should aim at reducing spending on imports in order to maximize the positive impact of remittances on GNP in Egypt. This can be accomplished through the encouragement of domestic industries that stand up to the level of foreign competition.

Finally, it should be emphasized that this study does not imply that Egyptian labor migration to Arab neighboring countries is without negative consequences for the Egyptian economy. Migrants' remittances have generated demand without contributing to productive capacity, for example, and inflation has been aggravated as a result. In addition, as Egyptian workers migrated, they left behind a market with excess demand for their skills. The results are low-quality and highly priced products and services that have created further inflationary pressures in the Egyptian economy.

Future research should consider these and other negative aspects of migration in order to provide a comprehensive evaluation of the consequences of labor migration in labor-exporting countries. More importantly, such studies will contribute to ongoing efforts that aim at the refinement of relevant bodies of economic theory, and thereby contribute to the development of analytical insights of more general applicability.

APPENDIX

Data Description and Sources

Sources of data are as follows:

1. *International Financial Statistics*, Yearbook, The International Monetary Fund, Washington.

2. *Migration of Egyptian Workers Abroad*, several issues, Central Agency for Public Mobilization and Statistics, Cairo (in Arabic).

3. *Statistical Yearbook: Arab Republic of Egypt (1952–1986)*, Central Agency for Public Mobilization and Statistics, Cairo.

4. Ikram, K. *Egypt: Economic Management in a Period of Transition*, World Bank, Washington, 1980.

5. Monthly and *Annual Bulletins* (Arabic), Central Bank of Egypt, several issues.

6. *The Economics of Egyptian Migrants Savings* (Arabic), National Specialized Councils, Cairo, Arab Center for Research and Publishing.

Data series employed and their sources are as follows:

• The migration rate: total number of Egyptian migrants to the AOPC divided by Egypt's population, source number 2.

• Egypt's Consumer Price Index, source number 1.

• The average per capita income in seven major oil-producing countries, source number 1.

• Per capita income in Egypt, source number 1.

• Egypt's population density, source number 4.

• Egypt's inflation rate, source number 1.

• Egypt's population, source number 3.

• The total value of private consumption spending, gross national product, exports, imports, government spending, and private investment spending, source number 1.

• The total value of income taxes in Egypt, source number 5.

• The total value of remittances made by Egyptian workers to their home country, sources number 5 and 6.

NOTES

1. These annual figures are for Egyptians leaving Egypt for Arab countries on government secondment or with "personal contracts." Accordingly, these figures include only Egyptians passing through the Ministry of Labor Power and Training and exclude private sector migrants who are not required to have work permits. The figures also exclude annual labor and craftsmen and the increasing number of Egyptian workers who leave the country before securing a job abroad or without being required to obtain work permits from Egyptian authorities.

2. Since the numbers reported in Table 3 are in nominal magnitudes, part of the observed growth over time is attributed to the inflation rate.

3. The patterns of consumption resulting from remittances have been subjected to several discussions. For example, Serag El Din, et al. (1983) explored this issue and concluded that the expenditure patterns resulting from remittances have been far from rational and the objectives of economic development in Egypt. Similarly, one can cite a quote from the Egyptian National Plan (1979–1982) that supports this idea, ". . . those individuals (referring to Egyptian migrants) return to Egypt possessed with huge purchasing power, which they usually direct not to savings and investments but to flagrant and luxurious consumption."

4. This issue has been discussed in some detail in Abdel-Fadil (1980) in which he bases his information on a questionnaire addressed to a sample of Egyptians who worked for some time in the Arab oil-producing countries. The sample included three major categories: construction workers, schoolteachers, and university academic staff.

5. Egypt is not unique in this experience. Others who have contributed to the international labor migration literature have noted the same thing. For example, Ecevit and Zachariah (1978) mention that a small portion of remittances that have resulted from international migration has been successfully channeled into productive investment while the bulk has been spent on consumer goods.

REFERENCES

Abdel-Fadil, M. 1980. "The Effects of Labor Migration to Oil Production Countries on Personal Incomes and Consumption Behavior in Labor Exporting Countries." *Oil and Arab Cooperation* 6: 97–109.

Amin, G. A., and E. Awny. 1985. *International Migration of Egyptian Labor: A Review of the State of the Art.* Canada: International Development Center.

Birks, J. S., and C. A. Sinclair. 1980. *International Migration and Development in the Arab Region.* Geneva: International Labor Organization.

Central Agency for Public Mobilization and Statistics. 1987. *Statistical Yearbook.* Cairo: CAPMAS.

Choucri, N. R. Eckaus, and A. Mohie El-Din. 1977. *Migration and Employment in the Construction Sector: Critical Factors in the Egyptian Development.* Cairo: Cairo University.

Dessouki, A. 1982. "The Shift in Egypt's Migration Policy: 1952–1977." *Middle Eastern Studies* 18: 53–68.

Ecevit, Z., and K. C. Zachariah. 1978. "International Labor Migration." *Finance and Development* 15: 32–37.

Fabricant, R. A. 1970. "An Expectation Model of Migration." *Journal of Regional Science* 10: 13–24.

Ikram, K. 1980. *Egypt: Economic Management in a Period of Transition.* Washington: The World Bank.

Kandil, M., and M. Metwally. 1992. "Determinants of the Egyptian Labor Migration." *International Migration* 30 (1): 39–56.

———. 1990. "The Impact of Migrants' Remittances on the Egyptian Economy." *International Migration* 26 (2): 159–181.

Khalifa, F. 1986. "The Economic and Social Effects of Egyptian Workers' Remittances on the Egyptian Economy for the Period 1970–1983." *Social Science* 14: 71–94.

Lee, E. S. 1966. "A Theory of Migration." *Demography* 3: 47–57.

Meade, J. E. 1955. *The Theory of International Economic Policy: Trade and Welfare.* Oxford: Oxford University Press.

National Specialized Councils. 1983. *The Economics of Savings of Egyptians Working Abroad* (in Arabic). Cairo: Arab Center for Research and Publishing.

Serag El Din, I., J. Socknat, S. Birks, and C. Sinclair. 1983. *Manpower and International Labor Migration in the Middle East and North Africa.* Washington: The World Bank.

Sjaastad, L. A. 1962. "The Costs and Returns of Human Migration." *Journal of Political Economy* 70: 80–93.

Willis, K. G. 1975. "Regression Models of Migration." *Geografiska Annalu* 57B: 42–54.

———. 1974. *Problems in Migration Analysis.* London: D. C. Heath.

7. Religion and International Conflict
An Individual-Level Analysis

Mark Tessler and Jodi Nachtwey

Defying all expectations of modernization theory, the 1970s and 1980s witnessed a reawakening of religious ideas and social movements. Moreover, the Middle East, which provided the setting for important early research on modernization, has played an important role in demonstrating that economic development and social change are not necessarily associated with an increase in secularism. In the Islamic countries of the Middle East in particular, but in substantial measure in Israel as well, it is today more important than ever to devote attention to religion and religious movements when examining social and political phenomena. This is another example of how theory-oriented inquiry needs to concern itself with developments on the ground in particular world regions.

Despite the increased attention that religion has received as an analytical concept, however, both within the Middle East and more generally, a systematic and coherent understanding of the connections between religion and politics remains elusive. First, studies are often highly descriptive, confined to particular cultural or sociopolitical settings and concerned with explicating the causes and consequences of specific events rather than contributing generalizable theoretical insights. Second, only rarely are studies cross-national and genuinely comparative, with a concern for discovering system-level conditionalities included as a prominent research goal. Third, and perhaps most important, there has been little research in which the individual is the unit of analysis, and accordingly very few systematic, data-based investigations that focus on the link between the religious and political orientations of ordinary citizens.

To these deficiencies may be added the paucity of information about the

The research reported in this chapter was supported in part by a grant from the United States Institute of Peace. The authors acknowledge this support with appreciation.

relationship between religion and international conflict, which is the focus of the research reported in this chapter. So far as the Muslim world is concerned, it is sometimes asserted that Islam threatens peaceful relations among states in the international system. This argument is advanced in the clash of civilizations debate, for example, and in some studies that challenge the applicability to the Middle East of the hypothesis that democracies do not go to war against one another. But such assertions usually involve overly simplified conceptions of Islam, if not outright stereotypes, and they are almost always unsupported by rigorous, data-based investigations.

A small body of research in the United States is beginning to address some of these deficiencies, and studies carried out in the Middle East can and should participate in this effort. While the impetus for this research is to be found primarily in the politically significant religious resurgence occurring in the United States, some hypotheses have been examined in European countries as well. Scholarship in the Middle East needs to be informed by this research, and it must also contribute to this cumulative analytical undertaking both through the refinement that comes with replication and by identifying the generalizability, limitations, and conditionalities associated with propositions that purport to be broadly applicable.

Toward this end, the present chapter explores the relationship between religion and international conflict at the individual level of analysis. It employs public opinion data collected in five Middle Eastern countries: Jordan, Lebanon, Egypt, Kuwait, and Palestine, the latter referring to the West Bank and Gaza Strip. To place the analysis within an appropriate conceptual framework and to connect this study to more general theoretical concerns, the conceptualization of key variables and hypothesized variable relationships will first be discussed in relation to the existing political science literature on religion and political behavior. Thereafter, to add an area-specific focus to these more general theoretical concerns, the interplay between religion and politics in the Middle East will be summarized briefly. Finally, informed by and seeking to contribute to both kinds of knowledge, that in the domains of disciplinary inquiry and "area studies" respectively, the data will be presented and analyzed in order to add to our understanding of whether, in what ways, and under what conditions religious ideas, in this case those associated with Islam, influence citizen orientations relating to international relations and international conflict.

RELIGION, POLITICS, AND INTERNATIONAL AFFAIRS

The theoretical importance of studying religion and international politics is based, in part, on the link between culture and politics. Religion, as a key component of culture, plays a critical role in creating and shaping the normative orientations of individuals and their understanding of the surrounding world. Religious beliefs provide answers in unpredictable surroundings; they guide behavior through compelling ethical or moral prescriptions; and they establish social identity by distinguishing religious adherents from nonbelievers (Goldstein and Keohane 1993, p. 16; Leege 1993). Indeed, although not all cultural values are of religious origin, religion is a particularly important source of the normative codes that influence attitudes and behavior. This is especially true among adherents and believers because, as Leege notes, religion "characterizes its answers as sacred, eternal, [and] implicated with the ultimate meaning of life" (1993, p. 10).

Since religion provides normative guidelines and behavioral prescriptions pertaining to many areas of human interaction, it is reasonable to assume that religious values and beliefs have implications for the way that individuals view political events and processes. At least three different kinds of roles have been suggested for religion so far as the world of politics is concerned: a priestly role, a prophetic role, and a mediating societal function (Wald 1992). In its priestly role, religion is a force which legitimates government action by justifying policies on the basis of a superior, transcendent, moral authority (Berger 1969; Leege 1993). If a religious belief system is widely shared, these common norms may be emphasized in order to build support for the government and its policies (Jelen 1996b). In a prophetic role, by contrast, religious ideals provide criteria by which to judge governmental authority and, in particular, to criticize political decisions or policies that are believed to be inconsistent with divine purposes. In this way, religion provides support for advocates of political change. Finally, as a mediating institution, religion offers protection from excessive government control and authoritarian tendencies. By providing a focus of identity that rivals state loyalties, and also through the provision of services that reduce dependence on the state, religious institutions contribute to the vitality of civil society and allow individuals to maintain an independent or even critical stance toward the government and its actions (Leege 1993).

On the other hand, it can also be argued that religion has little or no influence on political attitudes and behavior. This thesis, at least as applied to Western societies, rests in part on the assumption that religion has been privatized, that religion increasingly has meaning only in the private sphere of the individual. It also rests on the assumption that most individuals have embraced secularism as a model for state-society relations. As expressed in one recent study, if institutional modernization has routinized and specialized social relations and removed from the state any legitimate concern with maintaining a religious worldview, then the search for religious fulfillment becomes a personal quest for spiritual meaning and is quite detached from the daily functioning of political affairs (Casanova 1994, pp 16–17). Thus, to the extent these assumptions about privatized religion and secularism are correct, religious norms may be influential only in matters of personal ethics and morality.

These competing perspectives suggest that the utility of religious variables in explaining political attitudes and behavior may depend on the kinds of religious orientations that individuals hold and on the broader societal and cultural context within which they reside. Findings from a number of empirical studies, while not entirely consistent, also suggest a more nuanced and conditional relationship between religion and politics, one in which individual-level religious orientations are neither consistently useful nor consistently irrelevant in accounting for variance in political attitudes and behavior. Several opinion surveys report, for example, that personal religiosity is strongly and positively related to the nature and degree of importance that individuals attach to issues of public policy pertaining to personal conduct, especially, as in the case of abortion, homosexuality, and gender roles, if this conduct is deemed to involve an ethical or moral dimension (Hayes 1994; Jelen 1991, 1996a). Some of these studies are based on cross-national data.

In another study, using data from the United States, researchers constructed attitudinal scales measuring four different normative dimensions associated with religion and then examined the correlation between each and a series of political attitudes (Benson and Williams 1982). Two scales exhibited particularly strong correlations. One assessed whether respondents viewed the "human problem" primarily as a personal struggle or as a societal challenge. The other measured the degree to which respondents' religious behavior focused more on their private relationship with God or on relationships with other people. In each case, the more individualistic orientations were correlated with greater conservatism, as normally defined in Western countries, both in general and with respect to various public policy concerns. Although the data for this study are based on a survey limited to elites, the findings nevertheless offer additional evidence that religious factors sometimes may, but also sometimes may not, account for variance in political orientations. Moreover, the study is of particular interest because it offers a conceptualization of religiosity that is based on normative interpretation rather than church affiliation or other institutional considerations, thus making it readily applicable to the world of Islam.

A few opinion studies in the Middle East have also examined the relationship between religiosity and attitudes toward politics and public policy, and they, too, report that some religious orientations have more explanatory power than others. For example, a recent analysis of public opinion data from Egypt observed a negative correlation between religious activism, as measured by support for religious dress, censorship, religious instruction in schools, and Islamic revival, and support for economic liberalism in such areas as price controls and subsidies (Palmer et al. 1996). On the other hand, religiosity defined in terms of piety and measured on the basis of prayer and ritual performance bears no relationship to attitudes toward these issues of political and economic policy.

Other studies have explored the relationship between religious piety and partisan preferences using survey data from Egypt and Lebanon, and in each case there was at best a weak relationship not only between religiosity and political preferences in general but between religiosity and support for Islamic political movements in particular. In Egypt, more than one-third of those classified as more pious did not support Islamic parties, whereas approximately half of those who did support these parties were not personally observant and devout (Tessler 1997). In Lebanon, the relationship between religiosity and support for the Islamic political party, Hizballah, was only moderately strong (Harik 1996, p. 57).

Although there have been only a few studies that attempt to link religion to international concerns at the individual level of analysis, the research reports available once again suggest that relationships are complex and conditional. Guth and Green (1993), using data from the United States, looked at religiosity defined in terms of a tendency to seek religious guidance and biblical literalism and found a positive correlation with anti-communism and higher levels of support for military and defense-related spending. But while this finding suggests that religiosity pushes toward conservative and nationalistic political views, a study using European data found that greater religiosity was positively correlated with higher levels of internationalism, and specifically with more support for European integration and for aid to developing countries (MacIver 1989). In this case, religiosity was measured by the degree to which respondents reported that religion was important in shaping their political outlook.

The findings of yet another scholar are similarly diverse. In studies based on data from the United States, including a measure of attitudes toward the Gulf War, Jelen found that respondents with beliefs associated with Evangelical Protestantism were more likely to display hawkish foreign policy attitudes and, specifically, to support increased defense spending, the use of military power to achieve foreign policy goals, and the bombing of civilian targets in wartime situations. Roman Catholics, by contrast, took more dovish positions on a number of foreign policy questions (Jelen 1994). An even less consistent pattern emerged from Jelen's analysis of European data. With an index of attitudes toward NATO and the U.S. military presence in Europe treated as the dependent variable, and using church attendance, which was the only available indicator, to measure religiosity, he found (1) a direct positive correlation between religiosity and support for military security in three countries, (2) a direct but negative correlation between religiosity and support for military security in two countries, and (3) a positive but indirect correlation between religiosity and support for military security in seven countries (Jelen 1996b).

The findings by Benson and Williams (1982) illuminate further the complex role of religiosity as an independent variable. Of the four normative dimensions mentioned above, the two religious orientations associated with political conservatism were also correlated with conservatism in foreign policy attitudes. Specifically, using attitudes toward foreign aid and defense spending as dependent variables, support for defense spending and a reduction in foreign aid was associated with more individualistic orientations on both religious dimensions. In this instance, it is not the degree of religiosity but rather the type of religious orientation that accounts for variance in individual political attitudes, thus suggesting that it is not possible to draw simple and straightforward conclusions about an association between levels of personal religiosity and particular political attitudes.

The findings from these various studies suggest that religious orientations do play an important role in shaping political attitudes, including attitudes relating to foreign policy and world affairs. Further, more often than not, they suggest that religiosity pushes toward a more conservative and nationalistic view of politics and international relations. In addition, however, taken in the aggregate, this body of research also shows that religiosity can sometimes lead to a more liberal and internationalist political perspective, that the salience and direction of relationships vary as a function both of the particular dimension of religiosity treated as an independent variable and of the particular political attitude treated as a dependent variable, and, finally, that all of this variation is itself influenced by place- and time-associated conditionalities.

As the preceding indicates, the present state of knowledge about the relationship between religion and politics at the individual level of analysis is characterized by a diversity of findings and many apparent inconsistencies. On the other hand, since there has been relatively little systematic research in this area, and even less involving replication and a focused contribution to scientific cumulativeness, it is reasonable to hope that more coherent insights about relationships and conditionalities will emerge as additional studies are conducted and more data become available. This is a long-term prospect, of course, toward which progress will be made only incrementally. But each individual study strengthens the empirical foundation required for theoretical development, and this is precisely the contribution that the present research report aspires to make.

RELIGION AND POLITICS IN THE MIDDLE EAST

In the context of the preceding discussion, research about religion and politics in the Middle East is important in at least two interrelated respects. First, as with any empirical investigation, it provides additional data for the cumulative exercise described above, and, in particular, it expands the range of conditions under which salient variable relationships may be explored. Second, and equally important, it permits consideration of the possibility that the diversity and inconsistency noted in studies conducted in Western societies are at least partly a consequence of the ambiguous political role that religion plays in largely secular societies. This would be indicated should a different pattern, and especially a more coherent one, be observed in societies, such as those in the Muslim Middle East, where there has long been a much stronger connection between religion and political life. Reality may or may not conform to this possibility, but, in any event, studies in the Middle East will make it possible to compare findings from Muslim and non-Muslim countries, and this in turn will shed light on the degree to which the impact of religious orientations on political attitudes is itself dependent on the broader religious and societal environment within which individuals reside.

Only a brief summary of the aggregate and historical connections between religion and politics in the Muslim world is required in the present context. These connections are for the most part familiar, and the concern of the present report is in any event limited to an examination of variable relationships at the individual level of analysis. But since this also includes consideration of the differences and similarities between patterns observed in Arab and Islamic countries and those reported in studies conducted in more secular societies, it may be useful to offer a short and very general account of Islam's political significance in the Muslim Middle East. This portrait will provide a basis for informed speculation about some of the conditionalities associated with the comparative dimension of the analysis.

The association between religion and politics can be seen at several levels in the Arab and Islamic world. On the one hand, constitutions declare Islam to be the official state religion in almost all Arab countries and, accordingly, religious holidays are national holidays, religion is part of the curriculum in state-run schools, the government has responsibility for mosques and other Islamic institutions, and, most important perhaps, substantial segments of national legal codes are based on the Quran. Thus, as summarized recently by an Arab scholar, "secularism and the privatization of religion are alien to the Muslim conception. Muslims have continued to assume that only a 'religious leader' can provide good government for the Muslim community and that the main function of an Islamic government is to ensure obedience to God's law as explained in the Quran and the Sunnah" (Al-Suwaidi 1995, p. 87). This strong and historically validated connection between religion and politics contrasts dramatically with the established patterns of secularism that, however imperfect, characterize most Western societies.

On the other hand, Islam contributes significantly to both the ideological and the institutional axes according to which government and opposition play themselves out in Muslim countries of the Middle East. Although there is some variation across political systems, and also over time, it is common for governments to employ Islamic symbols in an attempt to shore up their legitimacy and to use government-appointed religious officials to justify the regime and its policies. In the latter connection, there are numerous examples of Islamic jurists and scholars issuing pronouncements that are deliberately designed to serve the interests of political leaders (Hanafi 1982, p. 65), such as the statement that Anwar Sadat obtained in 1979 from Islamic scholars at Cairo's Al-Azhar Mosque University to the effect that peace with Israel is compatible with Islam (Jansen 1986, p. 44; Hopwood 1982, p. 119).

Similarly, Islam provides a frame of reference and an institutional structure for political movements opposed to established regimes. This has been particularly apparent in recent decades, although it is not a new phenomenon. Indeed, nationalist movements often carried out resistance to colonialism during the pre-independence period under the ideological banner of Islam, and they often used mosques and brotherhood lodges for organizational purposes. More recently, Islamist groups have been in the forefront of challenging the governments of many Arab countries, sometimes working within the political system, as in the case of the Muslim Brotherhood in Jordan, for example (Tessler and Brand 1996), and sometimes using extra-legal or even violent means in pursuit of their objectives. These groups use mosques and other Muslim institutions to recruit followers and disseminate their message, the content of which is usually that the government is not only repressive and corrupt but has also deviated from Islamic principles and is therefore illegitimate (Waterbury 1994).

There are a number of reasons why Islamic opposition movements have assumed increased importance in recent decades (Tessler 1997). Some have to do with deteriorating economic and political conditions, which lead ordinary citizens to support for nonideological reasons those political movements they believe to be best able to put pressure on the government. In this instance, especially in view of the political vacuum that exists in countries ruled by authoritarian governments, the organizational and mobilizational advantages of Islamist movements are particularly important. So, too, is the fact that many of these movements carry out an extensive array of welfare and development activities at the grassroots level, especially in poorer neighborhods. As one Arab scholar reports in this connection, groups associated with political Islam use socioeconomic institutions and programs, particularly those that target the poor, to gain "greater access to the masses and through them access to power" (Kawaran 1992, p. 172). On the other hand, factors having to do with Islam itself are also important. These include the religion's strong emphasis on justice, equality, and assistance to those in need, as well as the fact that Islamic law is regarded by Muslims as a guide and blueprint for societal organization in all spheres of human activity, including the political sphere.

The obvious point of this summary discussion is that Islam and politics are intimately connected in the Muslim world, making it reasonable to expect that the influence of religion on political attitudes will be much stronger and more consistent than the ambiguous pattern of relationships observed by studies carried out in the United States and other Western societies. If this is indeed the case, as discussed earlier, the hypothesis which follows is that the utility of religious orientations in accounting for variance in political attitudes is itself dependent on system-level conditionalities, and that particularly important among these conditionalities is the degree to which a society is more or less secular. It will also follow, should this be the case, that global generalizations about the impact of religion on political attitudes will be of limited value, and that meaningful theory construction requires the incorporation of information about the historical, cultural, and societal characteristics of particular world regions.

Mark Tessler and Jodi Nachtwey

DATA BASE AND RESEARCH DESIGN

The task of the present analysis is to examine the influence of Islamic orientations on attitudes toward international conflict using survey data from Arab societies, and then to compare the findings from this research with those based on studies conducted in Western societies. The data to be utilized are based on public opinion surveys carried out in Egypt, Kuwait, Lebanon, Jordan, and Palestine.

The Egyptian and Kuwaiti surveys were carried out in mid-1988 under the direction of Jamal Al-Suwaidi of United Arab Emirates University. Based on stratified samples of 295 adults in Cairo and 300 adults in Kuwait City, respondents reflect the heterogeneous nature of the general population. Each sample includes an approximately equal number of men and women and, despite a slight underrepresentation of poor and less well-educated individuals, each is broadly representative with respect to age, education, socioeconomic status, and place of residence. Egyptian Christians and Kuwaiti Shi'ites were excluded from the samples for analytical purposes, in order to facilitate comparison of Sunni Muslim populations in other Arab countries. The same survey instrument was employed in each country.

The Jordanian and Lebanese surveys were carried out in 1994 by the Market Research Organization of Amman, Jordan. They are based on random samples in major cities—Amman, Zarqa, and Irbid in Jordan, and Beirut, Tripoli, and Saidon in Lebanon—and employ the same survey instrument in the two countries. All respondents are over the age of 18 and, as would be expected with representative samples, the 251 Jordanian respondents and the 252 Lebanese respondents are equally divided between men and women.

The Palestinian survey was conducted in mid-1995 by the Center for Palestine Research and Studies (CPRS) in Nablus, under the supervision of its director, Dr. Khalil Shikaki, and the head of its polling unit, Dr. Nadir Said. Multistage area probability sampling techniques were employed to select respondents, and the interview schedule was administered to 1,184 adults residing in the West Bank and Gaza.

Taken together, the five countries from which the data are drawn encompass much of the diversity of the Arab world, and they accordingly constitute what is sometimes called a "most different systems" research design. They represent both rich and poor Arab states, both monarchies and republican forms of government, both more competitive and less competitive political systems, and both states with substantial and states with limited religious diversity. There is also diversity with respect to temporal considerations, with some surveys conducted before and other surveys conducted after the Gulf crisis of 1990–1991 and the Israel-PLO accord of 1993. As a result, these five states are at least reasonably representative of the Arab Middle East taken as a whole, and there is accordingly a strong likelihood that any variable relationships observed in all five are applicable broadly throughout the Arab world.

The dependent variable in this analysis is attitudes toward the resolution of international conflict, and specifically toward a peaceful resolution of the Arab-Israeli dispute. For each country, these attitudes are measured by a scale composed of two intercorrelated items from the survey instrument. Table 1 lists the items used to construct these measures, all of which deal with the desirability or possibility of achieving Arab-Israeli peace through diplomacy and compromise. Table 2 presents the response distribution on these measures of the dependent variable for each of the five countries.

The ability of religious orientations to explain this variance is the focus of the present analysis. In order to examine this relationship with as much sensitivity as possible, efforts were first made to refine the measure of religious attitudes. Since several questions dealing with religion were posed in the surveys, and also due to the complexity of the concept of religiosity, a multidimensional scaling procedure known as factor analysis has been employed to identify the principal religious orientations relevant for the populations surveyed. Not only does factor analysis provide conceptual guidance, it also has several statistical and methodological advantages. On the one hand, it contributes to parsimony and increases the ability of a regression equation to stand up to cross-validation (Stevens 1996, p. 365). On the other, it increases confidence in the reliability and validity of the items selected to measure religious orientations.

In the Egyptian, Kuwaiti, and Palestinian samples, two theoretically distinct and empirically independent dimensions of religious attitudes emerge from the factor analysis. The first revolves around aspects of personal piety (i.e., frequency of prayer), while the second concerns the relationship between religion and sociopolitical life and includes support for Islamist political movements. The survey items that cluster together to measure each dimension are shown in Tables 3 and 4, and in each case these items have been combined to create an additive index for use in the multivariate analysis. It is noteworthy that a similar pattern was found in another study, which increases confidence in the results of the factor analysis in the present instance. Using survey data from Egypt, Palmer, Safty, and Sullivan found that religiosity may relate to private, or largely "passive" ritual experiences, or it may tap into a concern for how religious principles are actively followed in society (1996). It is also notable that some work in the United States has found a similar differentiation among religious attitudes. In particular, Benson and Williams report a distinction between attitudes concerned with an individual's personal relationship with God and views emphasizing the role of religion in creating societal harmony (1982). This suggests that there may be important similarities in the dimensional structure, if not necessarily the associated political attitudes, of religious orientations in the Muslim Middle East and the more secular West.

Unfortunately, the salience of these dimensions cannot be examined in the Jordanian and Lebanese cases since questions about religious piety were not

Table 1: Survey Items Used to Measure the Dependent Variable

Egyptian and Kuwaiti Surveys:

• Which is the best solution to the Arab-Israeli conflict: military, or diplomatic?
• Which of the following best describes your attitudes towards relations with Israel? Egypt: peace treaty should be canceled, or peace treaty should continue; Kuwait: peace is impossible, or peace efforts are desirable.

Palestinian Survey:

• Do you support the continuation of current peace negotiations between the PLO and Israel?
• I expect the achievement of a lasting peace between Palestinians and Israelis. Do you agree or disagree with this statement?

Jordanian and Lebanese Surveys:

• The PLO and Israel have recently signed an agreement on mutual recognition and on a transitional period of autonomy for Palestinians in the Occupied Territories, starting with Gaza and Jericho. Do you approve or disapprove of this agreement?
• If there is overall Arab-Israeli settlement, would you favor or oppose our country's having normal diplomatic and other relations with Israel?

Table 2: Attitudes toward Peace with Israel*

	Favors Peace	Somewhat for Peace	Opposes Peace	Missing
Egypt	66%	16%	13%	5%
Kuwait	22%	27%	40%	10%
Palestine	28%	41%	16%	15%
Jordan	23%	14%	29%	34%
Lebanon	39%	14%	33%	15%

The items listed in Table 1 have been combined to form an index for each sample. Favors Peace indicates a positive response on both items; Opposes Peace indicates a negative response on both items. Please note that figures may not add up to 100% due to rounding.

Table 3: Survey Items Used to Measure Religious Orientations in Egypt and Kuwait

Personal Aspects of Islam:

1. How often do you refer to religious teachings when making important decisions about your life?
2. How often do you read the Koran?
3. Do you fast during Ramadan?
4. Do you observe your five daily prayers?

Political Aspects of Islam:

5. Do you agree or disagree that religion and politics should be separate?
6. What do you think of the following statement: religious practice must be kept private and separated from sociopolitical life?
7. Do you support current organized Islamic movements?
8. What do you think of the religious awakening now taking place in society?

Factor Analysis Using Varimax Rotation of Survey Items
Regarding Religious Attitudes

	Egypt		Kuwait	
Item Number	Factor 1: Personal Aspects of Islam	Factor 2: Political Aspects of Islam	Factor 1: Personal Aspects Islam	Factor 2: Political Aspects of Islam
1	.65	.06	.58	.31
2	.77	.11	.72	.07
3	.65	.21	.70	.10
4	.78	.16	.79	.20
5	.06	.75	.05	.80
6	.26	.65	.14	.80
7	.07	.67	.14	.57
8	.15	.62	.29	.57

Note: The factor loadings listed above represent the correlation between each individual survey item and the cluster of items taken together.

Table 4: Survey Items Used to Measure Religious Orientations in Palestine

Personal Aspects of Islam:

1. A Moslem is considered a Moslem even if he does not pray the five times.
2. Do you describe yourself as religious?
3. To what extent does the phrase, "I Pray," apply to you?

Political Aspects of Islam:

4. How important is it for men of religion to have a leading role in the government?
5. Islam is the sole faith by which Palestinians can obtain their rights.
6. I support Islamic political parties.
7. I support the establishment of an Islamic Caliph state.

Factor Analysis Using Varimax Rotation of Survey Items

Item Number	Factor 1: Political Aspects of Islam	Factor 2: Personal Aspects of Islam
1	.07	.47
2	.20	.82
3	.19	.84
4	.66	.08
5	.69	.21
6	.62	.14
7	.72	.14

Note: The factor loadings listed above represent the correlation between each individual survey item and the cluster of items taken together.

asked in the surveys conducted in these two countries. Only questions about the political and societal dimensions of Islam, as well as questions about the Arab-Israeli conflict, were included in the survey instrument. The item used to measure attitudes toward political Islam in Jordan and Lebanon asks about the degree of importance attached to the proposition that "our country should always be guided by religious values and Islamic law."

While the explanatory power of religious orientations is the central focus of this study, other independent variables should also be included in the analysis. These include gender, age, education, and income. The inclusion of these demographic variables makes it possible to assess the analytical utility of religious orientations relative to other personal characteristics that may influence attitudes toward international conflict. They also permit the introduction of statistical controls, reducing the problem of multi-colinearity by examining the impact of religion with other factors held constant.

Table 5: Logistic Regression of Factors Influencing Attitudes toward Peace in Egypt and Kuwait

	Egypt	Kuwait	Palestine
Piety	−.15	−.01	.09
(Additive Index)	(.14)	(.14)	(.08)
Political Islam	−.53	−.29	−.45
(Additive Index)	(.15)**	(.11)**	(.06)**
Sex	−.49	.19	−.22
	(.32)	(.30)	(.15)
Education	.15	−.21	−.20
	(.11)	(.14)	(.06)**
Age	.62	.25	−.00
	(.20)**	(.24)	(.04)
Income	−.03	−.01	−.20
	(.05)	(.06)	(.10)*
Constant	1.04	1.12	1.21
	(.88)	(.97)	(.35)
Model Chi-Square	36.45	15.14	67.38
PRE	.13	.15	.00
N	247	241	925

Note: Standard errors are in parentheses.
*p<.05, **p<.01

ANALYSIS AND FINDINGS

In order to test the impact of religious orientations on attitudes toward a peaceful resolution of the Arab-Israeli conflict, logistic regression analysis has been employed. A separate model is analyzed for each country in order to detect possible differences at the systemic level. Regression analysis is often used when ordinal level data approximates interval level data. Because the dependent variables utilized here had ony a limited number of categories, the variables were dichotomized so that logistic regression could be applied in order to obtain more accurate coefficient estimates. The results of these analyses are presented in Tables 5 and 6.

The most pervasive finding is the explanatory power of political Islam in all five models. In the samples for Egypt, Kuwait, Palestine, Lebanon, and Jordan, attitudes favoring the application of religious principles in political life are negatively associated with support for peace with Israel. In other words, re-

Table 6: Logistic Regression of Factors Influencing Attitudes toward Peace in Jordan and Lebanon

	Jordan	Lebanon
Political Islam	−.92	−2.38
	(.38)*	(.43)**
Sex	.54	.24
	(.33)	(.32)
Education	.01	−.05
	(.12)	(.10)
Age	.10	−.06
	(.13)	(.11)
Constant	−.24	1.01
	(.94)	(.89)
Model Chi-Square	9.15	40.81
PRE	.14	.31
N	166	215

Note: Standard errors are in parentheses.
*p<.05, **p<.01

spondents are much less likely to support peace if they favor a prominent role for religion in political and public affairs, if they support recent religious political movements, or if they are less critical of Islamic militants. On the other hand, personal piety or greater religious observance has little effect on attitudes toward the Arab-Israeli conflict. Individuals who report high levels of religious devotion in their personal lives do not possess attitudes toward the conflict that differ from those held by persons with lower levels of religious devotion in any case where the available data permit examination of this relationship.

While the first of these findings is perhaps to be expected, the latter may be more surprising. It is also at variance with the arguments advanced by some scholars, to the effect that Islam breeds militant attitudes and antipathy toward the West and accordingly pushes toward international conflict (Huntington 1993). In the context of the present analysis, the findings reported in Tables 5 and 6 are also notable because they offer much more coherent and consistent conclusions about the attitudinal consequences of religious orientations than do those which emerge from studies done in the West. In particular, the present analysis finds that different dimensions of religiosity bear different relation-ships to attitudes toward international conflict, that dimensions pertaining to political and societal aspects of religion do possess explanatory power while those pertaining to personal aspects do not, and that these relationships are the same despite significant differences in the countries and time periods from which the data are drawn.

The results of the other independent variables are rarely significant and, in any event, they are of only limited relevance to the present study. Their inclusion is nonetheless important, in that they permit assessing relationships involving Islam with standard demographic attributes held constant. This reduces the possibility of spurious relationships due to multi-colinearity.

In addition, there are a few statistically significant relationships involving personal attribute variables that may be noted. Most of these are in Palestine, where lower levels of education and lower levels of income are both associated with greater support for peace. While these findings are subject to differing interpretations, this would seem to suggest that it is among individuals who are less traditional, and perhaps more ideological in orientation, that opposition to peace is greatest. If correct, this is consistent with the finding that political Islam, but not personal religiosity, is an important determinant of popular attitudes toward the Arab-Israeli conflict.

CONCLUSION

The main goal of this research report has been to assess the impact of religious orientations on attitudes toward international conflict using survey data from Arab countries, and then to contrast any patterns observed with the ambiguous and inconclusive findings that emerge from studies carried out in the United States and other Western societies. To the extent that religiosity is related to attitudes toward conflict in a more clear and consistent manner in the Arab world, it will follow that different dynamics are at work in this world region and that attempts to determine the explanatory power of religious orientations will accordingly produce valid insights only if informed by an area-specific as well as a general theoretical perspective.

And this is precisely what the present study suggests is the case. An empirical distinction between personal and political dimensions of religion emerges in all cases where the data permit relevant analysis, and the relationship between each dimension and attitudes toward the Arab-Israeli conflict is the same in all of the Arab countries examined. Specifically, in the multivariate analysis, support for political Islam is consistently associated with unfavorable attitudes toward a peaceful resolution of the conflict, and personal piety is consistently unrelated to attitudes toward the conflict. This suggests that religion does influence political attitudes in the Arab world, a conclusion that is hardly surprising to those familiar with the Muslim world. In addition, however, it suggests that not all dimensions of religion are equally important, a conclusion whose significance cannot be fully appreciated without knowledge of the region.

Finally, and most important in the context of the present discussion, the findings reported above strongly indicate that attempts to derive generalizable insights about the influence of religion on attitudes toward international affairs require the incorporation of societal and cultural conditionalities. The nature and salience of religion's explanatory power appears to be different in the Muslim Middle East and the more secular West. Accordingly, in the language of comparative analysis, attributes which differentiate these world regions must be incorporated as system-level variables into theoretical models of individual behavior.

The regional differences explicated in this analysis must be presented with a note of caution, however. Past studies have varied widely in terms of methodology, measurement, and sampling, which naturally limits the comparability of their findings. Religiosity, for example, has been measured according to denomination, behavior, self-rating, and world view, to name but a few indicators, and this may account, at least in part, for the inconsistent results. It is therefore difficult to know whether the sporadic findings of Western studies reflect actual norms and behavior patterns or whether they are epiphenomena resulting from the application of varying measurement techniques.

While these methodological considerations indicate that some caution is in order when comparing findings from studies in the Middle East to those from studies in the West, they also suggest that issues of methodology and measurement constitute another area where research in the Middle East can make a contribution of more general relevance. In contrast to the West, where religion and religiosity have tended to be marginalized in political science research, attitudes and behavior associated with religion are prominent among the concerns of political scientists working in the Middle East. These scholars have devoted substantial attention to conceptual and methodological issues pertaining to the study of religion, an example of which is the distinction between personal and political dimensions of religiosity, and their work may consequently be a source of insight for those seeking to study religion and politics in the West or other world regions.

In conclusion, then, the present study clearly demonstrates the need for comparative and cross-regional analysis in order to understand more fully individual attitudes and behavior across cultures. It also illustrates the need for more sophisticated and multidimensional conceptualizations of religion, in order to allow for meaningful comparisons and thereby encourage the development of generalizable theoretical insights. Collaboration and dialogue between social scientists and area specialists are required for the achievement of these goals. Only by drawing upon the expertise and scholarly perspectives associated with both social science and area studies can the connections between religious orientations and political attitudes be properly understood.

REFERENCES

Al-Suwaidi, Jamal. 1995. "Arab and Western Conceptions of Democracy: Evidence from a UAE Opinion Survey." In *Democracy, War and Peace in the Middle East*. Ed. David Garnham and Mark Tessler. Bloomington: Indiana University Press.

Benson, Peter L., and Dorothy Williams. 1982. *Religion on Capitol Hill: Myths and Realities.* San Francisco: Harper & Row.

Berger, Peter L. 1969. *The Sacred Canopy: Elements of a Sociological Theory of Religion.* Garden City: Doubleday.

Casanova, Jose. 1994. *Public Religions in the Modern World.* Chicago: University of Chicago Press.

Goldstein, Judith, and Robert O. Keohane. 1993. *Ideas and Foreign Policy: Beliefs, Institutions, and Political Change.* Ithaca: Cornell University Press.

Guth, James L., and John C. Green. 1993. "Salience: The Core Concept?" In *Rediscovering the Religious Factor in American Politics.* Ed. David C. Leege and Lyman A. Kellstedt. Armonk: M. E. Sharpe.

Hanafi, Hassan. 1982. "The Relevance of the Islamic Alternative in Egypt." *Arab Studies Quarterly* 4 (Spring): 54–74.

Harik, Judith Palmer. 1996. "Between Islam and the System: Sources and Implication of Popular Support for Lebanon's Hizballah." *Journal of Conflict Resolution* 40: 41–67.

Hayes, Bernadette C. 1994. "The Impact of Religious Identification on Political Attitudes: An International Comparison." *Sociology of Religion* 56: 177–194.

Hopwood, Derek. 1982. *Egypt: Politics and Society, 1945–1981.* London: Allen & Unwin.

Huntington, Samuel P. 1993. "The Clash of Civilizations?" *Foreign Affairs* 72: 22–49.

———. 1991. *The Third Wave.* Norman: University of Oklahoma Press.

Jackman, Robert, and Ross Miller. 1996. "A Renaissance of Political Culture?" *American Journal of Political Science* 40 (August): 632–659.

Jansen, Johannes J. G. 1986. *The Neglected Duty: The Creed of Sadat's Assassins and Islamic Resurgence in the Middle East.* London: Macmillan.

Jelen, Ted G. 1996a. "Religion and Public Opinion in the 1990s: An Empirical Overview." In *Understanding Public Opinion.* Ed. Barbara Norrander and Clyde Wilcox. Washington: Congressional Quarterly Press.

———. 1996b. "Swords, Plowshares, and Philistines: A Comparative Analysis of Religion and Attitudes toward Security Policy." Paper presented at the American Political Science Association, San Francisco, 29 August–1 September.

———. 1994. "Religion and Foreign Policy Attitudes: Exploring the Effects of Denomination and Doctrine." *American Politics Quarterly* 22: 382–400.

———. 1991. *The Political Mobilization of Religious Beliefs.* New York: Praeger.

Kawaran, Ibrahim A. 1992. "'ReIslamization Movements' according to Kepel: On Striking Back and Striking Out." *Contention* 2 (Fall): 161–179.

Leege, David C. 1993. "Religion and Politics in Theoretical Perspective." In *Rediscovering the Religious Factor in American Politics.* Ed. David C. Leege and Lyman A. Kellstedt. New York: M. E. Sharpe.

———, and Lyman A. Kellstedt. 1993. "Religious Worldviews and Political Philosophies: Capturing Theory in the Grand Manner through Empirical Data." In *Rediscovering the Religious Factor in American Politics.* Ed. David C. Leege and Lyman A. Kellstedt. New York: M. E. Sharpe.

MacIver, Martha Abele. 1989. "Religious Politicization among Western European Mass Publics." In *Religious Politics in Global and Comparative Perspective.* Ed. William H. Swatos, Jr. New York: Greenwood.

Palmer, Monte, Madhia El Safty, and Earl Sullivan. 1996. "The Relationship between Economic and Religious Attitudes in Egypt." Paper presented at the 1996 Middle East Studies Association, 21–24 November.

Stevens, James. 1996. *Applied Multivariate Statistics for the Social Sciences*. Mahwah, N. J.: Lawrence Erlbaum.

Tessler, Mark. 1997. "The Origins of Popular Support for Islamist Movements: A Political Economy Analysis." In *Islam, Democracy, and the State in North Africa*. Ed. John P. Entelis. Bloomington: Indiana University Press.

———, and Laurie Brand. 1996. "Democracy and Islam in Arab Politics." *Pew Case Studies International Affairs*.

———, and Linda Hawkins. 1987. "Acculturation, Socioeconomic Status, and Attitude Change in Tunisia." In *Political Socialization in the Arab World*. Ed. Tawfic Farah and Yasumasa Kuroda. Boulder: Lynn Reinner.

Wald, Kenneth. 1992. *Religion and Politics in the United States*. Washington: Congressional Quarterly Press.

Waterbury, John. 1994. "Democracy without Democrats? The Potential for Political Liberalization in the Middle East." In *Democracy without Democrats? The Renewal of Politics in the Muslim World*. Ed. Ghassan Salamé. New York: I. B. Tauris.

8. The Arab-Israeli Conflict
Lessons about Diplomatic Initiatives and Negotiations

Laura Zittrain Eisenberg

INTRODUCTION

After the end of the Second World War, the locus of conflict shifted from Europe to non-European areas. Many of these regional conflicts have proven intractable for decades. Primary among them is the Arab-Israeli conflict, whose origins reach back to the turn of the century, but whose repeated outbreaks have reverberated throughout the international system during the post World War II era. Recent and unexpected breakthroughs in that peace process, as well as continuing setbacks and stalemates, raise several questions: Why have negotiating attempts so often failed? And what must change before a protracted conflict moves towards resolution?

This essay discusses a project which aims to pull together disparate Arab-Zionist/Israeli negotiating episodes over time, creating a model for placing contemporary Arab-Israeli negotiations within the context of a historical continuum of peacemaking efforts dating back to World War I (Eisenberg and Caplan 1998; Caplan 1978). The approach holds that no negotiating experience is an isolated event, and seeks to discover a historically credible paradigm of Arab-Israeli conciliation efforts into which each encounter, successful or not, logically fits. The findings complement the abundant literature on negotiation and bargaining, specifically in the Arab-Israeli case, while contributing a fresh comparative element. This is not a work in negotiation theory, but rather a history of a specific set of ongoing negotiation efforts.

Although this study was designed to investigate the persistence of a negotiating pattern specific to Arab-Israeli encounters, the model itself does not assume any idiosyncratic "Arab" or "Israeli" element and is generalizable to other cases of prolonged conflict and repeated negotiation attempts elsewhere around the globe. The traditional pattern of negotiations (in the Arab-Israeli case, of failed negotiations) is the expression of a diplomatic political culture, a form of common political behavior practiced by elites similarly schooled in the art of diplomacy specific to the particular history of their region of the world. An excellent example of this phenomenon is L. Carl Brown's development of "The Eastern Question" as the origin of a distinctly Middle Eastern international relations subsystem (Brown 1984; cf. Binder 1964; and Brecher 1972, pp. 47–55). Obviously other subregions with their own unique histories also produce area-specific patterns of elite political behavior. The task is to establish the existence, and then the characteristics, of a longstanding regional negotiating model, and then to check current peacemaking efforts against it, blending the historian's long-range perspective with the political scientist's analytical approach. The hypothesis is that if diplomacy is to succeed where it has previously failed, leaders must choose negotiating behaviors which deviate from the traditional pattern in specific and positive ways. There are thus both descriptive and prescriptive elements to the paradigm.

An examination of the determinants and conditions associated with the numerous attempts to resolve the Palestinian-Israeli and Arab-Israeli conflicts does identify a traditional pattern of factors which have historically stymied negotiators in their attempts at Arab-Israeli conflict resolution. The futile diplomacy of the mandate period followed a pattern that lends itself to examination under eight headings: (1) a wealth of experience, (2) dubious purposes and ulterior motives, (3) problems of timing, (4) problematic status of negotiating partners, (5) generally negative impact of third party involvement, (6) a wide gulf between proposed terms of agreement, (7) dynamics of deadlock, and (8) psychological obstacles. Studied together, they cover multiple levels of analysis.

In focusing on a pattern of regional elite political behavior, we look for the conditions which cause leaders to choose diplomacy over force as a means, and to choose compromise over absolute victory as an end. Successful negotiations require the authorization of leaders firmly in power and capable of dominating the national policymaking apparatus. As individuals, they must come to believe that they can secure the national interest by negotiating with the enemy instead of fighting him; as leaders, they must persuade their constituents to make the same psycho-political conversion.

The timing element relies overwhelmingly on national and international factors, particularly domestic challenges to the leadership in power, third party involvement in the region, and shifts in the global balance of power, such as those brought on by the end of the Cold War and the collapse of the Soviet Union. If and when the national and international stars aligned in such a way as to favor a diplomatic resolution of the conflict, the status of the negotiator proved to be the most critical variable; the wealth or dearth of previous diplomatic interaction between negotiating partners proved the least relevant element in determining the outcome of negotiations.

Once research had identified the pattern of negative negotiating habits repeatedly exhibited by Arabs and Israelis, the resultant paradigm was applied to a series of six case studies of Arab-Israeli negotiations since 1978. The assumption was that the outcomes of recent negotiation attempts could be better understood (although not always predicted) by assessing the ways in which they diverge from—or mirror—the historical model. Obviously negotiations can fail for a variety of reasons. Research confirmed, however, that contemporary negotiations which failed succumbed to that particular set of circumstances which have been torpedoing Arab-Zionist negotiations since the start of the mandate.

THE HISTORICAL MODEL

Despite repeated failures to resolve the growing conflict over Palestine, and the early, widespread assumption among prominent Zionists and Arabs that even their minimal goals were irreconcilable, Arab-Zionist negotiations continued throughout the mandate period, begging the question why? The answer lies in the sometimes counterintuitive nature of the process. Analysis of the cumulative negotiating experience of Zionists and Arabs between 1918 and 1948 revealed the eight components of the model for failure, to which we now return. The following discussion of that paradigm, and later its application to contemporary Arab-Israeli negotiations, is drawn from a comprehensive examination of multiple negotiating episodes in the post 1978 Arab-Israeli peace process (Eisenberg and Caplan 1996).

Wealth of Experience

The record of multiple failed negotiations suggests that neither a lack of direct communication nor unfamiliarity with the enemy has been responsible for the persistent failure to produce an Arab-Zionist or an Arab-Israeli accord. The record also shows that merely increasing the amount of contact between the two sides does not increase the likelihood of negotiators actually achieving a working agreement. Many times direct negotiations only clarified for the protagonists just how far apart, even irreconcilable, their positions really were.

Purposes and Motives

Both sides in this conflict have tended to enter the negotiating process for purposes other than actually making peace with one another. Instead, they reinterpreted the standard definition of the term "negotiation." Negotiation commonly refers to a process by which parties in conflict engage in a process of making concessions to each other in order to reach a mutually satisfactory agreement. In the Arab-Israeli case, however, a mutually satisfying peace was rarely their purpose in the first place. Parties often came together when one or both wanted to forestall other, less appealing, initiatives. Most often they negotiated for appearances, trying to impress upon their constituents or upon a powerful third party the justness of their cause, and the righteousness of their interpretation of events, as opposed to the extremist, uncompromising posture of the other side. In the traditional pattern, Arabs and Zionists sought to inverse Von Clausewitz's dictum by employing "diplomacy and negotiation . . . as an extension of their basic 'war' by other (non-violent) means" (Caplan 1978, p. 8; cf. Klieman 1995, p. 29).

Timing

Both Arabs and Zionists proved reluctant to negotiate from positions of perceived weakness; unfortunately, they have similarly lacked the incentive to make concessions from positions of perceived strength, illustrating the Middle Eastern adage: "When I am weak, how can I compromise? When I am strong, why should I compromise?" (Friedman 1990, p. 194; cf. Saunders 1991, pp. 30–31, 49–51, 124). Historically, Arabs and Israelis have come to the table not so much when conditions seemed propitious for peace as much as when "the status quo seemed more painful or dangerous than a potential negotiated compromise" (Stein and Lewis 1991, pp. 14–15; cf. Saunders 1991, pp. 24–25, 121). This is I. William Zartman's "hurting stalemate," which can make the time "ripe" for diplomatic solutions (Zartman 1991, pp. 11–22).

Status of the Negotiating Partners

Too often, Arab-Zionist peacemaking has suffered from a "Groucho Marxian" dilemma: "Anyone willing to negotiate with me can't be worth negotiating with." Arabs and Jews have often refused to meet with one another's hawks, while eschewing contact with the doves on the grounds that they were not truly representative or capable of delivering the goods. Many times one or both of the people at the table simply did not have an adequate power base to carry out his side of a bargain.

A related problem has been asymmetry in the status of Arab and Jewish negotiators. When one side was clearly stronger than the other, it usually tried to impose an unacceptable solution upon the weaker, again with negative results.

Early Zionist diplomacy focused on non-Palestinian pan-Arab leaders, hoping to find someone prepared to concede Palestine to the Jews in exchange for certain services to the Arab world as a whole, and able to influence Palestinian Arabs to go along with this arrangement. Such plans invariably fell flat when prominent Arab personalities outside of Palestine proved unable to "deliver" Palestinian acquiescence in this sort of "exchange of services" (Caplan 1978, p. 13).

The Arab-Israeli Conflict

Third Party Considerations

There have always been powerful external forces intimately involved in the region, whether Turkish, British, French, Soviet, or American. Brown goes so far as to argue that, regarding the tension between any regional subsystem and the West, "nowhere has the political dimension of that fateful confrontation been more thorough and more consistent than in the Middle East. It is in this sense that the Middle East is the most penetrated international relations subsystem in today's world" (Brown 1984, p. 4). Obviously, however, other subregions of the world have also felt the weight of the Great Powers, and the third-party factor provides another element for comparative work among scholars in different fields of area studies.

It is a fact of Middle East politics that Arabs and Zionists have consistently expected to better advance their interests by turning to outside powers, instead of to one another. Historically, the third party was more often a hindrance than a help. It was, after all, the audience to which Arab and Zionist negotiators played for appearances. Prior to 1948, both sides regularly petitioned the British to impose a solution wholly favorable to themselves. To the extent that Britain allowed Arabs or Jews to believe it might impose their maximum demands upon the other, neither side felt compelled to make the hard choices and difficult concessions needed for a negotiated settlement.

Proposed Terms of Agreement

The historical record shows that, during the course of negotiations, Arab and Zionist leaders have allowed for little or no scaling back of their maximum demands. This refusal or inability to prioritize objectives and then compromise accordingly may reflect either the genuine incompatibility of the two sides' most basic goals, or the fact that the negotiators' aims were something other than a negotiated settlement. This zero-sum approach denied the opponent any benefit from an agreement, leading to recurrent instability marked by either constant deadlock or requests for an imposed settlement.

Dynamics of Deadlock

This is the leadership factor. The rigors of maintaining national cohesiveness and morale during their protracted conflict have encouraged the rise of Arab and Zionist leaders well suited to wage war, but not necessarily peace. Heroic leadership was measured by the ability to eliminate defeatism and foster optimism even when the realities of a situation dictated otherwise. By defining the conflict in existential terms, squelching dissent, and promising their people imminent victory, leaders failed to prepare their communities for the difficult choices and compromises required for negotiating with the enemy, as opposed to obliterating him.

Psychological Factors

This is the other side of the dynamics of deadlock coin. A leader who wanted to break the dynamics of deadlock and pursue an unfamiliar peace option is faced with the additional burden of justifying such diplomatic maneuvers to followers who have been conditioned to distrust and revile the enemy. Persistent insecurity, recurrent war, wanton destruction, and an enormous loss of life have psychologically scarred Israelis and Arabs, leading one observer to conclude that "the most important obstacles to the achievement of peace are attitudes, perceptions, fears and symbols, rather that the incompatibility of existential interests" (Tessler 1994, p. xv). Whole generations have grown up in fear and distrust of one another, tutored as to the virtue of their own cause and the evil intentions of the other side. There exists an enormous reservoir of mutual fear and hatred between Arabs and Jews in the Middle East, from which the opponents of peaceful compromise have drawn freely over the years. Proponents of peace have had little to encourage them in counteracting this legacy.

The conflict persisted after 1948, despite multiple negotiation efforts, because Arabs and Israelis continued to bargain in the unhappy diplomatic tradition of Arabs and Zionists during the mandate period. The armistice agreements of 1949 merely marked the end of the Arab-Zionist conflict and the start of the Arab-Israeli conflict. It was the Camp David Accords of 1978–1979 which introduced a new element into the longstanding parade of diplomatic failures: success. The Jordanian-Israeli peace treaty and several surprising Palestinian-Israeli agreements in 1993–1995 similarly challenge the past model. But Arab-Israeli violence persists in the Middle East, the Palestinian-Israeli peace process is in constant jeopardy, and the Syrian and Lebanese conflicts with Israel still resist resolution. Often it seems that Arabs and Israelis are doomed to endlessly repeat a cycle of open warfare, cold hostility, and futile negotiations. But how to explain the apparent, successful aberrations? And can the formula be bottled for application on other fronts, and to protracted conflicts in subsystems elsewhere?

METHODOLOGY

Research required an appreciation for the lengthy history of Arab-Israeli diplomatic encounters, since the whole point of the exercise was to simultaneously reach backwards and forwards, pulling far-flung episodes of conflict resolution attempts into a seamless continuum. The concept applies equally well to other regions of the world which have seen sustained, long-term conflict among more or less the same parties over a period of many years. In the Middle East, the fact that the same leaders have been involved in both war and diplomacy for well over twenty-five years made evidence of attitudinal and policy change a personal, as well as a national phenomenon. The textual aspect of the research refers to a preference for primary source material as the basis for discerning shifts or stagnation in several key areas, among them the parties' motivations for entering into (or abstaining from) talks, the terms of agreement, the role of extra-regional actors, the leaders' priorities, and the popular psyche. The dynamics of deadlock factor, for instance, is well examined through leaders' speeches. Content analysis speaks volumes about the stagnation or reorientation of a leader's priorities, and the strategy employed to lead the people to support government policy and stay the course. Sadat's speech to the Knesset on 20 November 1977 is a stunning example of a leader deliberately stepping out of the historical rut and consciously speaking to both Israeli and Egyptian sensibilities in a completely new way (Sadat 1977, pp. 330–343).

Close textual analysis of treaties and agreements permits us to chart the widening or narrowing of the gap between the parties' positions. Ideally, we can study a series of drafts, proposals, and counterproposals leading up to the final agreement, allowing us to reconstruct the give and take of negotiations. Works by William Quandt and Shibley Telhami on negotiating at Camp David are excellent examples of this type of scholarship (Quandt 1986; Telhami 1990). By determining which issues were nonnegotiable for each party and which were open to modification over time, we can discern changes in each side's terms for a minimally acceptable agreement, and tease out motives and purposes as well.

Archival material served as the basis for the original study of pre-1948 Arab-Zionist negotiations; it is obviously premature to expect similarly rich documentation for the contemporary period. Fortunately today's negotiators tend to sign book contracts before their signatures on an agreement have dried. Those who don't publish grant interviews. Conflicting accounts of negotiations, whether from opposing sides or opponents within one camp, can be juxtaposed to suggest the competing purposes, motivations, perspectives, agendas, and personalities which drove the encounter. Clearly this is source material which lends itself well to content analysis, bargaining, prenegotiation, negotiation, and conflict resolution applications.

Grids proved another useful tool in standardizing and analyzing a disparate series of negotiation attempts. This project employed a table listing the eight flawed components of the historical Arab-Zionist negotiating pattern. Students checked the elements of each subsequent case study against the model, filling in columns to indicate where the case repeated the old pattern, where it deviated, whether the deviation was positive or negative, and how important that characteristic was in determining the outcome of the negotiation attempt. Classroom discussion revealed discrepancies among the students' charts, wonderfully demonstrating how differences in interpretation and perception among individuals struggling with roughly the same issues and information can arise around the negotiating table.

CONTEMPORARY APPLICATION

The eight basic elements described above serve as a checklist of stumbling blocks over which successful negotiators must prevail. Some of those eight traits pose greater obstacles than others. The more malleable are not necessarily those with the greatest impact on the outcome of negotiations.

The status of the negotiator emerges as perhaps the most critical factor in determining an initiative's success or failure. The best intentioned of negotiators might shatter the precedent in terms of flexibility, moderation, and cooperation, but if they cannot persuade their peers and people to follow them down the peace path, their signatures on the dotted lines are meaningless. The archival morgue of Arab-Israeli diplomacy is replete with dead-letter agreements of this sort. Amin Gemayel, only nominally president of Lebanon, negotiated an inoperative treaty with Israel in 1983; as foreign minister in a government under the control of a disapproving Yitzhak Shamir, Shimon Peres reached a similarly impotent accord with King Hussein in 1987. Alternatively, leaders firmly and formally in power have been able to implement agreements despite opposition from domestic rivalries or hesitancy on the part of their people, as with Camp David, the Jordanian-Israeli Peace Treaty, and the early phases of the Israeli-PLO Declaration of Principles. The successful negotiations between Anwar Sadat and Menachem Begin, and later Jordan's King Hussein and Israeli Prime Minister Yitzhak Rabin, all enjoyed an unprecedented equal and authoritative status between the negotiators. Rabin's decision to deal with Yasir Arafat marked an immense departure from the traditional Israeli preference for negotiating around the Palestinians by dealing with non-Palestinian Arab leaders.

Rabin's direct contact with Arafat enhanced the latter's status as the de facto Palestinian representative; Palestinian elections in January 1996 legitimized Arafat's position as the de jure president of the Palestinian Authority [PA]. But if Arafat's status as a negotiating partner was partly a function of Rabin's and then Peres's readiness to accept him as an equal at the bargaining table, the new Prime Minister Benjamin Netanyahu's cold shoulder will mark a return to the traditionally flawed Israeli predilection for bypassing the Palestinians en route to agreements with the Arab states, or trying to dictate a settlement to them, rather than reaching a mutual compromise.

But recent events show that the Israeli prime minister himself is not immune to existential or electoral challenges to his agenda. Rabin's assassination in November 1995 by a rightwing Israeli Jew first revealed the depth of the divisions within Israel over his peace gambit; Peres's defeat in the 1996 elections, touted as a referendum over the Oslo process, similarly exposed the constraints on Israeli leaders in living up to their end of controversial bargains. Netanyahu's razor-thin victory and the virtually even split within the Israeli body politic for and against this particular peace process constrains Netanyahu as much as it did Peres; neither man could claim a clear mandate for his position vis-à-vis the Palestinians, and Netanyahu will have to work hard to persuade the other half of the population to follow his diplomatic lead, a feat which eluded his predecessor.

Purposes and motives other than peacemaking continue to draw reluctant Arabs and Israelis to the bargaining table, first among them the desire to please the United States and win tangible rewards for approved behavior. This speaks as well to the continued relevance of third party activity. Jimmy Carter's personal dedication to the Egyptian-Israeli peace process led to the first true breakthrough in Arab-Israeli negotiations in 1978. There are no guarantees, however. Similarly, sustained attention by Secretary of State George Shultz only prolonged laborious Israeli-Lebanese negotiations and led to the stillborn 17 May Agreement in 1983. Previously, the Cold War let the U.S. and the U.S.S.R. play Britain's traditionally unhelpful third party role, insofar as they fueled an arms race and allowed their clients to persist in the belief that they could yet achieve a lopsided solution to their own advantage.

The demise of the Soviet Union has given the United States a tremendous opportunity to act as intermediary. Wielding both carrots and sticks, the Bush administration convened the Madrid Peace Conference in October 1991, and the subsequent Clinton administration worked to sustain momentum in the bilateral Arab-Israeli negotiations which followed, with substantial movement on the Jordanian and Palestinian tracks. Norway's surprise foray into Arab-Israeli diplomacy served as a reminder that the United States is not the sole outside party with something to contribute to the Middle East peace process.

Contemporary diplomatic activity confirms the findings from the earlier period regarding the largely inconsequential impact of a wealth or dearth of past negotiating experience on the outcome of new negotiations. Frequent and intensive Syrian-Israeli negotiations since the Madrid conference have only highlighted the areas of contention between the two sides, without mitigating their immense distrust of one another. The lack of serious contact between Israeli and PLO elites did not preclude them from reaching an understanding once timing factors, in the form of domestic threats and external constraints, made cooperation more attractive than conflict.

That Israel and the PLO not only decided to cooperate but also found common ground for compromise indicates a vast scaling back of their traditional demands and zero-sum terms for agreement. Despite the difficulties with implementing the various Israeli-Palestinian agreements, for the first time the two sides simultaneously committed themselves to partitioning Palestine between them. Any ambiguity on this point not dispelled by the Oslo I, Cairo, and Oslo II Agreements of 1993–1995 should have been alleviated in April 1996, when the PLO voted to replace those elements in its national charter which called for Israel's destruction and the use of force for achieving Palestinian goals, and the Israeli Labor Party responded in kind by removing from its platform the plank specifically rejecting the establishment of an independent Palestinian state in the West Bank and Gaza. These reciprocal gestures went a long way towards closing the gap between minimal Israeli and Palestinian terms of agreement. With its absolute objection to the eventual creation of a Palestinian state, Netanyahu's Likud-led government appears to return to the historical pattern, and the chasm yawns wide once again. The new Israeli prime minister has vowed to uphold Israeli obligations assumed by the former government, however, and in endorsing a partition-based solution, the Oslo and Cairo agreements represent an important departure from the historical record of mutually exclusive Zionist-Israeli and Palestinian-Arab claims to the land.

Timing elements in the form of the 1991 Gulf War and the breaking of the taboo against dealing with Israel by the PLO itself propelled King Hussein into open negotiations with Israel. But once convinced that the time was ripe, Hussein and Rabin embraced peacemaking as a genuine purpose and motivation behind the Israeli-Jordanian initiative. They understood that breaking the dynamic of deadlock requires clear signals by Arab and Israeli leaders that they recognize one another's humanity, and demands explicit gestures indicating to their people that differences between their nations must be resolved in the boardroom and not on the battlefield.

The presence of Egyptian President Mubarak, King Hussein, and representatives from the Gulf states at Rabin's funeral in Jerusalem in November 1995 was one such gesture. The antiterrorism gathering at Sharm el-Sheik in March 1996 was another. These photo opportunities carry symbolic and psychological weight, sorely needed at a time when popular feelings lag behind the leaders' newly stated policies of mutual recognition and trust building. One waits for Syria's Assad to step out of the rut of history and explicitly communicate to his people that the only solution is a diplomatic one. Similarly, with extremists from both camps still fanning the flames of fear and distrust, Arabs and Israelis alike were anxiously watching after the 1996 Israeli elections for signals as to how the new Netanyahu government would approach the land-for-peace process already under way.

It is these ordinary men and women who must transform their visions of one another if this protracted conflict is to see resolution. A popular movement to expand Israeli settlements in the West Bank will confirm for many Palestinians their fears that Israel will never relinquish its control over their land or their lives. Continued terrorist attacks will confirm for many Israelis their fears that the Palestinians, indeed, the Arabs, will never relinquish the ultimate goal of destroying the Jewish state. While the new Israeli prime minister struggles to put his cabinet together, the peace process wavers in limbo, leaving Arabs and Israelis alike peering at one another suspiciously, wondering if the leopard has indeed begun to change his spots.

CONCLUSION

The purpose of this line of research has been to organize a decades-long history of erratic Arab-Jewish negotiations into a meaningful analytical whole.

The search for continuity suggests that the two most contentious and precious cards which the Zionists pressured the British to play are the same ones Palestinians now demand of Israel, namely, control over immigration and conditions for future independence. Then as now a companion concern is how to accommodate Israeli and Palestinian independence and also ensure security for the mutually suspicious and hostile populations, each harboring a dissident faction which resists compromise.

Over half a century ago, clever strategists devised a variety of ingenious albeit complicated principles for Arab-Jewish coexistence in Palestine, such as cantonization, nondenomination, parity, binationalism, formulae for determining the economic capacity of the region to absorb new immigrants, and partition. "The range of logical possibilities seems to have been fully probed and exhausted in Arab-Zionist negotiations prior to 1948, and it is difficult to imagine a scenario for the post-1948 situation which had not been proposed, in some form, in the earlier period" (Caplan 1978, p. 18). The problem has not been a lack of creative imagination in devising schemes for a solution to either the Palestinian-Israeli or Arab-Israeli conflicts, but rather a lack of flexibility in considering departures from entrenched positions, dubious purposes and ulterior motives, the problematic status of the negotiators, third party machinations, poor timing, uninspired leadership, and psychological obstacles.

It is said that the epitome of insanity is doing the same thing over and over and expecting different results. The techniques and attitudes which characterize the pattern of unsuccessful Arab-Israeli negotiations uncovered by this line of inquiry are, if not insane, clearly insensitive to the political and psychological requirements of compromise and peacemaking. Although any of the eight components of the model could and did change at different times, successful negotiations exhibit striking deviations from the traditional paradigm, especially in terms of purpose, leadership, and psychology.

The significance of the findings is both academic and practical. Inasmuch as the paradigm is generalizable, scholars in diverse fields can use it to organize their analyses of the sporadic diplomatic episodes which punctuate the turmoil of any region long engulfed in conflict. New negotiation attempts can be integrated and studied within the context of the historical continuum longtime combatants share. The model also facilitates comparative analyses among different area studies subregions.

There is also potential, however, for this type of research to traverse the divide which too often separates academic thinkers from political doers. A notable exception to this phenomenon was the timely publication by the United States Institute of Peace of the proceedings of a series of workshops on Arab-Israeli negotiations. The sessions brought together American scholars and diplomats with actual Middle East field experience. Senior U.S. diplomats took and consulted early drafts of the conference findings on their shuttles to the Middle East in the summer of 1991. The resultant publication (Stein and Lewis 1991) came off the presses just in time to be distributed to all of the members of the U.S. delegation at the Madrid Peace Conference in October

1991. Another recent example, focused on substance as well as process, is the work of two study groups composed of American, Palestinian, and Israeli scholars that was carried out under the auspices of the American Academy of Arts and Sciences. One group produced a report that was distributed to Israeli and Palestinian participants in the negotiations that followed the Madrid Conference (Lesch et al. 1992), and the other prepared reports for top Israeli and Palestinian security analysts which contributed to the Israeli-PLO agreement subsequently reached in Oslo (Makovsky 1996, pp. 17–18).

Such open intersections of activity between the academic and political communities are unusual, but these examples demonstrate that even in less obvious ways, those who work in the field of area studies can contribute to the political process, as well as observe and analyze it. While scholars cannot present a precise diplomatic roadmap to Arab-Israeli peace, we can at least identify for practitioners those potholes and hazards which have repeatedly obstructed their predecessors' efforts. The significance of the work takes on a new dimension if it can reach and inform leaders who are looking to break the bad habits of the past in favor of more positive approaches to finally negotiating a diplomatic resolution to the conflict.

REFERENCES

Binder, Leonard. 1964. "The Middle East as a Subordinate International System." In *The Ideological Revolution in the Middle East*. Ed. Leonard Binder. New York: Wiley.

Brecher, Michael. 1972. *The Foreign Policy System of Israel*. New Haven: Yale University Press.

Brown, L. Carl. 1984. *International Politics and the Middle East: Old Rules, Dangerous Game*. Princeton: Princeton University Press.

Caplan, Neil. 1978. "Negotiation and the Arab-Israeli Conflict." *Jerusalem Quarterly* 6: 3–19.

Eisenberg, Laura Zittrain, and Neil Caplan. 1998. *Negotiating Arab-Israeli Peace: Patterns, Problems, Possibilities*. Bloomington: Indiana University Press.

Friedman, Thomas L. 1990. *From Beirut to Jerusalem*. New York: Doubleday Anchor.

Klieman, Aharon. 1995. "Approaching the Finish Line: The United States in Post-Oslo Peace Making." *Security and Policy Studies* 22: 3–45.

Lesch, Ann, et al. 1992. *Transition to Palestinian Self-Government: Practical Steps toward Israeli-Palestinian Peace*. Bloomington: Indiana University Press.

Makovsky, David. 1996. *Making Peace with the PLO: The Rabin Government's Road to the Oslo Accord*. Boulder: Westview.

Quandt, William B. 1993. *Peace Process: American Diplomacy and the Arab-Israeli Conflict since 1967*. Washington: The Brookings Institution.

———. 1986. *Camp David: Peacemaking and Politics*. Washington: The Brookings Institution.

———. 1977. *Decade of Decisions: American Policy toward the Arab-Israeli Conflict, 1967–1976*. Berkeley: University of California Press.

Sadat, Anwar. 1977. *In Search of Identity: An Autobiography*. New York: Harper & Row.

Saunders, Harold H. 1991. *The Other Walls: The Arab-Israeli Peace Process in a Global Perspective*. Princeton: Princeton University Press.

Stein, Kenneth W., and Samuel W. Lewis. 1991. *Making Peace among Arabs and Israelis: Lessons from Fifty Years of Negotiating Experience*. Washington: The United States Institute of Peace.

Telhami, Shibley. 1990. *Power and Leadership in International Bargaining: The Path to the Camp David Accords*. New York: Columbia University Press.

Tessler, Mark. 1994. *A History of the Israeli-Palestinian Conflict*. Bloomington: Indiana University Press.

Zartman, I. William. 1991. "Conflict and Resolution: Contest, Cost, and Change." *The Annals of the American Academy of Political and Social Science* 518: 11–22.

9. | **Middle Eastern Alliances**
From Neorealism to Political
Economy

Laurie A. Brand

Several of the contributions to this volume make the point that comparative politics as a subfield of the discipline of political science has paid little attention to the Middle East/North Africa (MENA) region. While not disputing that contention, I would argue that until quite recently the subfield of international relations (IR) has shown even less interest in the area stretching from the Atlantic to the Persian Gulf. This is not to say that the MENA region did not receive its share of interest from the policy community, the group of specialists or nonspecialist pundits who concern themselves primarily with decision makers' responses to foreign policy challenges. Indeed, over the years the amount of attention devoted to the Arab-Israeli conflict alone by such specialists, while not rivaling the attention devoted to Kremlin-watching, has nonetheless been substantial. Similarly, geostrategists have written a great deal on the implications for U.S., Western European, and Japanese interests of the presence of oil in the region and the need to secure safe access to it.

But this is the world of the policy community, and for better or for worse, its concerns have not always found their way into the academy. I daresay most policy-makers would be at a loss, if not put off or bored by the types of questions many international relations scholars ask, or at the very least by the way in which they go about studying them. The debate about which side's failing this represents will be left for another occasion. Suffice it to say that, at least in its present form, much of the international relations literature is viewed by policy-makers as arcane or irrelevant.

My own work in graduate school had been in comparative politics, but when I joined a faculty of international relations, I entered a world for which a certain degree of retooling was required. What I soon realized was that this was a world of theory that in many ways replicated the U.S. view of the international system and itself; it was concerned almost exclusively with the great powers if one looked to the pre-WWII period, and with the superpowers or so-called system-defining powers—the United States and the Soviet Union—in the post-1945 era. Hence, in some ways, the lack of attention the Middle East received from students of international relations is not surprising, for when it came to areas of what used to be called the Third World, international relations was an equal opportunity ignorer.[1]

While the realism of Hans Morgenthau had at least assigned a place to smaller powers through consideration of power balancing and a variety of national attributes that contributed to overall evaluations of power, its successor, neorealism, privileged the existing bipolar construction of the international system by focusing on the two poles, the United States and the Soviet Union, and their immediate allied camps. Neorealism's drive for parsimony produced a model of international relations derived from microeconomic theory in which the lesser states of the international system were largely ignored, based on the fact that they played little or no role in the overall bipolar power balance.[2] Just as Americanists have held sway and defined what constitutes preeminent work in other parts of the field of political science, in the field or subfield of IR, no graduate student in his or her right mind would have thought of trying to build a career by applying or testing IR theory to areas outside of the United States and Europe. Senior IR scholars simply have not built their careers on work that draws empirical referents from outside the "big power" arena.[3]

For a scholar with strong developing-world area training, the IR literature is particularly off-putting and perplexing. Not only do its preeminent scholars ignore the regions of the world on which we focus our work, but the hegemony of the discourse, especially if evaluated on purely intellectual grounds, appears quite unwarranted, since it in fact explains so little. Indeed, now that the Cold War is over, a reexamination of neorealism certainly suggests that it was less a theory of international politics than an intellectual framework that was an adjunct to maintaining U.S. political domination. Moreover, if the current hegemonic paradigm in comparative politics tends to universalize a very particular form of Western "rationality" to non-Western individuals, the arrogance of international relations has been such that—with the exception of those scholars working on psychological approaches to foreign policy decision-making—individuals do not matter (or, dare I say, count) at all.

Given such a picture, where were/are the possibilities for an intersection of insights from international relations theory and an empirical grounding in the experiences of state interaction in the MENA region? In my own case, I had long been interested in the periodic reshuffling or shifting of alignments in the Middle East and was dissatisfied with the way in which that literature which did exist described or explained Arab interstate behavior. Never enamored of ideological or cultural explanations of politics in the Arab world or elsewhere, and with an inclination to look for explanations in material conditions and structures, I decided to undertake a project intended to explore the possible materialist bases of Arab alliance behavior. As the discussion that follows demonstrates, I first sought guidance from traditional works on security, narrowly defined, but quickly found myself drawn to what in the early 1990s was a growing body of literature dealing with the developing world, which argued for alternative or broader notions of what constituted security. While working with this burgeoning theoretical literature, I continued to consult both the historically descriptive as well as the more theoretically orientated works of Middle East specialists who had examined related topics.

As the project gradually evolved, it became a study of the inter-Arab relations of the Hashemite Kingdom of Jordan, and involved the construction of in-depth case studies of Jordan's relations with five key Arab states. As the contours became more clear, what emerged from this inductive work was a picture showing the critical importance of domestic economic imperatives in determining Jordanian alliance behavior. In the case of my project, the marriage of the international relations literature and careful area studies work helped produce a novel and, for some, controversial, argument regarding inter-Arab behavior.[4]

THE SECURITY LITERATURE

It was actually a book written by a neorealist—the first to my knowledge to attempt to explore the international politics of the Middle East—that initially drew me to the topic. In *The Origins of Alliances*, Stephen Walt argued for amending balance of power theory to include not just power, but also threats—an important distinction.[5] Nonetheless, in estimating threats and power, he used the traditional realist military, industrial, and technological criteria. Walt did stress the importance of aggressive intentions, and occasionally noted the role of domestic factors, but continued to hold to the realist/neorealist notion of threats, the catalysts for alliances, as emanating exclusively from outside a state's borders. Part of Walt's problem lay in his definitions, for he considered both formal alliances and looser alignments but continued implicitly to assume that the only goals of alliances would be directed toward *external* threats or balancing. Beginning with this faulty assumption, he then proceeded to categorize Middle Eastern alliances as constituting either balancing or band-wagoning (aligning with the threatening power) against an external threat. As a result, he mischaracterized Arab alliance behavior in a number of instances, such as the Baghdad Pact and the United Arab Republic, and left a great deal un(der)explained or misinterpreted.

This is not to say that Walt was wrong across the board. However, he tried to fit all such alignment or alliance decisions into the same mold. He himself realized that this did not work in all instances, but in order to save the argument, he was forced to argue that balancing in inter-Arab relations was of a type that differed from the common military power-acquiring model. "In the

Arab world," he contended, "the most important source of power has been the ability to manipulate one's own image and the image of one's rivals in the minds of other Arab elites. Regimes have gained power and legitimacy if they have been seen as loyal to accepted Arab goals, and they have lost these assets if they have appeared to stray outside the Arab consensus."[6] Here he committed a fatal error for a neorealist by engaging in reductionism, reaching below the system (and even the state) level for an explanation of state behavior. In so doing, he in fact empowered the Arab street, and entered, certainly unwillingly, into the realm of domestic politics.

It was just shortly after the publication of Walt's book that domestic politics began to force itself onto the IR agenda. Given the relationship between developments in the field of international relations theory and the place of the United States in world politics, it is not surprising that the intellectual space for challenging the prevailing state- or system-level assumptions of the literature on security came as the Cold War was ending. Although authors had previously drawn attention to security issues beyond those of the nuclear or conventional weapons balance, it was not until the late 1980s that a more extensive literature began to emerge reexamining traditional notions of security and suggesting new foci or emphases. The subjects of the new security literature—the environment, the economy, leadership, human rights, food, and the like—all opened the way for a consideration of domestic-level factors in the larger assessment of what constituted, threatened, or enhanced welfare.

This new literature also addressed what years of experience living and researching in the Middle East had taught me were the primary concerns of ordinary citizens and many leaders. While it is true that Israeli nuclear capabilities and a number of Arab states' nonnuclear nonconventional stockpiles do pose a threat to the region's peoples and states, security to many means being free of fear of a range of human rights violations at the hands of the very state that international relations theory (and classical political theory before it) viewed as the guarantor of men's (although never women's)[7] security.

With this domestic component of security emerging as an important bridge between comparative politics and international relations, I was drawn to the notion of rethinking security for my own work for two primary reasons. First, because it seemed to offer richer possibilities for understanding the concept of threat in a way that could greatly enhance our understanding of politics—domestic and foreign—in the Third World. But second, because it reintroduced human beings into the analysis: as victims not only of attacks from beyond their country's borders, but also of the coercive and predatory nature of the state.

Among the works that began to revive domestic components as explanatory factors in international politics, the work of Stephen David first caught my attention. David introduced the concept of "omnibalancing," a modification of balance of power theory which puts an emphasis on leaders, rather than the system or the state, and argues among other things that leaders may appease other states in order to counter a domestic challenge, and that the most frequent challenges to states in the developing world are internal challenges to the ruler or the ruling group. Since leaders may be expected to act in such a way as to keep themselves in power, they may pursue survival strategies that may not serve the larger interests of the country.[8]

Michael Barnett and Jack Levy also argued for including domestic and social variables in explanations of foreign policy.[9] Their focus was on the "impact of the domestic political economy on state trade-offs between alliances and international mobilization as alternative means for enhancing security." They looked to the domestic front for factors that might influence alliance formation, and they acknowledged the value of alliances as sources of military and economic resources as well as of security guarantees. Nonetheless, their interest remained focused on the repercussions of using different policy instruments to address *external* threats.

THE NOTION OF ECONOMIC SECURITY

My own tendency to look for political economy explanations for political phenomena, domestic and international, was reinforced by these authors' works. However, in discussions of the need to broaden the concept of security, no aspect has been as controversial as the economy. The range of opinion regarding the concept extends from those, generally students of the developing world, who clearly consider such economic topics as trade, foreign aid, and debt to be security issues,[10] to those who concede in passing that interstate wars may be caused by domestic economic or social stress but then go no further to try to determine whether or what kind of economic issues might, by implication, constitute a threat.

Indeed, while admitting of an economic component to security, most international relations literature spends a great deal of time arguing against an economic security component outside the military sector. Authors like Robert Rothstein and Walt have complained that such attempts threaten to broaden the concept of security so much as to render it useless, as potentially everything, they contend, could therefore be defined as a security issue.[11] One concern, voiced by economist Giacomo Luciani, is that while viewing problems related to economic crisis or prosperity as security issues might be appealing, this "line of reasoning will lead to the conclusion that events such as increases in the price of oil, increases in interest rates, and indirectly, even the deficit in the federal budget in the United States are forms of aggression."[12] He did not explain, however, why, conceptually, a threat must be understood only in terms of an identifiable, and presumably, punishable aggressor. Barry Buzan also made clear his skepticism regarding the concept of economic security, but on different grounds. He argued that since the international economy is a capitalist one and capitalism is a system based on competition and uncertainty, no unit could ever be meaningfully secure. "Relative security is possible, absolute security is not"[13]—as if absolute security in the military realm is possible.

I could cite others, but will close this brief review with my conclusions. The concern on the part of some scholars that attempts to redefine or broaden the concept of security threaten the field's coherence sounded less and less convincing with each rehearsal, especially since the traditional concept has been unable to capture the experiences and concerns of many states and much of the world's population. Beyond that, however, while redefinition may be problematic, the realm of possible solutions to the problem should not, it seemed to me, be circumscribed at the outset. Rather than thinking of innovation that would preserve coherence, they were content to broaden the term only in ways that continued to focus on the military or issues of territorial defense.

One of the problems in dealing with the notion of economic security concerned level of analysis. While both Rothstein and Buzan took levels of analysis into consideration, they did not do so systematically when it came to the question of economic security. For example, particularly in the post-1945 period, the emergence of new states out of colonial empires has been accepted; however, the disappearance or absorption of one state by another, a common feature during the process of state consolidation in Western Europe, is no longer accepted by the international community. Apparent economic or political nonviability has not led to the dissolution of these entities. Somalia and the former Zaire are cases in point. Hence, what we are concerned with in the developing world is really leadership or regime security, not national security as embodied in maintaining the territorial integrity of a state.

If one continues to make a careful analytical distinction between national security (defined in terms of preservation of territorial integrity and core values) and regime security (defined in terms of maintenance of power by the same leaders or ruling coalition), then a case can be made that while economic issues may prove slippery or more anomalous when confronting the former, they are much more easily applied to the latter. Price increases may lead to economic riots that force leaders to resign; neglect of the socioeconomic needs of particular regions or groups may lead to insurgencies that challenge the regime; or external debt may reach such levels that domestic solvency may be threatened, triggering major reforms and perhaps resulting in the ouster of a leadership.

A number of historical cases illustrate this point quite nicely and serve as additional empirical referents for what I term budget security: that is, the imperative to maintain state financial solvency as a key condition for leadership or national security. One of the best examples of how state and regime security may be threatened by insolvency is that of Egypt at the end of the last century, when in 1875, as a result of fiscal irresponsibility, the Khedive Ismail was forced to sell Egypt's shares in the Suez Canal Company to Great Britain. Ismail persisted in incurring additional debt until 1876, when he simply ran out of money. At that point, a European Debt commission was imposed upon the country to "safeguard foreign interests," and it gradually acquired such extensive economic and financial powers that it has been referred to as a "veiled colonial administration." Thus, it was leadership security that was first compromised. These developments, however, paved the way for a domestic revolt that ultimately led *national* sovereignty to be lost to British invasion forces in 1882.[14]

But, of course, one need not go back so far in history, as the debt crisis of the 1980s provides additional examples that underscore the importance of understanding and applying the concept of "budget security." Whatever the causes of the insolvency, government spending cutbacks of some sort have been a central part of any IMF rescheduling package. Combined with the other elements of conditionality, austerity measures have had the potential—at times realized—to trigger instability. Bread riots in Egypt in 1977, Tunisia and Morocco in 1984, and Jordan in 1996 are but a few examples of the security at risk at times of economic crisis.

Debt rescheduling also touches on another, more traditional aspect of security, that of sovereignty. In accepting IMF conditionality, leaders in effect surrender a degree of what was sovereign economic decision-making power. This, in turn, may threaten national "core values," such as long-standing notions regarding state distributional or welfare responsibilities vis-à-vis the citizen.

THE AREA STUDIES LITERATURE

As I perused the "redefining security" literature for guidance in conceptualizing my study, I also consulted existing relevant works on the MENA region specifically. As noted at the beginning of this essay, I had long been dissatisfied with explanations of the frequency of alliance and alignment shifts in the Middle East, put forward by both Western and Arab analysts, that attributed such moves to ideological affinities: between moderates and radicals, Nasirists and Ba'thists, U.S. allies versus those in the Soviet camp, and so on. Also discouraging are the writings of nonspecialists, generally journalists and pundits, who dismiss developments in the region as based on the whimsical or irrational behavior of what they portray as the wacky gang of thugs that rule our region, as if Middle Eastern leaders had the market cornered on inhumane or irrational behavior.

Another problem I encountered was that the few works by scholars of the region that addressed the question of alliances seriously, most notably those by Malcolm Kerr, Patrick Seale, and Alan Taylor, nonetheless were descriptive in nature.[15] They contained solid empirical material, but offered little conceptual guidance. Perhaps the most creative approach to explaining Middle East international politics was produced by L. Carl Brown, who introduced the concept of the "Eastern Question system."[16] Brown's argument was that the patterns of present-day Middle East international politics developed through the region's interaction with the European state system, and he contended that the extent of this penetration went a long way toward explaining the nature of politics in the MENA region. Nevertheless, despite enumerating a series of "rules of the game," his work did not address theoretically the driving forces behind alliance shifts.

Bahgat Korany and Ali E. Hillal Dessouki's *The Foreign Policies of Arab States* was closer to what I was looking for, as its first three chapters seek to establish a framework for analysis.[17] To the best of my knowledge, this was the first serious attempt by scholars of the region to examine different approaches to foreign policy and attempt to evaluate their relevance to the Arab world. Their emphasis on constraints that served to circumscribe certain options because of the generally weak power position of these states in the international environment caught my attention, precisely because—for reasons explained below—I had decided to focus my study on Jordan. Given its size, population composition, location, and the structure of its domestic economy, the theme of constraints seemed quite appropriate.

In all of the case studies in their volume except that of Egypt, however, economic factors were intervening variables, not independent sources of foreign policy. By contrast, rather than seeking to understand how economic factors might constrain what foreign policies could be pursued, I had begun to ask a different question: given a state's economic structure, what sort of foreign policy may be expected? In other words, contrary or supplementary to Korany and Dessouki, the argument that began to take shape from the evidence I was amassing suggested that a leadership's or a regime's estimates of its economic needs and weaknesses were in fact a *source* of foreign policy—the independent variable—rather than merely a measure of foreign policy capability constructed on the basis of, or constrained by, other factors.

GATHERING THE EVIDENCE, CONSTRUCTING THE ARGUMENT

I selected the Hashemite Kingdom of Jordan as the focus of my research for several reasons, among them the inertia and affection that Lisa Anderson mentions in her chapter in this volume. As for sounder social science reasoning, Jordan seemed to offer a number of possibilities for saying something new and interesting about alliances. To the extent that scholars and analysts paid attention to the kingdom—and little serious social science literature (outside the field of anthropology) existed when I launched this project—it was generally in the context of Jordan's long involvement in the Arab-Israeli conflict.[18]

In any case, if one examined the existing literature, it appeared that Jordan was unworthy of study in and of itself, unless of course one looked at the domestic component, which in the writings of the time always meant the Palestinians, who were generally blamed for King Hussein's failure to make the peace everyone knew he wanted. Hence, Jordanian foreign policy was understood exclusively through the Arab-Israeli lens and from the perspective of the presence of a subnational group that for years one could not mention if one wanted to get tenure in the United States. Several research trips to the kingdom for other projects had demonstrated what a stale and boring view of the kingdom such an approach represented. Moreover, since I first began to study the Middle East it seemed to me that much of what was taught as received wisdom was not in fact very wise and that we would do better to begin by discarding it and readmitting it only after serious scrutiny. Arguing that Jordanian foreign policy could be better understood outside a framework that privileged the Arab-Israeli conflict seemed sufficiently iconoclastic at the time.

I had also decided that whatever shape the final argument took, to make a convincing case, I needed to explore several significant bilateral relationships. Since Jordan's most intensive and extensive interaction over the years has been with Arab partners, it made sense to choose examples from among states of the Arab world. I selected Egypt, Kuwait, Saudi Arabia, Iraq, and Syria in order to cover differences in regime type and orientation (so-called radical versus moderate), economic structure and economic relationship to the kingdom (aid donor as well as fellow aid solicitor), as well as states with which Jordan had been in and out of alliances and looser alignments over the years. I also needed to study a long enough period of time so as to capture a substantial number of alliance changes in the context of shifting regional and international politics. I decided to begin just after the 1973 October war. Like all inductive projects, this one was a gamble. Intuition told me there was a theoretically and empirically interesting story to be found. Was I right, or would I end up with nothing more than a series of cases with no larger message or lesson (and with no hope of a book manuscript that would secure my tenure)?

With the help of a research assistant, I began plowing through mounds of FBIS reports and back issues of MEED. The idea was to construct two parallel chronologies for each bilateral relationship. The first would document strictly political ties—so-called "high politics"—while the second would look at "lower level" economic relations: trade ties, foreign aid and loans, joint ventures, and the like. Once I had completed that Herculean task, I began trying to digest it all. Did all my factoids add up to something larger? I was aided in this process by the fact that I was able to conduct interviews in Jordan with a number of high-level economic and political decision makers. Here my regional and language expertise was invaluable. First, the access I enjoyed was the result of the contacts and reputation I had developed over years of field research. Second, most of the interviews had to be conducted in Arabic, as I was dealing not just with upper-level decision makers, many of whom speak English, but also with many mid-level people who may speak, but are not comfortable in, a language other than Arabic. Without the information from these interviews, I simply could not have made the case that began to emerge from the evidence.

Finally, years of experience with and in the region enabled me to put the empirical material gained from the interviews and from other primary sources into context.

Slowly a picture began to develop of a series of alliance shifts undertaken to achieve rather specific domestic economic goals. In some cases it was to secure more aid or free oil, in others it was to try to open up opportunities for a hard-pressed private sector. In each case, I took great care to account for the timing of the shift, and indeed it was this concern with timing that first helped bring the explanation into focus. As I fleshed out the stories of the individual alliance shifts undertaken by the king over the years, it became clear that Hussein had used alliances, in some cases quite dramatically, at the very least to improve his realm's economic position, and in several more extreme cases to save its solvency. What remained was to develop the argument more fully and determine what potential it had for generalizability.

Two lines of theoretical argument gradually began to come together. The first concerned a state's/leadership's possible reaction to a security threat with its origins or primary manifestation in the domestic economy. In other words, what was the range of possible responses to challenges to financial solvency —what I had dubbed "budget security"? In theory, a number of options are available to any given leadership. IMF conditionality and domestic economic structure in large part dictate the *domestic* policy instruments selected to address debt crises. However, what if states also use *foreign* policy instruments, in this case alliances, to address challenges to the domestic economy? Since the argument has been made that domestic crises of capital accumulation may lead to decisions to undertake expansionary policies or go to war,[19] why not another foreign policy tool, an alliance, to address an economic crisis?

Barnett's classification of policy response to the need for war mobilization was helpful here. In *Confronting the Costs of War* he details three possible responses: accommodational, restructural, and international.[20] An accommodational strategy involves only minor changes or adjustments in existing policy instruments; a restructual strategy involves an attempt by what he calls state managers to restructure the existing state-society compact on finance, production, and conscription; and an international strategy is one that attempts to distribute the costs of war onto foreign actors.

It seemed that this same classificatory scheme could be applied beyond the framework of war preparation to the concept of budget security. The definition of the accommodational strategy remains the same; restructuring, on the other hand, would involve the state's/leadership's attempts to create a new mix of agriculture, commerce, and industry, and its efforts to raise revenues or perhaps cut state services and allocations (the IMF formula). Finally, an international strategy would involve seeking additional or diversified sources of loans or aid, attempting to open new markets or engage new suppliers, sharing the costs of increased industrialization through joint ventures, and the like.

The selection or mix of strategies depends upon a number of factors. If a leadership is facing an economic crisis, then the time for the accommodational strategy has probably already passed. The inward-looking or restructural strategy would appear to be soundest in the long term, by further developing the domestic economy so that its contribution to the state budget would gradually increase or be diversified so as to wean the state away from what might be described as its unhealthy dependence upon a narrow or unreliable resource base. Yet in the short term, this strategy is also the most subversive. In the first place, there may be insufficient time to await the outcome of the restructuring. Just as important, powerful forces are likely to have vested interests in maintaining existing political and economic relations, thus perhaps undermining the regime's power base. Hence, one may in fact be much more likely to see the international solution: attempts to secure aid, loans, and other forms of external support for the domestic economy. It is a less solid fix, but it would be less likely to threaten domestic stability. My empirical work showed that this was precisely the strategy that the Jordanian leadership pursued over the majority of the period under study.

To complete or strengthen my argument, I also looked into the process and nature of economic and political decision making in the kingdom. It seemed necessary to demonstrate that the leadership was aware of the budgetary imperatives, that it consciously worked to address them, *and* that the decision makers enjoyed sufficient autonomy from societal actors who might have argued for different policies. Here, while a modified state-centered model seemed best to capture the process in Jordan through much of the 1970s, by the early 1980s the state's waning distributional capabilities had left an opening of sorts that enabled the small, and until then largely parasitic, private sector to gradually expand its influence on policy-making, if through diffuse and individualist, rather than formal, associational channels. By the early 1990s, the degree of state autonomy in such decision making had been severely eroded. "Budget security" in the kingdom was gradually taking on new dimensions as the bases of regime solvency shifted away from a reliance on external rents and toward greater domestic extraction.[21]

In sum and in the end, I had unwittingly selected what could be called a "hard case" for making a domestic economic structure argument, at least from the point of view of those who focus on external security and system structure. Their argument would be that Jordan's myriad sources of vulnerability would make it subject to system constraints, a receiver or reactor to developments in larger and more powerful states, not a state whose leadership would direct its foreign policy based on domestic economic imperatives. Nevertheless, as my detailed case studies demonstrate, and as the theoretical literature helped to guide me, domestic economic exigencies and structures do a much better job of explaining and predicting Jordanian foreign policy behavior than do traditional explanations based on military strength or superpower politics.

CONCLUSIONS

The splash Walt's book made at the time of its publication in 1987 made clear to me both the power of the theorist "unburdened" by familiarity with the empirical phenomena he seeks to explain, and the clear need for those who do labor in the vineyards of intensive field research to spend time with the works of the more disciplinarily powerful in order to better explain what happens in our region, but also, ideally, to help enrich international relations theory.

Such a conclusion assumes that if those of us with a strong interest and familiarity with a region embrace and engage theory more consistently and effectively, we will force those whose sole or primary interest is theory to read our work and take it seriously. But such a conclusion assumes a level playing field, devoid of power considerations. There are, I believe, clear reasons why "intellectual" discourses become hegemonic and, as in the case of both neo-realism and rational choice, why the demands of such approaches tend by definition to exclude or marginalize many of the issues or questions that those of us who study the developing world seek to explore.

But it is not just a question of the hegemony of a particular discourse or paradigm. Politics and economics play a role in determining the regions of the world considered to be of greatest interest to funders, governmental and otherwise. For reasons that deserve fuller exploration, the most recent period has witnessed a flurry of publications and conferences comparing the Latin American and East Asian development experiences. It cannot be accidental that such interest has coincided with the economic growth records of many states of these regions, certainly enabling people to argue that these are the areas of greatest dynamism (at least until the 1997 East and Southeast Asian currency crises). However, such dynamism does not by definition make them any more theoretically interesting—explaining lack of dynamism should be just as theoretically challenging—but it does seem to give those who specialize in these regions more academic job opportunities, and greater hopes of marketing themselves as generalists than students of other regions.

Those of us who study the Middle East must continue, both in our own work and in guiding the work of our students, to engage and contribute to the broader social science theoretical literature. It is the only way to change the perception of many scholars outside our regional field that we work in a framework focused on description rather than explanation. Having said that, I must end on a pessimistic note. Precisely because there are larger political and economic issues involved in producing and defeating approaches and paradigms, it seems clear to me that our efforts to contribute to the theoretical debates are necessary, but far from sufficient, to lead to our full integration into and acceptance by the broader community.

NOTES

1. I remember being particularly astonished by the parochialism of a view put forward in a seminar given by a prominent political scientist who was visiting USC regarding the need, at the end of the Cold War, to study the institutions that had been put in place at the end of WWII, so that the long peace since 1945 could be replicated after the Cold War. "Long peace?" I remember asking the presenter, "What about regional conflicts elsewhere, the Arab-Israeli conflict or, if one wanted an example of American troop involvement, *Vietnam?*" The response was that he and those involved in his project were concerned only with peace in Europe, the implication being that that was the only peace that really mattered. The arrogance of power, combined with at the very least a lack of concern with loss of life in the Third World, seemed quite clear.

2. The classic neorealist work is Kenneth Waltz's *Theory of International Politics* (Reading, Mass.: Addison-Wesley, 1979).

3. Whether the indication of a gradual change or mere exceptions, three young and now associate level IR scholars did do their dissertation work "out of region." Stephen Walt and Michael Barnett, whose work is discussed below, both used Middle Eastern cases, while Michael Desch wrote on U.S. involvement in several Third World regions.

4. This work was published as my *Jordan's Inter-Arab Relations: The Political Economy of Alliance Making* (New York: Columbia University Press, 1994).

5. Stephen Walt, *The Origins of Alliances* (Ithaca: Cornell University Press, 1987).

6. Ibid., p. 149.

7. For a discussion of how women never figured into the social contract, see Carole Pateman, *The Sexual Contract* (Stanford: Stanford University Press, 1988).

8. Stephen R. David, "Explaining Third World Alignment," *World Politics* 43 (2) (January 1991): 233–256.

9. Michael N. Barnett and Jack S. Levy, "Domestic Sources of Alliances and Alignments: The Case of Egypt 1962–73," *International Organization* 45 (3) (Summer 1991): 369–395.

10. Caroline Thomas, *In Search of Security: The Third World in International Relations* (Boulder: Lynne Reinner, 1987).

11. Robert L. Rothstein, "The 'Security Dilemma' and the 'Poverty Trap' in the Third World," *The Jerusalem Journal of International Relations* 8 (4) (December 1986), pp. 9, 11–12; Stephen Walt, "A Renaissance in Security Studies?" *International Studies Quarterly* 35 (1991), p. 227.

12. Giacomo Luciani, "The Economic Content of Security," *Journal of Public Policy* 8, 2, p. 155.

13. Barry Buzan, *People, States and Fear: An Agenda for International Security Studies in the Post–Cold War Era*, 2nd ed. (Boulder: Lynne Reinner, 1991), p. 235.

14. Derek Hopwood, *Egypt: Politics and Society, 1945–1981* (London: Allen & Unwin, 1982), pp. 10–12.

15. Malcolm H. Kerr, *The Arab Cold War: Gamal 'Abd al-Nasir and His Rivals, 1958–1970* (New York: Oxford University Press, 1971); Patrick Seale, *The Struggle for*

Syria (New Haven: Yale University Press, 1965); and Alan Taylor, *The Arab Balance of Power* (Syracuse: Syracuse University Press, 1982).

16. L. Carl Brown, *International Politics and the Middle East: Old Rules, Dangerous Games* (Princeton: Princeton University Press, 1984).

17. Bahgat Korany and Ali E. Hillal Dessouki, *The Foreign Policies of Arab States: The Challenge of Change* (Boulder: Westview, 1991).

18. Returning to the issue of hegemonic discourse, it seems to me that Arab politics was long considered important only insofar as it affected Israel's security or U.S. access to oil. I remain convinced of something Joel Beinin, professor of history at Stanford University, said years ago when asked why there had been so little theoretical innovation in the field of Middle Eastern studies. Without missing a beat he answered, "The Arab-Israeli conflict." While this contention deserves full exploration elsewhere, I am convinced that because this conflict has been so central to U.S. interests in the region and because of the political minefield this conflict has represented in the United States, scholars have been loathe to pose certain questions and unwilling to broach particular topics.

19. See Fred H. Lawson, *The Social Origins of Egyptian Expansionism during the Muhammad 'Ali Period* (New York: Columbia University Press, 1992) and *Why Syria Goes to War: Thirty Years of Confrontation* (Ithaca: Cornell University Press, 1996).

20. Michael Barnett, *Confronting the Costs of War: Military Power, State, and Society in Egypt and Israel* (Princeton: Princeton University Press, 1992).

21. Such an analysis draws on the insights of the literature on the rentier state, first put forward in Hazem Beblawi and Giacomo Luciani, *The Rentier State* (New York: Croom Helm, 1987).

10. International Relations Theory
Contributions from Research in the Middle East

Bahgat Korany

INTRODUCTION

At a time when advances in technology and communication have brought countries together in what some have termed the "global village," the concept of area studies often evokes an impression of narrowness and parochialism. Moreover, the field of area studies is under pressure from the declining availability of research funds and, in particular, from the changing priorities of many funding agencies. It is against this background that Rashid Khalidi, president of the Middle East Studies Association (MESA) in 1994, used the occasion of his presidential address at the annual MESA conference to issue an unambiguous wake-up call concerning the future of area studies.

This challenge to area studies also provides the context for the present chapter, which in some ways is more nuanced and less defensive than the remarks offered by Khalidi in 1994. In particular, I wish to emphasize the dynamic and dialectical relationship that has for more than three decades characterized interaction between area studies and traditional academic disciplines. Even more specifically, I wish to advance three propositions about this relationship.

1. A longitudinal perspective is necessary to understand the dialectical relationship between area studies and disciplinary social science, including that in my own field, international relations. Area studies today is very different than it was in the 1950s or 1960s. It is much less impressionistic and descriptive than in the past. Thus, much of the criticism directed at area studies is outdated.

2. We should avoid creating inappropriate and unnecessary dichotomies in

the pursuit of scholarly knowledge, one of which is the unproductive separation of area expertise and analytical social science. Rather, the two perspectives must be integrated, with both kinds of knowledge and expertise brought to bear on the study of issues of international significance. In most instances, opposition to this kind of integration comes not from area specialists but from social science generalists.

3. Middle East specialists, like other area specialists, should continue to work within the traditions of established disciplines, but they should also bring a critical perspective. They must not blindly borrow social science concepts and methodologies. They must also refine them, in part by investigating their operationalization and applicability in particular social and cultural settings. This is necessary for the kind of comparative inquiry that is required for social science to make progress toward its declared goal of generalizable insights. The contribution of area specialists is not only valuable, it is indispensable.

I contend that the area specialists of today, and even more those of the future, are also discipline-oriented specialists (i.e., economists, political scientists, sociologists, anthropologists, etc.). Indeed, many have gone so far in establishing a bridge between area and disciplinary specialization that it is often their counterparts, those who regard themselves as social science generalists, who are in danger of parochialism. To illustrate and support these contentions, I shall draw upon two examples from my own research in international relations. In concluding, I shall also offer some ideas about the future of area studies, since my attempt to correct misconceptions about area specialization is not intended to obscure the need for continued evolution in the field.

MIDDLE EAST STUDIES UNDER FIRE— FROM WITHIN

Only a few years ago, the relationship between area and disciplinary studies was confronted by Khalidi during his presidential address at the 1994 annual MESA convention. Khalidi was responding to a recent article by Stanley Heginbotham, vice president of the Social Science Research Council, in which the possibility was raised that area studies have become obsolete in the post–Cold War period and that what is needed today is research which is global and thematic in nature. Taking up this theme, Khalidi voiced his concerns by posing a serious question to his colleagues: "Is there a future for Middle East studies?"

> Some may ask why I have chosen this ominous-sounding title. For most of us, the MESA Conference is a time for socialising, browsing among the latest books and hearing papers on recent research, generally in that order. It is certainly not a time for serious, introspective, potentially boring questions like this one. In the beautiful environment of this resort, it is even harder to

focus on such unpleasant matters. In one of my last acts as President of MESA, however, I have decided to spoil the party, if only for a few minutes.

Khalidi then continued by identifying what he believed to be the most important way to save Middle East studies from "stagnation, provincialism, and ultimately extinction."

> . . . be part of the internal discourse within the disciplines, whereby new ideas are resisted or accepted, instead of standing outside, in splendid isolation, turning up our noses at such ideas. In other words, it is time for people studying the Middle East to partake of some of the excitement which characterizes many of their respective disciplines, and to realize that the future of the field is ultimately there.

A MORE NUANCED VIEW

My counter argument is that Middle East studies, except for some Orientalist and purely descriptive historical works, is already doing what Khalidi asks. Many younger and middle-aged scholars have been studying what he qualified as the rising "trendy themes": the shift to market economies, the process of democratization, the growth of civil society, the resurgence of nationalism, national identities, and ethnic and religious rivalries. This is confirmed by a look at the contributions to this volume, as well as by the book-review sections of such area-oriented journals as *The Middle East Journal* and the *International Journal of Middle East Studies*. These scholars have managed to address the issues of concern to social science generalists, who themselves often develop their "universally applicable" theories and "law-like generalizations" without feeling a need to visit, or even consult basic books about, any of the world regions to which they believe their insights apply.

Briefly, then, we can agree that the advancement of knowledge requires familiarity with both disciplinary and area studies. What must be added is that most Middle East specialists, contrary to past practices and to Khalidi's extreme defensiveness, are today following this prescription. Their initial frame of reference is their own social science discipline; they read general disciplinary books and journals, and they conceptualize their research problems in disciplinary terms. Many generalists, by contrast, have not managed to avoid the trap of "contextual bankruptcy."

To support these assertions, I shall briefly discuss two general works on international relations and one book with a Middle East area focus. The first of these is a stimulating book entitled *Traditions of International Ethics* (1992), which draws attention to the normative dimension of the international relations field. The editors, Terry Nardin and David Mapel, deal with an extended array of topics, including international law, classical and twentieth-century realism, natural law, Kant, utilitarianism, Marxism, Liberalism, the Contractarian tradition, individual human rights, and biblical arguments pertaining to international ethics. Although they select representatives of the most important voices in relevant ethical debates, they also admit to "obvious omissions," most notably "the traditions of Islamic, Chinese, and other non-Western civilizations." To explain these omissions, they state that "we did not attempt to examine these partly because the debate about international ethics for many years has been so decisively shaped by Western ideas, and partly because we were afraid to take on a task so obviously beyond our abilities."

To their credit, Nardin and Mapel are at least aware of the limits of their work. Moreover, Nardin deserves praise for his subsequent efforts to rectify this situation. He thus brings a more contextual perspective to the study of ethics and international affairs in his 1996 work on *The Ethics of War and Peace*. This volume contrasts the attitudes toward war and peace found in various religious and normative traditions, including those associated with Islam and Judaism.

A second and more blatant example is a recent collection entitled *International Relations Theory Today* (1995). This volume has much to recommend it. It extends beyond any single national perspective and includes prominent authorities from Europe and North America. Its coeditor, Steve Smith, is the editor of the Cambridge University Press/British International Studies Association series on international relations, which is the most prestigious and influential in the field.

In the very first chapter, Smith himself analyzes in an encyclopedic and stimulating manner as many as ten self-images of the subdiscipline. Yet not one of the 108 references he cites refers to the Middle East, to any other region in the Third World, or even to the Third World as a whole. Thus, if the Third World exists at all, it does not appear to influence theory-building endeavors in the presumably universally oriented field of international relations.

The volume's fifteen chapters cover such varied topics as international political economy, the environment, security, identity, and gender. There are a total of 611 references to these chapters, yet of these only four pertain to the Middle East, only three to Africa, and only six to the Third World as a whole. Moreover, none of these references or their authors is deemed important enough to appear in the appendix, and this despite the fact that one of the contributing theoreticians, Fred Halliday, has frequently published on the Middle East.

The work of many Middle East specialists is different. This is illustrated by an important American-Egyptian research project, initiated almost two decades ago by the late Malcolm Kerr, a confirmed area specialist as well as a political scientist. The book that resulted from this project (Kerr and Yassin 1982) reflects the increasing enrichment of Middle East area studies that was already becoming evident. First, the project has a strong interdisciplinary perspective, bringing together three sociologists, six economists, and three political scientists, all of whom worked as a unified team. Second, the 615 notes and references, 69 tables, and 5 figures contained in the published volume not only confirm this interdisciplinary orientation, they also reflect the conceptual and methodological preoccupations of the research. Third, with respect to substantive considerations, the work at this relatively early time period addressed the themes of low politics and interdependence that are becoming increasingly central in present-day international relations research.

THE ACTOR LEVEL

Additional studies may be reviewed to reinforce my assessment, and toward this end I shall comment briefly on both earlier and more recent scholarship, including several of my own published works. I shall also make use of a consensual division among international relations theorists, the distinction between actor and system, agent and structure, or, as it is also sometimes described, between micro- and macro-level analysis, and between foreign policy and international system analysis.

In two surveys of more than two hundred periodicals for the periods 1975–1981 and 1982–1988, it was found that the field of Middle East international relations was still unclear about the "what" of foreign policy (Korany and Dessouki 1991, Chapter 1). Does this mean the consequence of a specific action or behavior, or, alternatively, a strategy and general orientation, or perhaps both? The field also frequently devoted itself to current affairs. With very few exceptions, then, the analysis of foreign policy during the 1970s was more chronological and descriptive than analytical and theoretical. Decision-making analysis in particular was noticeably absent. This state of affairs corresponded to the characterization of Middle East area studies offered by Khalidi.

One notable exception was Michael Brecher's three-volume study of the structure and outcomes of Israel's foreign policy system (1972, 1974, 1980). The importance of this work lies in the amount and quality of the data it presents, in the elaboration of an explicit and detailed framework for the analysis of foreign policy, in the systematic and consistent application of this framework to the Israeli case, and in the incorporation of foreign policy theory.

While Brecher's work on Israel illustrates the behavioral or "scientific" study of foreign policy, his study has not been replicated in other countries of the Middle East. One possible reason may be the huge commitment of time (and funding) required for such research. Brecher himself had hoped to add a comparative dimension and extend the application of his framework to the analysis of India's foreign policy, but subsequently shied away from this effort. On the other hand, his work has influenced and inspired quite a few younger scholars who study the Middle East. A notable example is Adeed Dawisha, who has studied Egyptian foreign policy (1976), that country's intervention in the Yemeni civil war (1975), and Syria's 1976 decision to invade Lebanon (1980). Moreover, because Dawisha had difficulty acquiring all of the data required for the application of Brecher's framework, he devised adaptations that made the use of the framework more "doable," and in this way contributed to the further evolution of foreign policy analysis. This is illustrated by the works of Abu

Diyya (1991), Khalidi (1986), and Gamal Zahran (1987, 1993) pertaining to political systems in the Arab East, and those of Mary-Jane Deeb (1991), Nicole Grimaud (1984), and Said Ihrai (1986) focusing on countries of the Maghrib.*

Despite their conceptual and methodological sophistication, these analyses were still single-case studies. Although their findings were potentially generalizable, the basis for this generalizability needed to be complemented by comparative, multi-case studies. Other researchers have subsequently tried their hand at comparative analysis in order to fill this void, and two studies, published at a seven-year interval, provide an illustration. Both explicitly undertake to bring a conceptual perspective to the study of foreign policy in the Middle East.

The first work, by R. D. McLaurin, M. Mughisuddin, and P. A. Wagner (1977), is a seven-chapter book that examines four cases: Egypt, Iraq, Israel, and Syria. The emphasis was on domestic sources of foreign policy, and to allow "maximum comparability" the authors focused on three elements: people, processes, and policies. One of this book's strengths is its attempt to link the political structures and processes of the four countries to their foreign policy outputs. It is only partially successful in this endeavor, but is nonetheless an important early attempt to apply a theoretical framework to the analysis of foreign policy in the Middle East.

Rather than limiting itself to domestic inputs, the second attempt, undertaken by myself and a colleague, was influenced by a political economy perspective and integrated global dynamics into the analysis of foreign policies in Third World countries (Korany and Dessouki 1984, 1991). In addition to elaborating the book's analytical framework, my coauthor and I, individually or together, wrote seven of its thirteen chapters. The six remaining chapters were written by Middle East specialists from Canada, the United States, and the Middle East. Since the comparative study of foreign policy is essentially a collaborative enterprise, the objective of the volume was for researchers to adapt and apply a conceptual framework that they had not themselves developed. The framework itself was based on the three building blocks of foreign policy theory: the *why*, or foreign policy sources; the *what*, or foreign policy outputs; and the *how*, or decision making processes (Korany 1983). In addition to dealing with some nagging problems of theory and method, such as the definition of foreign policy outputs and comparability, the book attempted to widen the range of Middle Eastern cases considered by bringing in the Maghrib (i.e., Algeria) and nonstate actors (i.e., the PLO).

In undertaking this study, we not only sought to contribute to the analytical understanding of foreign policy in the Arab states, we also wished to encourage the continuing evolution of research on the Middle East that employs conceptual and methodological tools from the disciplines of political science and international relations. The project was thus a collective endeavor in which

---

These last three paragraphs are taken from Korany 1988.

borrowing from a discipline was as important as, or even more important than, a contribution to that discipline. Indeed, while there was a concern for advancing theory construction by offering insights based on area-oriented research, my coauthor and I also offered a critical assessment of much of the work on foreign policy that had previously been carried out by area specialists. We noted, for example, that "much of it belongs to the tradition of diplomatic history of commentary on current affairs" (Korany and Dessouki 1984, p. 1). Our goal in this connection, as with the volume as a whole, was to encourage students of Arab foreign policy to draw upon disciplinary tools and to integrate their work into a disciplinary matrix.

THE SYSTEM LEVEL

Integration into a disciplinary matrix remained the objective when I shifted the focus of my research to the systemic or structural level. In this instance, however, a primary objective of my project on national security was to address some deficiencies in the existing conceptual literature on strategic studies, particularly the dual separation of domestic and international politics and of high politics and low politics. Further, the state was often "black-boxed" in this literature, meaning that there was inadequate attention to its historical evolution and social dynamics (Korany 1986, 1989).

It was, therefore, necessary to revise some of the literature's basic assumptions and to provide an alternative framework that took into consideration the characteristics of states in the Middle East and other regions of the Third World. More specifically, it was important to move beyond a perspective that reified domestic and external military factors in the assessment of national security, and to emphasize as well such issues as debt, ethnic fragmentation, and low regime legitimacy, all of which are in the domain of low politics and assigned only secondary importance in much of the disciplinary literature on strategic studies. In fact, however, these latter attributes are of central importance in the Middle East and need to be treated as key independent variables in the analysis of national security.

The task of testing hypotheses derived from this new framework exceeded the capacity of a single researcher, and I accordingly undertook a collaborative project with two colleagues from McGill University, Paul Noble and Rex Brynen. We established the Inter-University Consortium for Arab Studies, and in 1993 we published our first volume, *The Many Faces of National Security in the Arab World*.

In contrast to the project on Arab foreign policies, the national security project from the beginning sought not merely to borrow, but rather to refine, the dominant paradigm in the relevant disciplinary literature. In this instance, in other words, a critical eye was directed not so much at the previous work of area specialists but rather at generalists and at the state of discipline-oriented scholarship. Commenting on the basic literature on strategic studies and national security, the introduction to our book accordingly noted:

> . . . the discussion is still terribly US-centric. Moreover, the problems of the majority of the global system, the Third World, were not dealt with directly. Thus, in Stephen Walt's systematic review of the field, Third World problems do not impinge on the analysis nor appear in the references. Moreover, there seems to be little awareness among many specialists of security studies, even the most open-minded, of the specific historical-sociological context of issues of state-building in these countries and how they could affect the pattern of their conflicts.
>
> This is why this book takes as its starting point state properties in the Arab world. Rather than continuing the tradition by limiting itself to the inter-state wars, the book aims to investigate the link between the specificities of these states and various types of security problems existing in the region. The aim is not only to draw attention to other types of threat to national security, and thus widen the definition of this basic concept, but also potentially to add to the explanation of the various inter-state wars that plague the region (Korany, Noble, and Brynen 1993, pp. xvii–xix).

Eleven scholars subsequently joined our research team, providing expertise in different areas and hence a solid empirical base for testing our conceptualization. As noted, this conceptualization emphasized the impact on national security issues of the internal fragility and other characteristics of Third World states. In order to prevent our project from resulting in a "conventional" reader, the research team worked together to ensure that the volume we were preparing would possess analytical coherence. The first chapter of the book thus introduced and explicated our conceptual framework. Subsequent chapters were divided into three parts, each introduced by a discussion that explicitly linked the specific contribution of each chapter to the volume's overall theme. A concluding chapter provided additional integration and also picked up where the authors left off by discussing Arab security issues in the post–Gulf War era. Tables containing social, military, and economic data were annexed in support of the book's critical arguments.

While it is for others to evaluate the contributions of this research, a recent follow-up project suggests that our effort to bring area expertise to bear on disciplinary issues has been productive. This is a Harvard project on New Frontiers of National Security in the Middle East, which builds on the *Many Faces* study by developing a "comprehensive framework" that moves beyond the military focus of traditional national security research (Martin 1996). Similarly, an earlier project, focusing on Asia, was inspired by the political economy approach of the Arab foreign policies study described earlier (Wurfel and Burton 1990). All of this suggests that area specialists can contribute, and indeed have been contributing, to the analytical cumulativeness required for scientific progress.

CONCLUSION

None of this means that area specialists should be satisfied with their achievements and resist calls for the further evolution of their research agenda and perspectives. Not at all. This chapter's main concern has been to correct misconceptions about area studies, but certainly not to advocate an end to the field's evolution.

At the turn of the century, two directions suggest themselves for the future evolution of area studies research. Both are of value and hold promise.

First, there are dynamic subfields of international relations research where students of the Middle East and other world regions could both profit from and contribute to ongoing efforts at theory construction. One such subfield is concerned with international regime analysis (Krasner 1983; Rittberger 1993; Levy et al. 1995). Despite its salience, very little work in this area has been explicitly devoted to the Third World. In fact, however, Middle East regional specialists could make an important contribution by investigating the utility of analyzing Arab groupings and coalitions from the perspective of international regimes, and, if necessary, suggesting conceptual refinements to make insights from this subfield applicable more broadly.

Another example is the growing body of international relations research which focuses on the hypothesis that democracies do not go to war against one another. With both democratization and regional conflict prominent items on the political agenda of the Middle East, regional specialists are particularly well-positioned to examine this hypothesis with a degree of depth that goes beyond the aggregate studies that characterize much of the disciplinary research in the field. And indeed there have already been a number of important contributions along these lines by Middle East specialists (Hudson 1995; Tessler and Grobschmidt 1995).

Second, the other direction for the evolution of area studies research involves reaching out to specialists in other world regions, such as Latin America, Africa, or Asia, and designing collaborative projects. This would contribute to scholarly cumulativeness in the study of many important issues, including processes of state formation, political liberalization and democratization, and privatization and structural adjustment. By comparing patterns and processes across regions, it will be possible both to identify generalizable insights and to determine whether and when the political dynamics characterizing a particular region are unique. This is not to say that generalizability and breadth should be sought at the expense of accuracy and depth, a concern that has been properly raised by another MESA president (Kazemi 1996). But cross-regional comparison is important, particularly in an age of increasing globalization, and in this respect, as in others, area studies has no choice but to adapt to new conditions and continue its evolution.

The opportunities and benefits of this cross-regional approach to scholarly inquiry are evident in numerous areas, including, among others, ethnic conflict, international diasporas, the relationship between domestic politics and foreign policy, international migration, gender and international relations, the impact of the global communications revolution, and the nature and consequences of economic liberalization programs. This in no way reduces the importance of area studies knowledge, however. On the contrary, the investigation of these and other global issues, or themes, should be pursued by examining the relevant experiences of different world regions, in each case drawing both on the appropriate conceptual and methodological disciplinary tools and on the area studies expertise needed for their valid and reliable application to real-world situations. In this way, not only will currently fashionable terms like "globalization" and "thematic perspective" help to shape the agenda for future research, it will also be clear that such research will fulfill its potential only if informed by the kind of knowledge associated with area studies, as well as that associated with social science disciplines.

REFERENCES

Abu Diyya, Saad. 1991. *Decision-making Process in Jordan's Foreign Policy* (in Arabic). Beirut: Center for Contemporary Arab Studies.

Booth, Ken, and Steve Smith, eds. 1995. *International Relations Theory Today*. Philadelphia: University of Pennsylvania Press.

Brecher, Michael. 1974. *Decisions in Israel's Foreign Policy*. Oxford: Oxford University Press.

———. 1972. *The Foreign Policy System of Israel*. Oxford: Oxford University Press.

———, and Benjamin Geist. 1980. *Decisions in Crisis: Israel 1967 and 1973*. Berkeley: University of California Press.

Dawisha, Adeed. 1983. *Islam in Foreign Policy*. Cambridge: Cambridge University Press.

———. 1980. *Syria and the Lebanese Crisis*. New York: St. Martin's.

———. 1976. *Egypt in the Arab World: Elements of Foreign Policy*. London: Macmillan.

———. 1975. "Intervention in Yemen: An Analysis of Egyptian Perception and Policies." *Middle East Journal* 29 (Winter): 47–63.

Deeb, Mary-Jane. 1991. *Libya's Foreign Policy in North Africa*. Boulder: Westview.

Grimaud, Nicole. 1984. *La Politique Extérieure de l'Algérie*. Paris: Karthala.

Heginbotham, Stanley J. 1994. "Rethinking International Scholarship." *Items* 48 (2–3): 33–40.

Hudson, Michael. 1995. "Democracy and Foreign Policy in the Arab World" in *Democracy, War and Peace in the Middle East*. Ed. David Garnham and Mark Tessler. Bloomington: Indiana University Press.

Ihrai, Said. 1986. *Pouvoir et Influence: Etat, Partis et Politique étrangère au Maroc*. Rabat: Edino.

Kazemi, Farhad. 1996. "Changes for Area Studies: Impact Could Be Great." *MESA Newsletter* 18, 2 (May).

Kerr, Malcolm, and S. Yassin, eds. 1982. *Poor and Rich States in the Middle East*. Boulder: Westview.

Khalidi, Rashid. 1995. "Is There a Future for Middle East Studies?" *MESA Bulletin* 29, 1 (July): 1–6.

———. 1986. *Under Siege: PLO Decision-Making during the 1982 War*. New York: Columbia University Press.

Korany, Bahgat. 1998. "Middle East International Relations." In *Handbook of Political Research on the Middle East and North Africa*. Ed. B. Reich and M. Deeb. Westport: Greenwood.

———. 1989. "Vers une Définition des Etudes Stratégiques." In *Les Etudes Stratégiques: approche et concept*. Charles David, et al. Montreal: Méridien.

———. 1986. "Strategic Studies and the Third World: A Critical Evaluation." *International Social Science Journal* 38, 1.

———. 1983. "The Take-off of Third World Studies? The Case of Foreign Policy." *World Politics* 33 (April): 465–487.

———. 1974. "Foreign Policy Models and Thin Empirical Relevance to Third World Acts: A Critique and an Alternative." *International Social Science Journal* 26, 1 (March): 70–94.

———, and A. E. H. Dessouki, et al., eds. 1984. *The Foreign Policy of Arab States*. Boulder: Westview. 2nd ed. 1991.

———, Paul Noble, and Rex Brynen, eds. 1998. *The Many Faces of National Security in the Arab World*. New York: St. Martin's.

Krasner, Stephen D., ed. 1983. *International Regimes*. Ithaca: Cornell University Press.

Levy, Mark, Oran Young, and Michael Zurn. 1995. "The Study of International Regimes." *European Journal of International Relations* 1, 3 (September): 267–330.

Martin, Lenore. 1996. "Towards a Comprehensive Approach to National Security in the Middle East." Paper presented at the second meeting of the project, New Frontiers of National Security in the Middle East, Bellaggio, Italy, 24–28 June 1996.

McLaurin, R. D., M. Mughisuddin, and P. A. Wagner. 1977. *Foreign Policy-Making in the Middle East*. New York: Praeger.

Nardin, Terry, ed. 1996. *The Ethics of War and Peace: Religious and Secular Perspectives*. Princeton: Princeton University Press.

———, and David Mapel, eds. 1992. *Traditions of International Ethics*. Cambridge: Cambridge University Press.

Rittberger, Volker. 1993. *Regime Theory and International Relations*. Oxford: Clarendon.

Sprout, Harold, and Margeret Sprout. 1965. *The Ecological Perspective in Human Affairs*. Princeton: Princeton University Press.

Tessler, Mark, and Marilyn Grobschmidt. 1995. "Democracy in the Arab World and the Arab-Israeli Conflict." In *Democracy, War, and Peace in the Middle East*. Ed. David Garnham and Mark Tessler. Bloomington: Indiana University Press.

Wurfel, David, and Bruce Burton, eds. 1990. *The Political Economy of Foreign Policy in South East Asia*. London: Macmillan.

Zahran, Gamal. 1993. *Who Governs Egypt? A Study in Political Decision-Making in Egypt and the Third World* (in Arabic). Cairo.

———. 1987. *Egypt's Foreign Policy* (in Arabic). Cairo: Madboli.

CONTRIBUTORS

LISA ANDERSON is Dean of the School of International and Public Affairs at Columbia University. She has served as chair of the Political Science Department and director of the Middle East Institute. Her works on politics and the Middle East include *Transitions to Democracy*.

ANNE BANDA is a doctoral student in urban studies at the University of Wisconsin–Milwaukee, where she has served as assistant director of the Center for International Studies and administrative coordinator of the American Institute for Maghrib Studies.

LAURIE A. BRAND is Associate Professor of International Relations and Director of the Center for International Studies at the University of Southern California. She is author of *Palestinians in the Arab World: Institution Building and the Search for State*; *Jordan's Inter-Arab Relations: The Political Economy of Alliance Making*; and *Women, the State, and Political Liberalization*.

LAURA ZITTRAIN EISENBERG is Visiting Associate Professor of History at Carnegie Mellon University. She is co-author (with Neil Caplan) of *Negotiating Arab-Israeli Peace: Patterns, Problems, Possibilities*.

JOHN P. ENTELIS is Professor of Political Science and Director of the Middle East Studies Program at Fordham University. His most recent publication is *Islam, Democracy, and the State in North Africa*.

Contributors

CLEMENT M. HENRY is Professor of Government at the University of Texas at Austin. He is author of *The Mediterranean Debt Crescent: Money and Power in Algeria, Egypt, Morocco, Tunisia, and Turkey.*

MAGDA KANDIL is Professor and Chair of Economics at the University of Wisconsin–Milwaukee. Her research interests and publications are in the areas of macroeconomic theory, labor and market fluctuations, and business cycles.

BAHGAT KORANY, currently Visiting Professor at the American University in Cairo, is Professor of Political Science at the Université de Montréal and Director of the Inter-University Consortium of Arab Studies. He is co-editor (with Paul Noble and Rex Brynen) of *The Many Faces of National Security in the Arab World* and *Political Liberalization and Democratization in the Arab World.*

JODI NACHTWEY is a doctoral student in political science at the University of Wisconsin–Milwaukee. She has published articles on gender, politics, and international relations in the Middle East and North Africa.

AUGUSTUS RICHARD NORTON is Professor of International Relations and Anthropology at Boston University. He is former director of the Civil Society in the Middle East Project at New York University and is editor of the two-volume work *Civil Society in the Middle East.*

MARK TESSLER is Professor of Political Science at the University of Wisconsin–Milwaukee, where he is also Director of the Center for International Studies. He is author of numerous works, including *A History of the Israeli-Palestinian Conflict* and *Democracy, War, and Peace in the Middle East.*

INDEX

Algeria: bureaucratic authoritarianism in, 16–17; civil society and, 12, 14, 16–17; colonialism in, 17, 22–23; democracy in, xvii, 18; economic development of, 17, 18; FIS, 8, 18, 20; FLN, 16; military, 21; political culture in, 17–18, 23; socialism and, 23; state-society relations and, 12–13, 16–17, 18

Algerian Revolution, 22–23

Arab-Israeli conflict, xviii, 131, 141, 142; attitudes toward peace, 112, 114, 115, 117; economic impact of, 81, 90; historical model and, 123–126; June War, 51; negotiation pattern, 121–122, 123–126, 128–130; war of 1947–1948, 126

Arafat, Yasir, 128

Area studies controversy: communication revolution and, 148; current status of, ix–xi; Middle East scholarship and, viii; political science, vii; response to, xi–xv; sources of, vii

Assad, 19, 130

Associational life, 16, 17, 26, 33, 44. *See also* Civil society

Attitudes: culture and, 103; in diplomacy, 126; factor analysis and, 112; political and role of religion, 102, 104–105, 107, 109; political science and, 118

Authoritarianism, 1, 22, 30–31, 37, 45, 49, 59; civil society and, 42, 44; crisis of, 14–15; democratic dialectic, 12–13; Islam and, 109; liberalization and, 20–21, 31;

political economy and, in MENA, 12, 13, 14–15; religion and, 104

Ba'athism, 140

Balance of power, 122, 135; in alliance formation, 136; omnibalancing, 137–138

Bank of England, 71

Banking: Anglo-Saxon model, 71–72; Berlin system, 74; bourgeoisie and, 70–72; commercial, 71–72; financial reform and, 73–74, 75; political patronage and, 75; in Tunisia, 75

al-Banna, Hasan, 52

Begin, Menachem, 128

Ben Ali, Zine el-Abidine, 25, 75

Benjedid, Chadli, 20

Boumediene, Houari, 23

Bourguiba, Habib, 75

Bureaucratic authoritarianism, 13–14; Algerian case, 16–17; banking and, 75–76; human rights and, 13; legitimacy of, 13, 15. *See also* Two-state system

Bush, George, 129

Camp David Accords, 7, 84, 85, 98, 126, 128

Capitalism, 79, 150; banking and, 72; civil society and, 70; international, 71–72, 138; Islam and, 77

Carter, Jimmy, 129

Case studies, xii; multiple, 153; thick description, xiii; values of, xiii–xiv

Civil society, 5, 17–18, 25, 26, 38–40, 44,

Index

Index

politics and, 137; in MENA scholarship, 7–8, 122, 134, 135–136, 151–152, 153, 156

International security. *See* National security

Intifada, 25

Iranian Revolution, 25; Islamists and influence of, 51–52

Islam, 21, 32, 33, 52, 151; civil society and, 37, 39, 41–42; cultural determinism and, 12; democracy and, 37; gender relations and, 54; role in national government, 108; values, 51, 65; women and, 53, 56, 62, 65

Islamic banking, 76, 77–78, 79

Islamism, 19, 34, 41, 48, 51, 53, 56; ideology and, 55; mothering theory and, 54. *See also* Political Islam

Islamist movements, 18, 25, 31–32, 44, 49, 56, 68, 108–109; gender equality and, 61–62, 65; ideological success of, 33; religiosity and, 60–61, 65, 105, 106; support for, 31–32, 49–52, 64, 65; women and, 48, 52, 53, 54–55, 56, 57, 65, 67. *See also* Political Islam

Israel-PLO Accord of 1993, 110, 128

Israeli-Palestinian conflict, 25, 122, 123, 126, 130, 131; British role, 125; early diplomacy, 124; Palestinian statehood, 130. *See also* Arab-Israeli conflict

Jordan, 128, 130, 141; foreign policy in, 141–144; international alliances and, 136, 141

Khedive Ismail, 139

Law of associations, 20

Law 93 (in Egypt), 43

League of Nations, 8

Legitimacy, 20, 25, 34–35, 46, 51; in Arab world, 11, 14, 15; international political economy and, 11; Islam and, 108; structural, 35. *See also* Political legitimacy

Liberalization, xi, 36–37; consequences of, 20–21; economic pressures, 14–15, 16, 17; in MENA, 4, 8, 11; political pressures, 12, 15–16. *See also* Economic liberalization

Low politics, 142, 152, 154

Madrid Peace Conference, 129

Migration: of Egyptian labor, 81–82, 83–87; government policies on, 85–87; liberalization impact on, 83; political relationships and, 84–85; push and pull factors, 82,

90–93, 98; rural-urban, 51, 58; theory of labor, 89–90; world energy crisis and, 83

Military, 138, 154; in Algeria, 21; in alliance formation, 136, 143, 144; national security and, 139

Modernization, 6, 7, 49; of institutions, 2; methodological liberation and, 77; religious movements and, 102; theory, 2, 102

Moallah, Mansour, 75

Morgenthau, Hans, 135

Mubarek, Hosni, 19, 34, 130

Muslim Brotherhood, 9, 52, 53

Muslim Sisters, 53

Nasser, Jamal Abd, 34, 86

Nasserism, 73, 140

National Defense Education Act, x

National security: alliances and, 136; budget security and, 139–140, 143; economic components, 138–140; end of Cold War and, 137; external threat, 138; in MENA, 12, 154; in Palestinian-Israeli conflict, 131; regime security and, 139; strategic studies and, 154–155

Nationalism, 8, 49; in Algeria, 22; Arab regimes, 50; feminism and, 55; National Liberation Model, 50

Netanyahu, Benjamin, 128–129, 130

Neocolonialism, 55, 56

New institutionalism, 8

Negotiation: Arab-Israeli conflict and, 121, 123–126, 128–130, 131; definition of, 123; patterns, 122; zero-sum approach, 125, 129

Neo-realism, 135, 137, 145

October 1973 war, 83, 142

October 1988 riots, 20, 21

OPEC (Organization of Petroleum Exporting Countries), 51

Orientalism, x, 12, 71, 150; civil society and, 76; Hegel and, 71, 76–77

Oslo process, 128, 129

Ottoman Empire, 8

Ozal, Turgut, 74

Pact of Monocloa, 4

Persian Gulf crisis, 110. *See also* Persian Gulf War

Persian Gulf War, 6, 34, 130; religion and attitudes toward, 106

PNA (Palestinian National Authority), 59, 63, 128

Political culture, 17–18, 35, 38, 40; in Alge-

Index

ria, 17–18, 23; authoritarianism and, 32; democratic, 38; diplomatic, 122; hegemony of ideology, 35, 36; Maghribi, 25; solidarism, 34, 35

Political economy, 7, 32–33, 36, 44, 71; alliances and, 138; authoritarianism and, 12, 13, 14–15, 31–32; commercial banking in, 78–79; democratization and, 79; foreign policy analysis and, 153; religion and, 79

Political Islam, 37, 38, 60; appeal to women, 53; civil society and, 76–78; support for, 49–51, 63, 64, 65; religiosity and, 60–61, 105–106

Political legitimacy, 25; in Arab regimes, 11; erosion of, 15; formula for, 35; of mukhabarat state, 14, 15

Political pacts, 4

Political participation, 2, 58; legalization of, 17

Political repression, 12, 14

Political science, 70, 122; influence of American politics, 2, 7, 9; in Middle East scholarship, 1–2, 3, 4, 5, 6–9, 12, 153; need for empiricism, 12; role of attitudes and behavior in, 103, 118

Post-modernism, ix–x, 70; reflexivity in, ix

Prophet Muhammed, 33

Public opinion, 1, 57; civil society and, 71

al-Qaddafi, Mu'ammar, 6

Rabin, Yitzak, 128, 130

Rational choice, ix, 135, 136; culture and, xii–xiii, xv; in MENA scholarship, 7, 8

Realism, 135

Religion: activism, 48; conservatism in foreign policy, 106; secular role, 107; women and, 48; world politics role, 104

Remittances, 78; GNP and, 93–97; impact on Egyptian economy, 82–83, 87–89, 98–99; types of, 87

Research methodology, xiv, xv, xix, 157; application in MENA, 6–7, 118; comparative politics and, 149; levels of analysis, 152, 154; most different systems design, 110; normative commitments and, 3; quantitative methods and, xiv, xv; regression analysis and, 115; textual analysis, 127

al-Sabah, 34

Sadat, Anwar, 74, 84, 86, 108, 128

Scientific cumulativeness, viii, ix, 107; area studies and, 156

Secularization, 49; of Arab regimes, 50; modernization and, 102

Shamir, Yitzhak, 128

Schultz, George, 129

Social science theory, viii–ix, xi, 150; and Arab politics, 12; construction of, xii; integration with area studies, 148–149, 150–152; in MENA scholarship, 13; role of culture, xiii, xiv; role of paradigms, 145

Socialism: in Algeria, 23; relation to Islam, 21

Society of Muslim Women, 53

Sovereignty, 9; colonialism and, 140; economic restraints on, 140; Islam and, 37–38

State-society relations, xviii, 12, 20, 38–39, 43, 44, 70; in Algeria, 12–13, 16–17, 18; authoritarianism and, xvii; civil society and, 14, 16, 18; conspiracy approach to, 18; in MENA, xvii, 13–14; role of state, 13; secularism, 104

Suez Canal Company, 140

Survey research, 142. *See also* Public opinion

"Thaw" principle, 21

Third Worldism, 23

Tunisian National Pact of 1988, 4

Two-state system: features of, 13–14; human rights and, 14; crises in, 14

United States: conflict resolution and, 120; influence on political science, 2, 7, 9

Universal banking, 73; in Imperial Germany, 71–72

Veiling, 57

Women, 60; education and, 52; Islamist movements and, 48, 52, 53, 54–55, 56, 57, 62, 65–67; organizations, 53; participation in public life, 52

World Bank, 73

World War II, 121; Arab-Israeli conflict, 121; post-war international system, 121

Yemen Civil War, 152

Zeroual, Liamine, 25

Milton Keynes UK
Ingram Content Group UK Ltd.
UKHW052042270324
440206UK00007B/565